Beyond the Congregation

Beyond the Congregation

The World of Christian Nonprofits

CHRISTOPHER P. SCHEITLE

OXFORD
UNIVERSITY PRESS

2010

OXFORD
UNIVERSITY PRESS

Oxford University Press, Inc., publishes works that further
Oxford University's objective of excellence
in research, scholarship, and education.

Oxford   New York
Auckland   Cape Town   Dar es Salaam   Hong Kong   Karachi
Kuala Lumpur   Madrid   Melbourne   Mexico City   Nairobi
New Delhi   Shanghai   Taipei   Toronto

With offices in
Argentina   Austria   Brazil   Chile   Czech Republic   France   Greece
Guatemala   Hungary   Italy   Japan   Poland   Portugal   Singapore
South Korea   Switzerland   Thailand   Turkey   Ukraine   Vietnam

Copyright © 2010 by Oxford University Press, Inc.

Published by Oxford University Press, Inc.
198 Madison Avenue, New York, New York 10016

www.oup.com

Library of Congress Cataloging-in-Publication Data
Scheitle, Christopher P., 1981–
Beyond the congregation : the world of Christian nonprofits / Christopher P. Scheitle.
   p.   cm.
Includes bibliographical references and index.
ISBN 978-0-19-973352-1; 978-0-19-973351-4 (pbk.)
1. Church charities—Societies, etc. 2. Nonprofit organizations. 3. Religious institutions.
I. Title.
HV530.S33 2010
361.7'5—dc22   2009053361

9 8 7 6 5 4 3 2 1

Printed in the United States of America
on acid-free paper

Acknowledgments

This book would not have been possible without the support of many individuals. The data collection forming the basis of the book was made possible through a grant from the College of Liberal Arts at Penn State University and from Dr. William Form and Dr. Joan Huber. The Department of Sociology at Penn State provided many forms of support that are all too easy to take for granted. Tom Pollak at the Urban Institute was also incredibly generous and provided access to the National Center for Charitable Statistics' data. I benefited from some exceptional undergraduate research assistants, namely, Jessica Markle, Andrew Moore, and Kimberly Mayers. A special thanks to Jessica who not only took on the monotonous tasks of assisting with the data collection but also provided her own ideas and suggestions about the project. John McCarthy, David Baker, and Timothy Pollock provided guidance and suggestions throughout this project. The book also benefited from comments provided by Jaime Harris and Jennifer McClure and statistical advice provided by Kimberly Daniels. I am also appreciative of Theo Calderara at Oxford University Press for his support.

I must also acknowledge several others who have had important direct and indirect roles in creating this book. First, I am not sure where I would be without two great mentors. As an undergraduate student, Michael Kearl inspired me to pursue my sociological imagination, and as a graduate student, Roger Finke helped me succeed in that pursuit.

Lisa, the period of my life encompassed in these pages and the memories attached to it will always be influenced by how you made it some of the happiest years I have experienced. Finally, I thank my parents who have always quietly done whatever it takes for me to succeed, and that is really the most children can ask from their parents.

Contents

Beyond the Congregation

1

Christian Nonprofits

The Religious Market's Other Supplier

> These kinds of special purpose groups seem to be gaining importance in American religion. Students of American religion have generally paid little attention to these kinds of organizations, relative to the extraordinary interest that has been devoted to churches and denominations.
> —Robert Wuthnow, *The Restructuring of American Religion*

Think for a moment about the last news story you read or heard about Christianity. Maybe it was a *Washington Post* article about "a nationwide Christian ministry for teenagers with disabilities." Or it could have been a CNN feature on a Christian organization serving men addicted to pornography. Then again, it might have been *USA Today*'s article on a ministry trying to preserve "girls' chastity by building healthy father-daughter relationships." Or it could have been one of several stories in *The New York Times*, such as the one about a faith-based organization providing chaplains for corporations or the story about a youth ministry causing controversy for a proposed event in San Francisco or the article describing the acquisition of decommissioned coast guard ships by a Christian medical relief organization.[1]

While the specifics undoubtedly varied, one fact likely remained— there is a very good chance that the story was not about and did not involve any congregation or denomination. Instead, it was likely about a type of Christian organization entirely independent from those "traditional" structures. While these organizations use many of the keywords we associate with churches or denominations . . . "faith," "Christian," "ministry" . . . they differ greatly in both appearance and action.

Their buildings consist of warehouses and cubicles instead of sanctuaries and pews. They are lead by CEOs, not ministers. They are focused on everything but weekly worship services.

Who or what are these organizations? They are Christian nonprofits, and they are widely recognized as representing a seismic shift in the structure of American religion. They have become the public face of Christianity in the United States and abroad. They represent billions of dollars in annual revenue. Their wide-ranging activities reach into our backyard and to the other side of the world. Well-known names include sociopolitical organizations like Focus on the Family and the American Family Association, fellowship groups such as Young Life and Promise Keepers, relief and development agencies like World Vision and Compassion International, publishing houses such as the American Bible Society, radio and television broadcasters such as the Christian Broadcasting Network, and thousands of other organizations of varying sizes and missions.

Within Christian circles, these organizations are said to be part of the "para-church" sector consisting of organizations existing beyond the boundaries and authority of congregations and denominations. The rise of these parachurch organizations has meant that there is an increasing likelihood the phrase "religious organization" *would not* be in reference to a church or a denomination. Symbolic of this fact, the media, politicians, and academics have come up with a variety of ways to discuss the growing organizational complexity of American Christianity. Names like "voluntary associations," "religious nonprofits," "faith-based organizations," and "special purpose groups" are now commonly used to account for the presence of these organizations.[2]

Understanding Christian nonprofits and the parachurch movement they represent is of vital importance in appreciating contemporary American Christianity.[3] It is not surprising then that they have been a serious point of discussion among churchgoers, denominational leaders, and Christian writers. However, despite representing what would seem to be a significant development in American religion, these organizations have not garnered much systematic research from social scientists. Removing this blind spot in our perception of the American religious landscape is the next logical step in understanding the "dynamic character" of religious marketplaces.[4]

Religious Change

For much of its history, social science held a fairly simple view of religious change.[5] Most scholars believed that religion was a remnant of a less modern age. It was assumed that with science, pluralism, economic security, and "modernization" in general, people's interest in or demand for religion would steadily decline.[6] A long list of well-respected psychologists, sociologists, and anthropologists fell into the trap of predicting the end of religion. Max Weber, one of the "founders" of sociology, wrote in 1918 that "[t]he fate of our times is characterized by rationalization and, above all, by the 'disenchantment of the world'."[7] Fifty years later, the esteemed sociologist Peter Berger argued that in "the 21st century, religious believers are likely to be found only in small sects, huddled together to resist a worldwide secular culture."[8] The problem was that the great secularization of society never seemed to fully occur, particularly at the level of individuals' desire to believe or participate in religion. Every time there was a sign of religious decline, either in the United States or abroad, there would be some other contradictory development. For example, just as one might have been willing to put a point in the column for secularization in the 1960s with the apparent rise of a "counterculture" hostile to religion, an active conservative Christian movement appeared in the 1970s.[9]

About 25 years ago, a new perspective on religious change began to emerge.[10] Some social scientists, questioning the assumption of linear decline, asked how our view of religion would change if we instead assumed that religious demand has been and will be more or less constant over time. Instead of looking for signs of systematic decline and trying to explain away the obvious exceptions, social scientists began to see decline as only one side of a much more complex process of religious change. It was realized that the fall of one congregation, denomination, or religion is often accompanied by the rise of another. The Presbyterians and Congregationalists of the 18th century gave way to the Baptists and the Methodists of the 19th century who gave way to the Pentecostal and other "upstart" denominations of the 20th century.[11] While the names change, religion persists.

Suddenly, social scientists began to see religious change as a much more dynamic process. While there are still debates about whether overall religious demand is rising, declining, or staying constant, this dynamic view of religious change has fundamentally altered the way academics and even the general public think and talk about religion. We no longer see religion as a stagnant and slowly dying phenomenon, but instead, we see a vibrant and ever-changing *religious market.*

The Religious Market

The social scientists who began to question the secularization model of religious change drew upon economic thinking not only to challenge the existing model of religious decline but also to propose numerous hypotheses of their own concerning religious behavior.[12] The guiding principle of this economics of religion is that there is a market for religion that functions in a way quite similar to that for any other product or service. In this market, there are consumers, or potential consumers, of religious goods. As with any good or service, not everyone will be equally interested in participating or purchasing these offerings, and some will not be interested at all. Even among those who are "in the market" for religion, there is great variation in what they are looking to buy. These religious preferences can be shaped by a number of factors, including ethnicity, social class, and just an implicit desire for a particular form of religion.

What exactly are these religious goods and services? Well, some are not inherently religious at all, such as the opportunity for friendships or support. Others are uniquely religious, such as an afterlife, miracles, or a personal, involved deity. Some fall somewhere in-between, such as a sense of meaning or purpose. Despite any ancillary secular benefits that may be acquired in the religious market, the purpose for its existence is for facilitating the exchange of the otherworldly or supernatural goods, whether these goods are ultimately received during or after life. These goods address human needs that, on some level, can never be entirely satisfied through anything society or the natural world can offer, hence the reason these scholars suggested that there would be a relatively constant demand for religion regardless of how much society became modernized. While individuals can find social support or even philosophical explanations for the world in other marketplaces, one can only find these uniquely religious goods in the religious market.

Of course, a market needs more than consumers. It also requires someone to produce the goods and services or in this case the religious suppliers. The primary religious supplier is the congregation, of which there are somewhere around 350,000 in the United States.[13] Most of these congregations are quite small. More than 70% have fewer than 100 regular participants, while more than one-third have fewer than 100 people affiliated with the congregation in any way regardless of how frequently, or at all, these people attend the congregation.[14] These congregations serve the most basic and primary function of a religious supplier, which is to "support and supervise" individuals' relationship with a god or gods.[15] Indeed, in most cases, it is somewhat inaccurate to refer to congregations as a religious supplier since they serve more as a middleman or distributor.

Many of these congregations are associated with a second major supplier of religious goods, specifically denominations. One could simply think of denominations as the aggregate of all the congregations and individuals within them, but denominations are not just the sum of their parts. Denominations serve two primary roles as a religious supplier. First, they serve an "authority" role, helping guide their member congregations on theological and administrative issues.[16]

As described by Gibson Winter, this "pastoral structure" of a denomination is "responsible for faith and discipline in the confessing community."[17] Beyond this authority function, denominations directly engage the religious market by organizing and supporting mission work, publishing, humanitarian work, and other activities. The denomination not only uses congregations as a resource base for these direct engagement efforts but also serves them by providing goods and services along with potential new members. One might think of congregations as local car dealerships within a particular brand (e.g., Ford) and the denomination as the manufacturing plant or corporate office of that brand. Most people may buy a car based on the brand, but they rarely interact directly with the corporate office.[18] However, the corporate office acts in the background for both the buyers and the dealerships through its marketing, financing, and so forth.

These consumers and suppliers together compose the religious market. The suppliers attempt to attract the consumers' resources, such as their time, money, and loyalty. Consumers examine the suppliers available to them and decide which provides the type of goods and services they prefer. If they become unhappy with their current supplier, which could occur due to short-term circumstances (e.g., a new minister) or broader long-term trends (e.g., changing theology), these consumers may decide to seek a new supplier. Resources are constantly shifting from congregation to congregation, denomination to denomination.

But what happens when these resources leave a congregation or denomination but do not end up in another congregation or denomination? Would this be the long-sought after evidence of secularization or is it possible that we are missing a part of the religious market? Is there another supplier?

Restructuring of the Religious Market

A focus on congregations and denominations as the religious market's main suppliers is entirely natural. Congregations are unquestionably the "fundamental unit of American Protestant organization" and "denominationalism is a central characteristic of American religion."[19] However, there have been signs over at least the past 20 years that there is another type of supplier that does not fit into these categories of traditional religious organizations, and these signs have become increasingly difficult to ignore.

One of the first social scientists to raise awareness of a possible other supplier was Robert Wuthnow. In an important 1988 work, Wuthnow examined the broad changes that have shaped American religion since World War II. While he pointed to a number of significant trends, such as the decline of denominational boundaries and the realignment of religion around liberal and conservative positions, he devoted one chapter to the "literally scores" of what he called "special purpose groups" that have appeared in this period.

> Their causes range from nuclear arms control to liturgical renewal, from gender equality to cult surveillance, from healing ministries to evangelism. They address issues both specific to the churches and of more general concern to the broader society. Yet they are clearly rooted in the religious realm. They take their legitimating slogans from religious creeds. And they draw their organizational resources, leadership, and personnel largely from churches and ecclesiastical agencies.

Wuthnow argued that these organizations tend to specialize around one activity or one demographic group and are often inter- or nondenominational. He summarized this development by stating that "the growth of special purpose groups constitutes a significant form of social restructuring in American religion."[20]

These special purpose groups have since received occasional mention by other social scientists but typically in the context of examining other phenomena. For instance, the more politically active special purpose organizations, such as Focus on the Family and the American Family Association, have frequently received attention in relation to their role in mobilizing the religious right.[21] In recent years, there has been a great deal of interest in special purpose organizations providing social services motivated by legislation that created greater opportunities for these organizations to receive public funding.[22] These discussions reinforce the presence and relevance of these other religious suppliers, but they do not capture the full scope or influence of these organizations.

One of the few works since Wuthnow's to present a broad vision of these organizations' importance is D. Michael Lindsay's examination of evangelical leaders working in the public spheres of business, media, education, and politics. The very premise that one must look outside of churches or denominational offices when looking for the power brokers of evangelical Christianity is itself quite eye-opening. However, Lindsay's conclusion that the evangelical "movement's center of gravity today is not found at the level of the local congregation" but instead within special purpose "organizations with national constituencies and organizational practices that resemble, in many ways, corporations" is even more striking.[23]

At the same time social scientists have been considering these special purpose groups in an often casual or peripheral manner, Christian leaders and laypersons have been grappling with what they have been calling the "parachurch" sector. These parachurch organizations are described as being typically specialized around some activity, ranging from international mission work to magazine publishing. They are not directly linked by finances, structure, or authority to congregations or denominations. They are "independent, entrepreneurial, [and] innovative," and in recent decades, Christians have been watching them "sprout and flourish."[24]

It becomes clear after a quick glance that this parachurch sector consists of the same organizations that social scientists have been referring to as special purpose groups. The same names are offered as evidence . . . Young Life, Focus on the Family, Billy Graham Evangelistic Association, World Vision, Prison Fellowship Ministries, and so on. Furthermore, the discussions taking place in the pews and in the Christian literature have reached a similar conclusion about the role these organizations are playing in the restructuring of the religious market. As Wesley Willmer, J. David Schmidt, and Martyn Smith state in their book, *The Prospering Parachurch*, the parachurch sector "is dramatically reshaping the religious world— and taking religion beyond the walls of the traditional church."[25]

Shared Conclusions, Shared Needs

What social scientists, Christian leaders, and laypersons have all concluded is that the religious market has been altered by the presence of a new supplier of religious goods and services. Whether we call them special purpose groups, parachurch organizations, or some other name, these organizations have become central players in American Christianity. For social scientists, the significance of this conclusion rests in what it means for accurately interpreting religious change. If we ignore a significant and growing segment of the market we are obviously going to miss trends within that segment, but we are also likely to misinterpret the market as a whole.

The rise of the parachurch sector and the restructuring of American Christianity is an intellectual or a theoretical curiosity among social scientists, but it has produced anxiety and consternation among many congregational and denominational leaders. Among these individuals and organizations, it represents a material change in their lives. The idea of a religious market is often seen as a useful metaphor for thinking about religion, but for congregations and denominations, it is a strongly felt reality that has become even more real with the increasing size and influence of parachurch organizations. Even if one objects to the idea of a religious market when it comes to individuals' decisions about the very nature of their faith, the market dynamics are difficult to ignore when it comes to parachurch organizations.[26] These organizations are explicitly pitching specialized goods and services in glossy brochures and elaborate Web sites. "Let us organize your short-term mission trip." "Buy your religious education supplies from us." "Sponsor a child through our agency." Individuals or congregations are explicitly purchasing these goods and services in financial transactions. And many of these products and services are (or were) also offered by congregations and denominations.

Competing with other religions, denominations, or churches for members and their resources is a game that everyone understands, but suddenly, there is a new group of competitors that does not seem to be following the long-standing rules of the market. They are ignoring ecclesiastical boundaries, operating outside of established institutions, not following the normal chain of command, and engaging in activities or methods that were previously unheard of, and by all accounts, they are doing so with resounding success. The position of congregations and denominations is not unlike that of any industry facing a paradigm-changing technology or business model, like the newspaper or recording industry in the digital age.[27] Until new roles, boundaries, and routines are established, there is an understandable feeling of uncertainty, even among those who generally support the creation of these organizational forms or practices.

While their motivations might be somewhat different, both social scientists and those in the Christian community would benefit greatly from systematic research on these parachurch organizations. However, such research has been lacking. There have been several obstacles. Because they raise numerous questions both broad and specific and in a range of academic fields, there has likely been some uncertainty about whose territory parachurch organizations fall into. Are they a case for religious studies, sociology, political science, business, communications, history, or some other field? There are aspects of these organizations that undoubtedly raise questions in all of these areas, but they are not fully contained within any one. When no one can decide who goes through the door first, then no one ends up getting through (a little like an intellectual version of the Three Stooges). There has also been a historical focus among social scientists on congregations and denominations as the primary organizational unit of analysis, a focus that is not unwarranted by any means, but which may have distracted us from recognizing other developments.[28]

More problematic might be the difficulty in acquiring information on these organizations in any systematic form.[29] While some of this difficulty can be attributed to the actual logistics of collecting such information, a much larger problem might simply be conceptual. You cannot begin to collect data on something unless you know exactly what these data should represent. What precisely are we talking about when we refer to special purpose or parachurch organizations? Everyone seems to have a vague sense of what is being talked and might be able to throw out a name or two as illustrations. But are we talking about a single type of organization? If not, what exactly does this umbrella term contain? These questions have very practical consequences as their answers shape if and how more systematic research would be undertaken. Before you can study anything, you must first create some boundaries around what is and is not of interest.

Parsing the Parachurch

To try and decompose both the meaning and the content of this parachurch sector, we could utilize two strategies. A more literal strategy could use the very word "parachurch" as a starting place. For example, let us assume that the local congregation is, as most would argue, the most basic unit of organized American religion and the "church" in "parachurch" refers to this basic unit.[30] That which is para-, or beyond or beside the church, would then consist of all external religious organizations and associations interacting with a local congregation.[31] The most obvious group falling into this category would be denominations and all their various components (e.g., publishing houses, education programs). This would strike many as a sign that such a literal approach is flawed. Most people implicitly or explicitly consider denominations as part of the Church, not the parachurch.[32] After all, the parachurch phenomenon is considered new, while denominations are seemingly old. Despite violating common definitions of parachurch, we will see in the following chapters that recognizing the shared functions and intertwined histories of denominations and the parachurch sector provides some important insights into the changes that have occurred in the religious market, both in the past and present.

For now, though, we can utilize a more observational strategy by examining what has been written or said about parachurch organizations to see if a more specific category or categories can be identified. Using this method, we would bypass denominations and go directly to nondenominational organizations that are supplying services or goods to individuals, congregations, and even denominations. The "non-" here refers to structural and financial independence from denominations rather than any necessary lack of a theological or historical identity. There are some of these organizations that are entirely separate from a denomination but still claim some specific affiliation or tradition (e.g., Methodist). However, as we will see, most of these organizations do not claim any specific tradition by design.[33]

Beyond specifying their structural and financial independence from denominations, this observational approach would find that most of these organizations hold a specific legal status. Indeed, Willmer, Schmidt, and Smith explicitly define a parachurch organization as an "organized nonprofit."[34] It seems that if we are to zero in on the parachurch phenomenon that most people mean, we should begin an examination of this larger nonprofit population.[35]

The Nonprofit Sector

The past 20 years have seen immense growth in the nonprofit sector. Its expansion has far outpaced growth in business and government organizations. In 1995, there were just over 1 million nonprofit organizations registered with the Internal Revenue Service (IRS). A little over a decade later, this had increased by almost 40%, bringing the total to just under 1.5 million.[36] The nonprofit population consists of several different types of organization. The largest and most well-known type is known as 501(c)(3)s, which refers to the part of the tax code that defines them. These nonprofits are engaged in one of several broad types of activities that qualify for 501(c)(3) status, including educational, charitable, scientific, or, most importantly for our interest, religious activities.[37] This status exempts the nonprofit from federal income taxes and also provides contributors a deduction on their own taxes. In return for their tax-exempt status, these nonprofits must follow a few primary rules. First, they cannot do any campaigning or "electioneering" for a political candidate. Second, they cannot engage in substantial lobbying activity aimed at opposing or favoring legislation. Third, their activities cannot benefit any individual or individuals who are part of the nonprofit. Any excess earnings must be used toward the operations and purpose of the nonprofit, not toward the benefit of individuals in the nonprofit.[38]

Within the 501(c)(3) category, there are two subgroups. The first group consists of private foundations, which are funded by one or two sources like a wealthy individual or corporation—hence the reason that they are often named

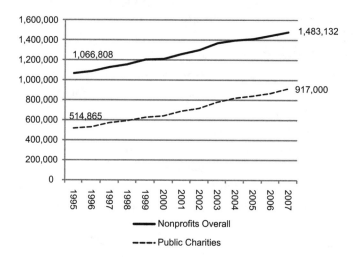

FIGURE 1.1. All Nonprofits and Public Charities Registered with IRS, 1995–2007.
Source: National Center for Charitable Statistics (IRS Business Master Files).

after their benefactor. There were approximately 100,000 private foundations in 2007. Most private foundations are in the business of giving money away to others and do not typically "do" anything beyond writing checks.[39] The second group of 501(c)(3)s consists of public charities. Public charities solicit support from a wide range of people, corporations, and private foundations. Unlike private foundations, public charities typically provide services or goods. There were more than 917,000 public charities in 2007. Given their large numbers, their grassroots support, and world-engaging nature, it is clear that most scholars, churchgoers, and denominational leaders are really talking about public charities when they refer to parachurch organizations as nonprofits, so it is worth exploring these public charities further.

Religious Public Charities

One of the justifications for receiving 501(c)(3) status is that an organization is religious in nature. Indeed, this was among the earliest justifications for tax-exempt status. How many public charities fall into the religious category? A quick answer is 193,356 or about a fifth of the total and the largest single category.[40] But this quick answer can be deceptive. One problem, which would apply to an enumeration of any type of public charity, is that a religious organization may not fit neatly into any particular category. So, if anything, this number is likely an undercount since some organizations with an explicit religious identity might be categorized, for example, in the "Housing, Shelter" category if their activities have something to do with housing.

When it comes to enumerating *parachurch* religious public charities, there are additional complications that result from the way in which the law and the IRS treat congregations, denominations, and parachurch organizations. The crux of the problem is that these 193,356 religious public charities include congregations and denominational agencies that have voluntarily registered with the IRS even though they are not required to do so. In short, this number mixes church with parachurch. The good news is that the IRS does try to separate out these numbers by offering a separate classification for nonprofits claiming to be a church. Seventy-five percent of these organizations, or 146,475, are registered as a church.[41] This would mean that the remaining 46,881 organizations are noncongregational religious public charities or parachurch organizations. However, some nonprofits that almost everyone would view as parachurch claim church status in IRS records. So, this 46,881 is at best a conservative estimate since it does not include any parachurch organizations that are hiding in the "church" number. This issue will be explored in more detail in chapter 7.

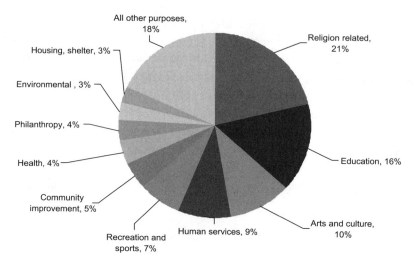

FIGURE 1.2. Most Common Exempt Purposes of Public Charities.
Source: National Center for Charitable Statistics (September 2007 IRS Business Master Files).

A different quirk of the IRS' rules provides an alternative way of estimating the number of parachurch organizations included in the total number of religious public charities. While some congregations and denominational agencies have registered with the IRS to ensure contributors that their donations will be tax deductible or because they mistakenly thought they were required to do so, very few take the additional step of filing annual financial returns with the IRS. Filing these forms is not required of these church organizations and has no impact on the ability of donors to deduct their contributions. However, religious public charities that are not a congregation or denomination or integrated into a congregation or denomination are required to file annual tax returns. As a result, this filing requirement filters out most of the church while leaving the parachurch. This is why more than 20% of registered public charities are religious, but only 7% of public charities filing financial returns are religious.

Of the 193,356 registered religious public charities in 2007, 23,260 filed a financial return. There is another complication, though. Only public charities with more than $25,000 in gross receipts are required to file in the first place, meaning that this 23,260 only represents parachurch organizations that are relatively large. Among all public charities, about 40% file financial returns, so we could assume that there is another 60% of the parachurch total that we are not seeing. Taking this into account would mean that there are approximately 58,000 religious public charities that are not congregations or denominational agencies.[42]

To summarize, the 193,356 registered religious public charities in 2007 would then consist of somewhere between 47,000 and 58,000 parachurch organizations.

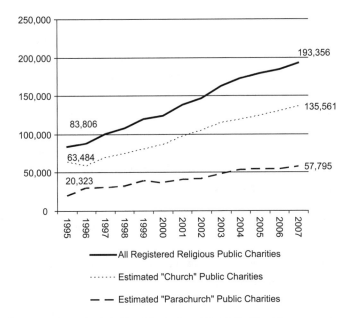

FIGURE 1.3. Religious, "Church," and "Parachurch" Public Charities, 1995–2007.
Source: National Center for Charitable Statistics (IRS Business Master Files). Estimates of "church" and "parachurch" public charities based on author's calculations as described in text.

Taking the latter estimate would mean that the parachurch sector represents about 7% of all public charities.[43] If we apply this same method to past years, we find that the estimated number of "church" public charities has grown 92%—from about 70,000 to 135,000—between 1995 and 2007, while the number of "parachurch" public charities has grown 190% from 20,000 to 58,000 in the same time. Both populations have grown, but the parachurch population has grown at a faster rate. However, such a comparison is somewhat deceptive and only diminishes the large growth in the parachurch sector because much of the growth in the number of registered church organizations is a statistical illusion. Many of the congregations or denominational offices choosing to register are not new in any real sense. The observed numbers are simply catching up with a population that has existed for a long time as congregations feel pressure to register for administrative or bureaucratic reasons. On the other hand, there are many reasons to believe that the parachurch trend represents actual growth in that population.

All nonprofits have grown during this period, so one might be tempted to just pass off the parachurch trend as an overall nonprofit trend. However, the overall number of public charities has only grown 78% from 1995 to 2007 compared with the 190% of parachurch organizations. This becomes even more remarkable considering that the typical explanations given for the growth of the overall nonprofit sector are not as applicable or satisfying when applied to that of parachurch nonprofits. For example, many scholars argue that a central reason the number of nonprofits has grown is that "the modern welfare state has largely been subcontracted to nonprofits."[44] That is, in the last few decades, federal and state governments have shifted from directly providing services to instead offering money for other organizations, typically in the nonprofit sector, to provide those services in its place. While it is true that some religious nonprofits receive government funding and that this issue has received a great deal of attention in recent years, the reality is that the overwhelming majority of religious nonprofits are not engaged in any activities that would receive government funding. Although it should not be surprising, most of these organizations are focused explicitly on religious activities that the government is not interested in or legally able to fund.

Others point to modern society's heightened awareness and discovery of new causes and the ease with which people can organize around them as a driver of nonprofit growth.[45] But we must remember that the religious sector already had an infrastructure for pursuing the activities of these parachurch organizations, making their presence and rapid growth even more remarkable. While a nonprofit organization may have been a natural strategy for pursuing some newfound cause in, say, the environmental sector, it would seem more natural that religious causes would have been funneled through the already existing congregational or denominational structure. All of this suggests that the growth in the parachurch sector is being fueled by some other force within the religious market itself, a hypothesis that will be explored in the following chapter.

— my "religion etone" paper relevant here?

The Parachurch 2000

Social scientists, Christian leaders, and churchgoers have identified a significant reorganization of the religious market in the past few decades driven by the rise of a new supplier of religious goods and services. Various names have been given to describe these new suppliers, but they have most commonly been called special purpose or parachurch organizations. Beyond agreeing upon their existence, we know very little about this population. What explains its apparent growth? In what activities are these organizations involved? How are they funded and operated? How do they fit into the religious market and how do they relate to other suppliers within it? The first step toward answering these questions is to try and corral what has been a somewhat nebulous phenomenon into a more defined and workable population of organizations so that we can begin to gather more information about them. We took that first step here by recognizing that these special purpose or parachurch organizations seem to be highly concentrated in the nonprofit population or more specifically the population of 501(c)(3) public charities.

Now that we know where to look, the next logical step in our attempt to understand this restructuring of the religious market is to gather more detailed information on these organizations. It is exactly this type of information that this book presents. Using a variety of sources, I have identified the largest U.S.-based Christian nonprofits operating on a national and/or an international level. These are the most well-known, influential, and well-funded parachurch organizations. When parachurch organizations are discussed or written about, it is from this group that examples are typically drawn. This is the segment of the parachurch world where organizations are as well known in urban Miami, FL, as they are in small-town Cody, WY. These are the nonprofits where churches and individuals in both California and Maine purchase products or hold memberships. This is the segment where revenues rival that of some denominations and the nonprofits' influence among churches and individuals is similarly powerful.[46] You might think of them as the Fortune 500 of the parachurch sector, although there are actually about 2,000 organizations identified and examined in this book. As figure 1-4 shows, examining when these organizations acquired their exempt status from the IRS, referred to as their "ruling year," reinforces the story of parachurch growth.[47]

In the next chapter, we will explore the history of the parachurch sector, which extends much further back than many people realize, and how this history can shed light on the mechanisms underlying its success in recent decades.

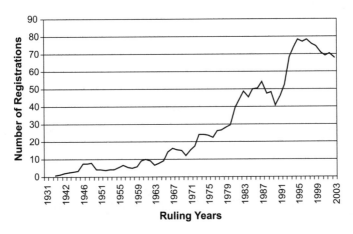

FIGURE 1.4. IRS Ruling Dates of Largest National and International Christian Nonprofits.
Source: IRS ruling dates of organizations (*N* = 1,941) included in data collection.

2

From Religious Societies to Public Charities

A Parachurch History

Moral societies, Sunday schools—tract societies—Bible societies—
missionary societies, and funds to educate and make preachers, are now
in the full tide of operation . . .

—John Leland, 1826

Christian nonprofits and the parachurch movement they represent
first gained serious attention over two decades ago.[1] Since those early
articles and books, the number of organizations, the variety of their
activities, and the amount of money supporting them have only grown.
It is not surprising then that the public, media, and scholars tend
to present a consistent, if somewhat vague, historical description of
Christian nonprofits. Namely, they all tend to take the position that this
is a new phenomenon that has been defined by recent and rapid growth.[2]
Adjectives such as proliferating and burgeoning are commonly used
in such descriptions. The numbers examined in the previous chapter
confirm these impressions.

However, the story becomes more complicated once we expand
our window of observation beyond the past few decades. The reality is
that this is not the first occurrence of a large parachurch sector
in American Christianity. As we will see in this chapter, recognizing this
provides a key insight in understanding the rise of the contemporary
parachurch sector.

Rise or Revival?

As scholars have come to recognize Christian nonprofits and the parachurch sector, we have come to further appreciate the "structural adaptability" of an institution often associated with tradition and stability.[3] It would be easy to conclude that this flexibility is a recent development. Like love triangles in romance novels, declaring something a new phenomenon is one of the most popular plot devices in social research.[4] The only problem is that such claims are almost never entirely accurate. So it is with Christian nonprofits. It would be tempting to say that the proliferation of Christian nonprofits occurred ex nihilo and constitutes the discovery of a brand-new type of religious organization. However, this argument would have some obvious flaws given that a few of the organizations discussed in the following chapters are more than 200 years old.

Individuals and groups have frequently created new types of organizations to help accomplish their religiously inspired goals. Indeed, many of the organizations that we have come to take for granted as traditional, such as denominations, were themselves innovations at one time. Although still an underappreciated part of American religious history, several scholars have traced the creation of denominational agencies, such as publishing houses, relief agencies, and education programs, to their origins in the mid-19th century.[5] Prior to this point, denominations were limited to dealing with issues of intragroup authority and theology and lacked the action or outreach-oriented organizational structures they have today.

However, individuals and congregations did not just sit around and do nothing just because they lacked denominational organizations to help them. The late 18th and early 19th centuries were actually a booming time for religious outreach, but these pursuits were organized in an entirely different manner. Instead of centralized denominations serving as the coordinators of religious outreach, various voluntary associations or "religious societies" were the main facilitators. These societies were typically specialized around a single goal, such as publishing Bibles and religious tracts, conducting domestic and international missionary projects, or advancing sociopolitical issues like temperance and abolition. These organizations served as the outreach arm of the church.

As with contemporary parachurch organizations, it would be a mistake to dismiss these 19th-century organizations as insignificant in either size or importance. The 19th-century parachurch organizations were some of the largest creators of printed material during their time, producing "millions of tracts, pamphlets, hymnbooks, and devotional books, as well as journals, magazines and newspapers." The "flood" of material created by religious societies has been pointed to as the origin of mass media in the United States.[6] Similarly, antislavery or temperance moral societies represented the "birth of the American social movement," and Sunday school societies played a central role in education in the early United States.[7]

All of this makes the burgeoning and proliferating nature of contemporary parachurch organizations seem like a case of déjà vu.[8] However, the 19th- and 21st-century parachurch sectors are not disconnected instances of history repeating itself. The rise, fall, and rise again of the parachurch sector represent a continuous narrative in the changing structure of the religious market.

The First Coming

While one could clearly trace their history back further, the direct inspiration for and ancestor of parachurch organizations in the United States were the British religious societies that were dedicated to missionary work and distributing scripture. The earliest example was the Company for the Propagation of the Gospel in New England. Founded in 1649 and later renamed as the New England Company, it worked among the Native Americans in the American colonies.[9] It still exists today as a grant-making agency to students and pastors in Canada and the Caribbean. Another example was the painfully self-descriptive Society for the Conversion and Religious Instruction and Education of the Negro Slaves in the British West India Islands, which was founded in 1691.

It may not have been the first, but few of British religious societies would match the size or influence of the Society for Promoting Christian Knowledge (SPCK). The SPCK was a voluntary association founded in 1698 with the goal of producing and distributing Christian literature to alleviate the "gross ignorance of the principles of the Christian religion" both in Britain and overseas. The SPCK was joined in 1701 by the Society for the Propagation of the Gospel in Foreign Parts (SPG). Both the SPCK and the SPG were the brainchild of Thomas Bray, making him the first multiorganizational founder in the parachurch sector. Bray began his career by establishing libraries in America and England. This work provided the inspiration for the SPCK. Bray wrote *A General Plan of the Constitution of a Protestant Congregation or Society for Promoting Christian Knowledge*, which would serve as the organizational plan for the SPCK and SPG. His vision was for a "corporate body empowered to receive gifts and legacies, and charged both to send missionaries to the plantations, provide them with libraries, and care for the maintenance of themselves and their dependants." This vision would accurately describe many contemporary Christian nonprofits.[10]

From Thomas Bray's "A General Plan of the Constitution of a Protestant Congregation or Society for Propagating Christian Knowledge," which became the inspiration and business plan for many later missionary societies.[11]

First.—That it consist both of Clergy of the chieftest note, and of such Lay Gentlemen as are eminent for their worth, and affection to Religion.

As to the Plantations abroad.

1st. That it be under their care to provide and support such Missionaries as the Lord Bishop of London shall think necessary to be sent into those parts, where no establishment or provision is yet made for the support of the Clergy. . . .

4thly. That it be their care to make some provision for such of our Missionaries' widows and children as are left unprovided; especially for the widows and orphans of such as by their zeal and industry in converting souls may have occasioned the loss of life or goods.

As to the Propagating of Christian Knowledge at home.

3rdly. To enable the Congregation pro Propaganda Fide to discharge these forementioned trusts, that they be empowered by their charter to receive gifts, grants, legacies, etc. . . .

The British missionary, Bible, and religious tract societies would serve as the inspiration for similar societies that began to flourish within the United States in the late 18th and early 19th centuries.[12] A 1796 letter to the editor in the Boston-based *Columbian Centinel* responded to the creation of a Bible society in London by asking as follows:

Might not a Bible Society in America, be very useful in counteracting the effects of Anti-Bible Societies, who are industriously circulating in every part of our country, the poisonous works of Tom Paine?[13]

It did not take long for this call to be answered. Soon, announcements about religious tract and Bible societies began appearing in newspapers across New England: the Massachusetts Society for Promoting Religious Knowledge in 1803, the Connecticut Tract Society in 1807, the Philadelphia Bible Society and the Vermont Religious Tract Society in 1808, the New York Bible Society in 1809, and so on. These societies modeled themselves after their British counterparts and their activities were provided legitimacy through those earlier organizations. The 1811 report of the Connecticut Tract Society argued that distributing tracts had

> peculiar advantages. It has, for a number of years past, been pursued
> with great success in Great-Britain. Several millions of tracts have been
> there distributed. The salutary effects have been clearly perceived.[14]

At the same time that these Bible and tract societies were being founded in New England, American mission societies modeled after their British counterparts were appearing. A 1796 article in the *Centinel of Freedom* noted that the clergy and laity of several churches had created the New York Missionary Society to "send the gospel to the Indian tribes."[15] Sometime after the appearance of the mission and publishing societies, religious societies began to form around certain social issues, particularly combating slavery and immoral behaviors.[16]

There is much discussion about the novelty of contemporary parachurch organizations. Ironically, this is not the first time these discussions have occurred. Despite having precedents in England, these early American parachurch organizations viewed their activities as being cutting edge and potentially controversial. The 1797 Report of the Directors of the New York Missionary Society noted the innovative nature of their organization.

> An institution so novel in this country, and so much beyond the
> ordinary habits of religious enterprise as the present Missionary Society,
> could hardly expect to enjoy immediate and universal support. Yet it is
> not without peculiar satisfaction, that the Directors find, that in
> proportion as it is understood, it recommends itself to the *approbation*
> *and affection of Christians of different denominations.*[17]

Market Opening

Grassroots and independent religious societies took advantage of a significant opening in the religious market. There was obviously a demand for a service or product that was not being met by any existing religious supplier. Just like today, these large-scale outreach activities were beyond the ability of individual congregations. Importantly, though, denominations were not in a position to conduct such outreach either as they lacked the structure and resources that we have come to associate with contemporary denominations. Staffing and spending were very sparse for most denominations, meaning that there were no official publishing houses, mission agencies, education offices, or other denominational structures.[18] These would not begin to form until the mid-19th century. Ben Primer described the transformation for one group as follows:

Because they shared members and officers, many of the various 19th century religious societies would coordinate their annual conventions so individuals could attend multiple events in the same place and time. This "Anniversary Week" was a "season of interest to thousands." The **Gazetteer of the State of New York** *from 1860 (Syracuse: Pearsall Smith) listed the following "Religious, Literary, and Benevolent Societies" as active in the state:*

The American Bible Society . . . has for its object the publication and distribution of the Bible . . .

The American Tract Society . . . for the purpose of disseminating tracts and books upon moral and religious subjects . . .

The American Board of Commissioners for Foreign Missions . . . for the purpose of supporting missions in foreign lands . . .

The American Home Missionary Society . . . for the purpose of supporting the ministry in feeble and destitute Presb. and Cong. churches . . .

The American Sunday School Union . . . for the purpose of encouraging the establishment of Sunday schools. . . .

The American Seamen's Friend Society . . . distributing Bibles and tracts . . . promoting the moral welfare of seamen.

The American Bethel Society . . . for the purpose of opening chapels for boatmen and mariners . . .

The American and Foreign Christian Union . . . for the special object of counteracting the influence of Romish and other churches opposed to the class usually denominated "evangelical."

The Central American Education Society . . . for the purpose of assisting young men preparing for the ministry . . .

The American Colonization Society . . . for the colonization of free colored persons in Africa . . .

The National Compensating Emancipation Society . . . for its object of purchasing slaves for the purpose of giving them freedom . . .

The American Anti Slavery Society . . .

The American Missionary Association . . . has a slaves' Bible Fund, and labors for the extinction of slavery. The Association publish The American Missionary (paper) and American Missionary Magazine . . .

Young Men's Christian Association . . . These associations embrace within their objects a library, reading room, lectures and prayer meetings.

The Young Men's Christian Union . . .

Young Men's Association . . . usually includes a library, reading room, cabinet, lecture course, and debating club.

The New York State Temperance Society . . . to suppress intemperance and limited the traffic in intoxicating liquors.

In 1876 the Disciples of Christ supported three independent missionary societies. Each was located in a different city, and only one had a full-time administrator. Together they spent less than $20,000 annually to maintain a small number of missionaries at home and abroad.

A half-century later startling changes had occurred . . . Work was now divided into various departments. More than one hundred "experts" and "office workers" were needed to direct the expenditure of a two million dollar budget. . . . The total number of missionaries was larger than ever . . . [and] now included such new functions as Christian education, social service and promotion.

The Disciples of Christ were actually somewhat of a late bloomer when it came to bureaucratizing itself. By the time they began this process, other denominations had already established centralized offices and greatly increased their spending at a national level.

Why denominations in the early- to mid-19th century lacked the elaborate agencies and offices we are accustomed to today is itself an interesting question. Two hypotheses clearly present themselves. First, the lack of denominational structures could simply reflect a larger historical pattern by which many sectors did not come to be dominated by large-scale bureaucracies until the late 19th century. Second, there is the possibility that church-state relations had an impact on the structure of denominations in the early United States. Since at least some denominations were officially supported by particular colonies, their motivation to create organizational structures to conduct outreach may have been hampered.[19]

Regardless, in the absence of such denominational structures, individuals and congregations channeled their outreach efforts through these grassroots religious societies. This was particularly true for some groups, such as Presbyterians and Congregationalists. In the early 18th century, these groups enlisted the assistance of voluntary missionary organizations to fight off perceived competition from Catholic missionaries. By the 19th century, the threat had changed as competition from upstart Methodists and Baptists increased, but the response was similar. In 1801, Presbyterians and Congregationalists entered into an agreement called the Plan of Union that, in part, was designed to facilitate cooperation in mission efforts. But because neither had their own denominational agencies, they once again utilized religious societies and voluntary associations as their outreach organizations. Michael Young notes that religious societies "emerged through the creative and coordinated interaction between Presbyterians and Congregationalists." The societies were so dominated by Presbyterians and Congregationalists that many refer to them "Presbygational." This outsourcing of Presbyterian and Congrega-tional outreach, along with the same lack of denominational structures in other groups, provided the fuel for the 19th-century parachurch sector. This favorable environment, however, did not last long.[20]

Rise of Denominational Agencies

A sign of the declining market opening for religious societies was the increasingly rocky marriage between the Presbyterians and Congregationalists. Each became perturbed with what they perceived to be the dilution of their identity and/or ineffectiveness within the union and the religious societies. By 1840, both sides began to resign their membership from the Plan of Union. To replace the activities they previously organized through the religious societies, denominations began to create their own publishing and missionary agencies. For example, the Presbyterians created the Presby-terian Board of Domestic Missions, the Board of Church Erection, and the Presbyterian Publishing House. Other denominations had also begun forming their own denomina-tional outreach organizations. Often, denominations would simply envelop the various religious societies they had previously utilized on a less formal basis. Methodists, for instance, took over the Missionary and Bible Society and the Church Extension Society, renaming the latter to the Board of Church Extension.[21]

Religious societies of all types felt this shift in the religious market. The American Bible Society (ABS), for example, had always had issues with free-riding local societies. However, the ABS began to realize that their list of auxiliary local societies was increasingly dominated by nonactive and/or nonsupporting societies. At several points starting in the 1830s, the national society discussed ending their reliance on local societies but decided against it for a lack of good alternatives.[22] By 1900, though, the lack of activity and support at the local level led the ABS to take steps to become a much more centralized and self-sustaining organization rather than rely on many local societies.

A laundry list of explanations was given for the decline of the local Bible societies, including

> immense changes in transportation . . . the development of the use of mail . . . the distribution effected by great department stores and mail order establishments . . . the change in character of American communities . . . the moving about from place to place of families . . . the demands upon churches for the support of new enterprises . . . and the spirit of the times.[23]

While some of these reasons may have had a role, they miss the larger story that was occurring. The organizational center of American Christianity had shifted. Religious societies were the product of a time when denominations did not have their own agencies and utilized religious societies as de facto denominational agencies. As denominations began to create their own agencies, the individuals and churches that had formed the basis of the religious societies were drawn into them and away from the societies. The structures that had been developed on a grassroot and an independent level "had largely passed into denominational hands."[24] Not all religious societies, especially large national organizations, went away due to the rise of denominational agencies. However, they could no longer count on being a pseudodenominational agency for individuals and congregations. Instead, they were competitors to those agencies.

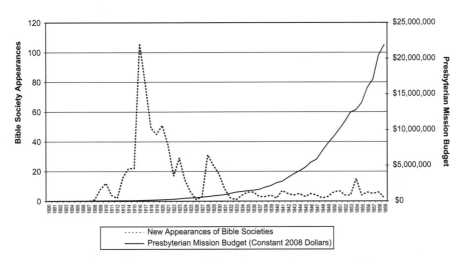

FIGURE 2.1. Appearance of New Bible Societies Compared to the Growth of Denominational Mission Work. The figure shows the number of appearances of new Bible societies based on newspaper records from 1800 to 1859 compared to the amount spent by Presbyterians on mission work. New appearances saw sharp decreases as denominational spending increased.

Source: Data collected by the author from America's *Historical Newspaper* database, produced by Readex; Presbyterian data taken from *Presbyterian Statistics through One Hundred Years 1826-1926* by Rev. Herman C. Weber. 1927. The General Council of the Presbyterian Church in the United States includes combined numbers from the Old School and New School Presbyterians after their 1937 schism. To extend these data to missing years, the trend for the observed years was used to predict the unobserved years. This was done by modeling the natural log of the amount spent as a function of time and taking the exponentiated predicted values. The correlation between the imputed variable and the observed variable is .97. Conversion to constant dollars was done using Consumer Price Index data from the Federal Reserve located at http://www.minneapolisfed.org/research/data/us/calc/hist1800.cfm.

The Second Coming

It is possible that there never would have been a rise of a 19th-century parachurch sector if the absence of denominational structures had not created an opportunity for the many religious societies to fill that market niche. But this raises a question about the current parachurch sector. If denominations created their outreach structures in the 19th century, thereby undercutting the parachurch resource base, how have Christian nonprofits and other parachurch organizations managed to turn the tide of history? Furthermore, how can the rise and decline of 19th-century religious societies shed light on the mechanisms driving the rise of parachurch organizations we are witnessing today? The 19th-century parachurch sector was driven by the void created by the lack of denominational organizational structures, and its eventual decline was driven by the filling of that void. Today, however, we are seeing significant changes in the denominational nature of religion in the United States, which is fueling a renewed parachurch sector.

Growth of Unaffiliated Resources

One of the most significant yet underappreciated religious developments in the United States has been the rise of a non- or postdenominational Protestant identity.[25] This is reflected in the increase in nondenominational congregations and the corresponding increase in individuals claiming nondenominational or "just Christian" affiliations. According to the General Social Survey, the percentage of Protestants claiming no denomination or nondenominational has increased from about 4% in the early 1970s to 15% in 2006.[26] The 1998 National Congregations Study estimated that nondenominational churches represent 19% of all congregations and contain 11% of all attendees. As a collective, this group would represent one of the largest denominations in the United States.[27]

How is this trend related to the growth of Christian nonprofits? From a practical perspective, just because a congregation is or becomes unaffiliated with a denomination does not free it from needing the goods and services typically obtained from denominational structures. Independent congregations still need worship supplies, church and leadership consulting, ministry education and training, missions support, and so on. Independent congregations, though, have no preexisting relationship with a supplier of these goods and services. Therefore, a congregation without denominational allegiances represents money looking for a place to be spent. Many signs seem to suggest that Christian nonprofits are responding to fulfill this demand. In interviews with 73 independent churches, Scott Thumma found that nondenominational

churches rely on the parachurch sector to "strengthen the nondenominational identity much like an established denomination's resources, programs, publications and
seminaries reinforce a denominational culture."[28]

Figure 2-2 compares the percentage of Protestants in the United States stating
they do not have a denominational affiliation in the General Social Survey over the
past 30 years with the ruling dates of the Christian nonprofits examined in this
book. Ruling dates represent when the nonprofit received recognition of their
exempt status from the Internal Revenue Service and typically come soon after the
organization is founded.[29] The percentage of unaffiliated Protestants has gone from
about 4% in the early 1970s to more than 15% in 2006. This has corresponded to a
similar doubling of the rate of Christian nonprofit filings. Even more telling is the
apparent lag between increases in unaffiliated individuals and nonprofits. The
jumps in nonprofits seem to follow about 5 years after those in unaffiliated individuals. An increase in the mid-1970s in unaffiliated individuals was followed by an
increase in the early 1980s in nonprofit filings. Another jump in nondenominational identity in the late 1980s was followed by an increase in nonprofit filings in
the mid-1990s. This lag is not surprising because it takes time for the market to
respond to changes in demand and resources. Before a nonprofit can survive, there
must be people and congregations willing to support it.

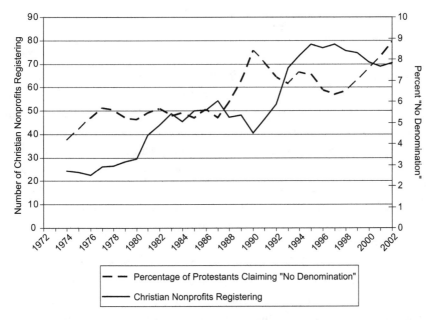

FIGURE 2.2. Growth of "No Denomination" Protestants Compared to Registrations of
Christian Nonprofits.
Source: General Social Surveys, 1972–2006; ruling dates of 1,941 organizations in Christian nonprofit data.

Independent congregations and individuals only represent the most visible part of a much larger trend in the weakening of denominational boundaries. Not coincidentally, immediately before discussing the rise of special purpose groups in his book on the restructuring of American religion, Robert Wuthnow argued that we were witnessing a "declining significance of denominationalism." He pointed to decreasing social and demographic differences across, increasing rates of switching between, and less hostile attitudes toward different denominations as signs that these boundaries were being weakened. Responding to similar trends, Wade Clark Roof and William McKinney observed a "new religious voluntarism" emphasizing individualism as weakening the importance of denominational structures and loyalties. Churches, they argued, would need "to adapt to this new milieu" if they were to "inspire commitment." It might just be this prescription that the parachurch sector is filling. As Alan Wolfe noted, parachurch organizations thrive off of those who are "oblivious to denominational boundaries."[30]

In addition to responding to these trends, Christian nonprofits are likely accelerating them. By creating options for outreach outside of denominations, Christian nonprofits are making it easier and more attractive for other congregations and individuals to go outside of denominational structures. By framing this outreach in a non- or postdenominational identity, Christian nonprofits are also reinforcing one of the key mechanisms underlying their growth.

Denominational Outsourcing

The growth of nondenominational identities and affiliations is a major source of growth for Christian nonprofits, but even within denominations, there are signs of decreasing loyalty from congregations and members. For example, there has been a growing concern among denominations about the decline in the proportion of church income provided back to the denomination. These so-called benevolences are used for the denomination's mission and outreach work. At the same time, there has been a parallel decrease within denominations in the percentage of a person's income given to the church. People are giving proportionally less of their income to the church, and churches are giving less of their income back to denominational structures.[31]

Once we factor in the rise of Christian nonprofits, the story becomes more complicated. As seen in figure 2-3, the decline in benevolences has been offset by the increasing numbers of nonprofit organizations.[32] These nonprofits must have money to survive, and not surprisingly, most of their supporters are the same as those of congregations and denominations. When faced with competing demands for their time and money, individuals must either increase their overall

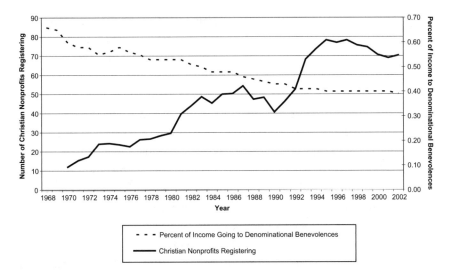

FIGURE 2.3. Decline of Denominational Benevolences Compared to Growth of Christian Nonprofits.

Source: Emptytomb.org, "Per Member Giving as a Percentage of U.S. Per Capita Disposable Personal Income, and U.S. Per Capita Disposable Personal Income, 1968–2004." Ruling dates of 1,941 organizations in Christian nonprofit data.

support or choose one over the other. It seems that at least some of the growth in the population of Christian nonprofits has come at the expense of their denominational competitors. This means that the decline in denominational finances is probably more of a transformation than an overall decline in religious philanthropy.[33]

Why have individuals and churches have shifted their support from denominations to the parachurch sector? There may be some competitive and organizational dynamics that provide certain advantages to parachurch organizations, allowing them to simply win resources from denominations. We will explore these issues in the next chapter. However, there have been changes in many denominations that have made competition a nonissue, particularly among the mainline denominations. Many of these groups have all but stopped their missions programs, church planting, and other domestic and foreign outreach. The largest mainline denominations, including the Episcopal Church, the United Methodist Church, the United Church of Christ, and the Evangelical Lutheran Church in America, all have fewer than one foreign missionary per 10,000 members. This compares with more than 9 for the Southern Baptist Convention, 26 for the Christian and Missionary Alliance, and more than 100 for the Church of the Nazarene.[34] It is true that there is probably lower demand within these denominations for outreach programs, but it is unlikely that there is absolutely no demand.

Nancy Ammerman provides the following quote from a pastor of an Episcopal church, "We used to have missionaries. . . . Now there are no missionaries of the Episcopal Church. . . . The need hasn't disappeared. . . . Some of us are saying, 'We've got to do better!'"[35]

Surveys of these denominations have found some disconnect between the beliefs and attitudes of the denominations' leadership and its members, often with the latter being more conservative than the former. So there is likely some demand for certain religious services and goods not being satisfied by the denominations.[36] It is not surprising then that many of these denominations have faced internal movements aimed at remobilizing the denominations' outreach, education, and evangelism programs. One such movement in the Presbyterian Church (U.S.A.) explicitly stated that while reforming the denomination itself was one strategy it was pursuing, it was also open to working with "para-church missional organizations" to serve its needs.[37] In sum, the retreat of mainline denominations from these areas has provided many open spaces in the market for parachurch organizations to utilize. This has not gone unnoticed among mainline leaders:

> These [parachurch] organizations are not made up of free-floating, unaffiliated evangelicals. *The mainline evangelicals themselves are the backbone of the massive parachurch organizations dominating much of American Christianity.* The mainline liberal establishment should not delude itself on this point. . . . The parachurch dollars are coming from mainline pockets.[38]

These open spaces within the religious market are not unlike those created by the lack of denominational structures in the early 19th century that fueled that era's parachurch sector. So, in some ways, the story of America's religious organizational structure has come full circle. From parachurch, to denominations, to parachurch.

The intertwined histories of denominational and parachurch organizations show that in many ways the two are united by the same social forces. The exclusion of denominational agencies from the parachurch population is not entirely warranted from a sociological perspective. This is not to say that there are not important differences between denominations and parachurch organizations. The next chapter will explore these differences along with the complex relationship between church and parachurch organizations. Restructuring a market often displaces some people and organizations temporarily or permanently, and the growth of religious outreach being conducted through Christian nonprofits has been met with mixed reviews among more traditional suppliers of religious outreach.

3

Competition and Collaboration

The Market Dynamics of Church and Parachurch

There was a day when newspapers would summarize Sunday's sermons of prominent ministers in their Monday editions; today the media interview and quote from parachurchmen—Bill Bright, Billy Graham, Charles Colson and the celebrity figures. *Time* magazine's cover story on the evangelicals quoted no pastor. Television specials interview "leaders," which usually are not pastors. . . . Official and unofficial grumbling has begun about the shift.

—Stephen Board, "The Great Evangelical Power Shift"

As we saw in the previous chapter, understanding the functional similarities between church and parachurch organizations can go a long way toward explaining the historical ebb and flow between the two. Understanding their similarities, and maybe more importantly their differences, is also crucial in explaining the often complicated relationship between the church and parachurch organizations. The term "parachurch" hints at some of the underlying tension. The prefix "para-" could be defined as something existing "beside" or "alongside" of a related entity. However, it could also be defined as something "beyond" or "aside from" a related entity. The difference is subtle, but it represents the crux of the problem. Is the parachurch sector a partner working cooperatively *alongside* churches and denominations or is it a rogue agent working *beyond* the reach of them?

Parachurch organizations have many of the same goals and motivations as denominations and congregations—supporting believers, spreading the faith, and generally promoting Christianity. On some level, they are all on the same team. This obviously provides reason for at least some inherent affinity among churches, denominations, and parachurch organizations. In fact, most ministers, denominational leaders, and churchgoers will say positive things about parachurch organizations. After all, these individuals undoubtedly interact with the parachurch sector on a fairly regular basis; otherwise, these parachurch organizations would not have the resources to exist. Still, these positive comments are often followed, either cautiously or forcefully, by a "but I wish they . . ." or a "but I don't like that . . ."

This ambivalence is clear in much of the writing on the contemporary parachurch sector. Jerry White spoke of an "uneasy marriage" between the church and parachurch. Providing an even harsher assessment, David Fitch threw parachurch organizations in the same category as big business, consumer capitalism, and other "modern maladies" (apparently if the first two left you unsure of his opinion of the parachurch sector, the latter was meant to leave no doubt). One pastor noted that descriptions of parachurch organizations vary from "God's gift[s] to His church to necessary evils." But what is the source of this ambivalence?[1]

The Church Perspective

The charges against parachurch organizations range from theological to material. Some critics simply argue that parachurch organizations are unnecessary and redundant for fulfilling the purpose of Christianity:

> If the parachurch is so essential and necessary to Christ's church, where was it in the 2nd century? 12th century? 16th century? Why in the 21st century (and why in North America especially?!) can't the church function without professional help from "outside"? Does the same truth the church has proclaimed for 1900+ years all of a sudden become more believable or "doable" when Promise Keepers shares it? Or is the issue the church faces one of unbelief in the pulpit and pew? There is no need for the church to look to contemporary trends or the latest innovative brainstorming technique to fulfill its God ordained mandate.[2]

This relates to doubts that some express concerning the religious authenticity or genuineness of those who participate in parachurch organizations. The flashiness of many parachurch organizations and their specialized offerings makes some question whether the motivation for individuals to participate is "emotional, secular, spiritual, or some uneasy, and perhaps unstable, combination of all three."[3]

Others say that organizations working outside of traditional church structures have no biblical legitimacy. The argument is that while the activities of parachurch organizations may be worthy pursuits, those pursuits should be initiated and overseen by local churches. As the focal point of Christianity, all work of the "Church" should radiate from congregations given their "theological priority."[4] Denominational organizations, being composed of and at least indirectly accountable to churches, work within this system. Parachurch organizations, however, are said to ignore this structure. While, in theory, they work in collaboration and within church structures, in reality, they work outside of those structures.[5] In the words of one writer:

> The major criticism, and one that is easiest to make stick, is that they
> lack accountability to anyone but themselves. Parachurch groups are
> religion gone free enterprise.[6]

This has led some to argue that it should be "the local church commissioning those who serve in the parachurch."[7]

But let us think about these statements for a minute. Since when has religion *not* been defined by free enterprise, especially in the United States where the history books are littered with schisms, new religious groups, and charismatic leaders forging their own path? A careful listener will quickly realize that these complaints are not simply about scriptural interpretation. At their heart, these theological arguments are ultimately about power. What we must recognize is that innovation and free enterprise tend to challenge the status quo. Local churches and their larger denominational networks hold large amounts of resources, and they naturally do not want to give those resources up. The problem is not with free enterprise but with enterprise that challenges the territory of the current powers. It is a little like a corporation praising the virtues of an unregulated market system until they become the dominant player in the market. Then, all of a sudden, they praise the virtues of laws protecting their patents and copyrights and other mechanisms limiting the ability of competitors to challenge it.[8]

A similar turf issue stems from the nondenominational identity of most parachurch organizations. Individuals and churches coming from a denominational affiliation accuse parachurch organizations of watering down or ignoring historical, theological, and cultural differences they view as crucial. For instance, the United Methodist General Board of Discipleship issued a warning in 1995 that Promise Keepers, a major men's parachurch organization, was "not in keeping with United Methodist theology and practice."[9] This is actually a long-standing point of tension between traditional church structures and the parachurch. When publishing and mission societies were created in the early 19th century, religious authorities complained that these "clergy independent of the churches" were

TABLE 3.1. Stated Affiliations of the Largest National or Internationally Focused Christian Nonprofits ($N = 1{,}941$).

Affiliation	Organizations	%
No stated affiliation	1,795	92.5
Adventist	2	0.1
Baptist	27	1.4
Catholic	79	4.1
Episcopal	3	0.2
Lutheran	12	0.6
Methodist	5	0.3
Orthodox	3	0.2
Presbyterian	7	0.4
Other	8	0.4

ignoring the "ecclesiastical order." The sociologist Michael Young notes how even in their earliest days during the start of the 19th century, many of the religious publishing and mission societies were very careful not to "excite sectarian differences," taking steps such as excluding prayers from meetings. Many of the interdenominational national religious societies formed in the 19th century, such as the American Sunday School Union, would slowly see their support fray because participants felt denominational differences were being ignored.[10]

From a February 21, 2006, posting on the "Out of Ur" blog of *Leadership Journal*, a publication of *Christianity Today*.

Perhaps you have had this conversation before with someone in your church. I had one recently.

FRIEND   I'm thinking about starting a parachurch ministry.

ME   Oh yeah, what sort of ministry?

FRIEND   Well, from my perspective the local church isn't doing its job with [fill in the blank].

ME   Well how do you propose we fix that?

FRIEND   I'm going to start a paraministry that focuses on [fill in the blank].

ME   How is that going to help the local church with its problem?

FRIEND   It's going to address [fill in the blank] so the local church doesn't have to.

ME   That doesn't really sound like you are helping the local church at all.

We cannot ignore the material issues surrounding the relationship between church and parachurch. Despite all the discussion of biblical legitimacy and denominational integrity, the actual conflict tends to "lie largely in non-theological, 'practical' confrontations." This includes competition for volunteers and leadership talent, but in particular, it refers to competition for money. While "no one ever complains that the parachurch is taking up prayer time that ought to be devoted to the church," finances are often a point of contention. Parachurch organizations are accused of using "local congregations as easy avenues to raise funds without regard to the effect on the local congregation."[11]

It is fairly safe to assume that parachurch organizations, congregations, and denominations all draw support from a similar population of individuals and organizations. Granted, there is not a perfect overlap as individuals may patronize a parachurch organization without ever participating in a congregation. Nevertheless, growth in the parachurch sector means one of two things for the total available pool of money and labor to churches and denominations. It is possible that there has been an overall increase due to higher levels of giving and participation on the part of religious consumers or due to an increase in the number of religious consumers. That is, there are more Christians and/or more money going to Christian causes. This would allow parachurch organizations to increase in number while church and denominational organizations see their resources hold constant or grow. Maybe the proverbial pie has just gotten larger thereby allowing everyone to have their fair share.

If there has not been an overall increase in the pool of money and customers, and the parachurch sector draws significantly from the same pool as churches and denominations, then the situation represents a zero-sum game in which one actor's gain is another's loss. Unless the pie is getting bigger, more slices means smaller slices. Indeed, as we saw in the previous chapter, there is evidence that individuals and churches have shifted some of their contributions from churches and denominations to the parachurch sector. Even if the total amount of resources is increasing, the resources going to the parachurch sector might have gone to churches and denominations if the parachurch sector did not exist. In other words, even though their slice did not change, they know that they could have had a bigger one if they had not been forced to share. So regardless of how much parachurch organizations actually take away from the resources of churches and denominations, their very existence is enough to raise concerns that resources are being lost to them.

The Parachurch Perspective

The tension between traditional church structures and parachurch organizations is reciprocal. From the perspective of parachurch leaders, it is exactly these theological and administrative turf wars that prevent churches and denominations from being able to engage the world effectively.[12] As one executive with a Christian nonprofit prison ministry summarized the situation, "if anyone is unable to work with us then it is due to *their* issues and inability to overcome doctrinal divides, not ours."[13]

Another observer stated this point in the following way:

[Parachurch organizations] are not doing or saying anything the churches should not have been saying or doing all along. So long as the churches live in a subliminal, subnormal level, then there are going to be parachurches that arise . . . and I say "God bless them."[14]

Similarly, the theologian Edmund Clowney argues that "parachurch groups have often accomplished what the Lord designed the church to do" and that "in an undivided church," such organizations would not be seen as unusual. "That such ministries may be regarded as irregular in denominational polity may reveal more about sectarian assumptions in the polity than about violations of New Testament order."[15] A leader with Promise Keepers argued, in reference to denominational boundaries, that "no one is shooting over the walls at the real enemy. Rather, everyone is shooting at each other."[16] These are not new observations. The entry for "Missions" in the 1904 *A Protestant Dictionary* described the motivation for nondenominational missionary organizations as a product of denominations' weaknesses:

Where a Church is in a sluggish state spiritually, the few individuals who are in earnest find the task a hard one to rouse it to action. It is also to be borne in mind that official bodies are inevitably slow in their movements, and often slow also by reason of internal differences.[17]

Christian nonprofits and the parachurch sector have created an organizational structure uniting individuals and churches across denominational lines and in doing so have accomplished many of the philosophical goals of the 20th-century ecumenical movement through an entirely different strategy. While that movement sought an elimination of denominational boundaries through the merging of denominational institutions, the parachurch sector has made those boundaries less relevant by creating an alternative that bypasses those institutions altogether. They market their products and services directly to churches and individuals across denominational lines and to the unaffiliated population.[18]

There are a number of ironies to be found within this story. The institutional ecumenical movement was primarily driven by more liberal or modernist leaders and denominations. On the contrary, the parachurch movement and its grassroots ecumenism is driven by more conservative or evangelical leaders and organizations.

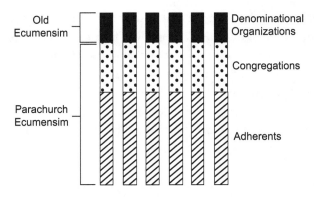

FIGURE 3.1. Old Ecumenism versus Parachurch Ecumenism.

Many of these people may be coming out of liberal mainline denominations, but these individuals are looking to the parachurch sector as a "second home" that provides religious elements absent in their churches and denominations.[19] Indeed, the fact that people turn to an intentionally nondenominational organization for a more distinctive religious product provides its own sense of irony.

Given the overall evangelical nature of the parachurch sector, we must be careful not to take the grassroots ecumenism analogy too far. In interviews with parachurch organizations, which he calls "special purpose groups," Robert Wuthnow found that despite their transdenominational base, they still are quite theologically exclusive and resistant to language and actions that would compromise their religious worldview.[20] Even parachurch organizations that are theologically liberal tend to exist exactly for the advancement of that position, so true cooperation across denominational *and* theological lines could undercut their very purpose for existence. This ecumenism is more of a conscious business decision, as it avoids denominational turf wars and provides a much larger base from which to draw support, than a philosophical one concerning cooperation and harmony.

A Sociological Perspective

The issues described above are well known among church and parachurch leaders. However, missing from this dialogue has been a sociological analysis of these issues and the church-parachurch relationship underlying them. This is unfortunate for both sociologists and those on the front line of these debates. Underlying the squabbles of the church-parachurch relationship are significant questions about the role of religion in society and how that role is organized. To think about this, we must take a few steps back to think about the nature of religion itself.

Academics have spent a great deal of time trying to define religion. If you look in most sociology textbooks, you will find two schools of thought.[21] Functionalist definitions take the position that religion is anything that fulfills a particular function in society. For instance, a classic argument in the functionalist vein is that religion is anything that binds people together. Substantive definitions, on the other hand, state that religion is defined by some particular feature, such as a belief in some supernatural being. It is a favorite pastime of religious studies students to debate the weaknesses of both positions (e.g., "Can sports be a religion? It binds people together, but it does not have supernatural content.").

To be honest, these debates and even their underlying definitions tend to be a little overly intellectualized. While academics are debating what is and is not religion, individuals and organizations are busy living and acting in the name of their religion. It is a little like a Keystone Cops routine where the police debate what should or should not be a crime while they are watching someone get mugged or as they arrest the victim.

When you move beyond trying to say what is or is not religion and simply look at the wide range of things done in the name of religion, you will begin to see two broad categories of behavior.[22] The first, and arguably most accepted as "purely" religious, is *worship*. This includes all the behaviors an individual does to contemplate and experience their faith internally. These behaviors can be done privately or publicly, alone or with other believers. Prayer, religious services, scriptural study, private devotionals, and similar behaviors all fall under this category.

The second category of religious behavior can be generally labeled *outreach*. In the words of the sociologist Mayer Zald, all religious groups hold "theological and ideological beliefs about the relation of individuals and groups to each other, to society, and to the good and just life."[23] Unless those beliefs call for a complete retreat from the world, the believer is usually inspired and compelled to try and shape the world into the vision described by their beliefs. This is the role of outreach, which consists of four themes or goals: conversion, community, communication, and charity.[24]

As one might expect, activities aimed at *conversion* attempt to increase the number of believers to a particular belief. This can mean winning nonbelievers or members of other groups. *Community* outreach efforts are those activities meant to provide nonworship opportunities for fellowship. Women's and men's groups, youth ministries, and other similar activities are all examples of outreach efforts for building community. In this sense, community outreach is more internally focused than conversion outreach. *Communication* outreach, however, can be both internally and externally aimed. It can mean providing publications or other media for adherents, or it can mean advocating for sociopolitical issues informed by the beliefs of the group. Finally, outreach efforts with the goal of *charity* are those activities where a religious individual or group is inspired to change the world in a more material form. Indeed, most if not all faiths call for believers to perform charitable acts, such as giving to the poor both locally and afar.

As already hinted at, these four types of religious outreach are not exclusive of each other by any means. They overlap in various ways, and each has their own subcategories. Consider missionary work. On the one hand, most missionary projects involve a form of charity, such as building schools or digging wells. But most of these projects also contain some hope for conversion. Similarly, communication could mean publishing resources aimed at community building, but it could also mean publishing religious tracts and other material aimed at conversion, which could be used during charitable activities. We will explore the various activities of Christian nonprofits and how they map onto these four goals in a later chapter.

It is also important to note that while comprising a different set of religious behaviors, outreach is not entirely disconnected from worship. Indeed, outreach would have no impetus without worship. Worship serves as the energy that pushes outreach in these four directions. As the manifestation of faith, worship is the core of religious behavior. Outreach also serves as a support role for worship. For example, conversion efforts bring in new members to worship, and communication efforts help fulfill some of the administrative needs of worship.

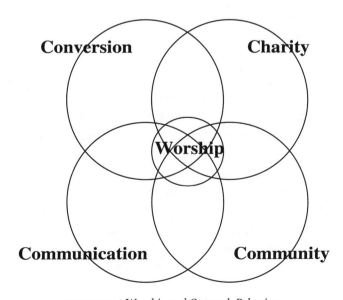

FIGURE 3.2. Worship and Outreach Behaviors.

Organizing Religion

The four goals of religious outreach are not simply philosophical or theological categories. They are categories of human activity done in the effort to accomplish those goals. Whenever a human activity reaches a certain level of complexity, such as the coordination of a few people, organizations will be created to facilitate and support those activities. Religious behavior is no different.[25] Since worship and outreach constitute two forms of religious behavior, it is not surprising that each has developed its own corresponding organizational forms. Others have recognized such a dichotomy in religious organization.

The theologian Ralph Winter argues that the "church" has always consisted of a local church arm and a missionary or parachurch arm. He calls the former the "modality" and the latter the "sodality." In the language being used here, we can think of the modality as the worship component of Christianity while the sodality is the outreach component. This dichotomy is traced back to the earliest days of Christianity. Paul, for instance, is pointed to as the father of independent mission agencies. He founded and "strengthened" several congregations during his travels, providing the biblical basis from which many contemporary church planting agencies cite in their mission statements.[26]

> Paul was "sent off" not "sent out" by the Antioch congregation. He may
> have reported back to it but did not take orders from it. His mission band
> (sodality) had all the autonomy and authority of a local congregation.

Organizing Outreach

When it comes to worship, the overwhelmingly dominant organizational form is the local congregation.[27] Much like worship is the behavioral anchor and driving force of outreach, the local congregation lies at the center of religious organization. It probably should not be surprising that the one strategy for organizing outreach is to simply use the local congregation. Since it is the primary unit of religious behavior and the impetus for religious outreach, it is natural that the local congregation is the place people turn to first for outreach activities. Even today, most congregations have some outreach component . . . vacation Bible schools, community sports leagues, supporting a community shelter, and so forth. These tend to be more localized in scope, but they are still driven by the same four goals of conversion, community, communication, and charity.

The characteristics of local congregations that make them ideal organizational structures for worship often make them less than ideal for outreach. In short, they are small and have limited resources. For worship, this smallness tends to help people know each other and build a supportive community. Even so-called mega-churches attempt to create this same feeling through small groups or cells.[28] However, the relative smallness of a local congregation limits how much it can do in terms of outreach. It is difficult to mount world-changing operations with 75 people who are typically all volunteers and the budget that goes along with such a small workforce. As a result, outreach efforts have often produced other organizations that go beyond the congregation.

Pooling Resources

The limitations of most local congregations when it comes to outreach have led people to devise other outreach strategies. The most common strategy, outside of creating larger congregations, is for groups of people and their congregations to pool resources together.[29] This larger resource base provides the opportunity to tackle goals that would normally be out of reach for a single congregation.

Identity versus Activity

History has provided examples of two ways to pool resources for the purpose of religious outreach. The first method is for people and congregations with similar theological, historical, or cultural ties to join together in outreach. This could be called an identity pool. Identity pools are essentially what we call denominations. Denominations are umbrella organizations for groups of people and congregations with a similar theological, historical, or cultural identity. Those people and congregations provide support for the denomination, often called benevolences, which are utilized at least in part for large-scale religious outreach.

The alternative to an identity-based pooling of resources is an activity- or interest-based pool. This is where individuals and congregations with a particular interest, say Bible publishing and distribution, pool their resources regardless of their particular theological or cultural background. For the most part, this is and always has been the outreach strategy of the parachurch sector, both in its 19th-century religious society and contemporary Christian nonprofit incarnations. Indeed, complaints about the parachurch sector ignoring the "ecclesiastical order" are entirely true and a result of this activity-based strategy of pooling of resources. The parachurch sector has always been dominated by a nondenominational streak, and you can see this in the relative lack of stated theological or denominational affiliations within the Christian nonprofit population.

Pros and Cons

There are advantages and disadvantages to either pooling strategy. When it is based on a very strong in-group/out-group mentality, the identity-based pool can command high levels of loyalty and commitment from individuals and congregations. A strong identity leads people to fiercely stick to in-group activities and organizations and avoid anything else outside of the group since it would threaten their identity and possibly even their membership in the group. Indeed, if a religious group believes that *only* their type of outreach is legitimate, then they will likely create identity-based resource pools, and the organizations resulting from those pools will also be limited to that particular identity when it comes to who can participate and in some cases who can be served in the outreach.

There are downsides to identity-based outreach, however. The most obvious issue is that the size of the outreach effort will partially be a factor of the group's size.[30] If your religious group only has 1,000 people and your entire outreach effort is strictly based on those individual's resources, then you are going to be limited relative to an organization cutting across identity groups (assuming, of course, the activity would be attractive to multiple groups).

The other downside to identity-based organizations is that they have the worst combination of service and customer range. Specifically, they are generalists when it comes to activities but specialists when it comes to audience. What this means is that outreach organized around identity groups attempts to do everything for a small segment of the total population. It would be like saying you are going to run a restaurant that serves every possible type of cuisine, but you are only going to serve customers between the ages of 35 and 45 years. Not only are you going to have huge overhead costs since you have to maintain supplies for a wide range of food, but you will have a very limited customer base as well. High costs and low sales rarely lead to an effective business model. This is not to mention the likelihood that such a wide-ranging menu will produce lower quality food across the board than in an organization that focuses on perfecting one type of cuisine.[31]

As identity-based organizations, denominations essentially have such a model. They try to provide a wide range of outreach services, such as publishing, education, and relief and development, while at the same time relying on a specific support and customer base (i.e., the individual and congregational members of the denomination). Denominations are not specialists in any particular outreach area, but they have their hand in all of them. What unites them is not any particular activity but a shared identity.

The activity- or interest-based pooling of resources has its own advantages and disadvantages, many of which have already been mentioned. First, organizations

TABLE 3.2. Organizational Characteristics of Church and Parachurch Organizations.

	Denominations and Congregations	Parachurch Organizations
Resource pool	Identity based	Activity based
Audience	Specialized	Generalized
Activities	Generalized	Specialized

that focus only on one activity can often become more specialized and effective at that activity than those trying to cover many activities. They spend more time and resources focusing on one specific issue, so they are more likely to come up with innovative ideas. This applies to both the secular and the religious world. New ideas in technology often come from small companies focusing on one or two projects. Large multifaceted companies are often simply maintaining their current activities and have little time for developing new ones. The same is true with religious groups. Small sects are often the source of innovation in the religious market, not large and established denominations.[32]

Specializing around one activity can be risky, though. Think of an organization's activities as its stock portfolio. If you only hold stock in one company, and that company goes bankrupt, you are in serious trouble. If you have a diversified portfolio, then you can deal with sudden shifts in demand and market fads. The same risk applies to many parachurch ministries. If tract publishing becomes seen as an obsolete form of religious outreach, a Christian nonprofit devoted to tract publishing will need to quickly reevaluate its goals or become obsolete itself. Even if the activity is still viable, a downturn in the economy can threaten specialists more than generalists.[33] Recessions often cause donors to lower contributions and choose their benefactors more carefully. If they rank the specialist's activity as a lower priority, then this could be a severe blow. Generalists, though, have multiple offerings so it is likely that at least one of them will still take in some money during hard times.

The Primacy of Identity

So how does a religious group, or any social group for that matter, go about deciding whether to organize itself by identity or activity? There are few real sociological laws, at least of the same certainty as those in the natural sciences. However, one of the closest things we have to a sociological law is that of social homophily. This is a technical term for the common saying that "birds of a feather flock together." People like to associate with those who look, act, and believe like they do.[34] Even if they are really passionate about a particular activity, they tend to find similar people to do that activity with.[35] So, in short, people tend to favor identity-based organizations.

Given the strength of identity-based groups in the rest of society, it should not be surprising that the natural tendency for religious groups is to organize their outreach efforts based on identity first. After all, if the group did not view their identity as the most important factor in whom they do outreach with and how they do it, then why would the group exist in the first place? The more a group views itself as distinctive from other religious groups, the more likely they are going to want to limit cross-group activities. The main motivation for religious groups to come together for an activity is for the activity of coming together (i.e., ecumenical events, councils of churches). Otherwise, they tend to stay within their religious identity groups. When you look at the four goals or motivations in religious outreach, most of them have some role in identity. You usually want to convert people to *your* particular brand of faith. You want to build a community with *your* fellow believers. Charity-focused outreach is probably best suited to activity-based outreach as opposed to identity-based efforts.

Whether a group allows flexibility for *groups of members* to organize their own activity-based outreach within the boundaries of the identity group is a secondary issue and a product of how centralized or bureaucratic the group is. For instance, the Latter-day Saints (Mormons) have produced centralized outreach structures and limit how much independence is given to members to create or organize their own. On the contrary, the Catholic Church allows relatively independent activity-based outreach through religious orders and other internal mechanisms, but these activities are held together under the larger identity of Catholicism. The group is flexible enough to allow independent activity-based outreach, but the group identity is still the primary basis for those activities.[36]

The Protestant Exception

The existence of thousands upon thousands of activity-based parachurch organizations is evidence enough that some groups are not as committed to identity-based outreach as are others, and this is especially the case with Protestants. Protestants have never been completely married to making group identity the primary basis of their outreach organizations. As a result, Protestants have formed the basis of the parachurch sector throughout history. Even today, Catholics represent about one-quarter of the population but only 4% of the largest Christian nonprofit organizations.

Some have pointed to theological aspects of Protestantism as the source of this ambivalence. Telford Work states that the Reformation was rooted in a suspicion of church structures and an emphasis on personal salvation.

> Ecclesiology takes a back seat to soteriology, and the Church becomes merely an external instrument—perhaps even a dispensable instrument—of salvation. The earthly Church is to salvation as wineskin is to wine; its job is to dispense grace to needy souls and stay out of grace's way.

This produced an "action-oriented" view that sees churches as stagnant and ineffective, which has led Protestants to find activity-based outlets for outreach instead of sticking to their particular congregation or group of congregations. Ralph Winter calls this "the other Protestant schism."[37]

A related issue is the complicated nature of Protestantism as a religious category. On some level, Protestants could be considered to be a group, but there are obviously also many different groups (i.e., denominations). On the one hand, independent denominations want to maintain that independence and identity when it comes to their outreach efforts. On the other hand, the boundaries between many Protestant denominations are fuzzy at best. Many share strong theological and historical ties, so it is tempting to conduct outreach on a shared "Protestant" basis and focus on specific activities instead of identities. As the famous itinerant minister George Whitefield once put it, "Don't tell me you are a Baptist, an Independent, a Presbyterian, a Dissenter . . . tell me you are a Christian, that is all I want."[38] In short, Protestants are not quite committed to religious outreach based strictly on denominational identities since they share much in common across those identities, but they are also not entirely committed to religious outreach focused on pan-Protestant activities.

Overlapping Niches

When both identity- and activity-based outreach are being conducted in the same group, as is often the case with Protestants, conflicts such as those detailed earlier are bound to occur. Let us pretend you could get all the Protestants interested in religious outreach together in a room. You then want to sort them into groups that will focus on religious outreach. A purely identity-based sorting system would sort them all by their particular identity group or denomination (e.g., the United Methodist outreach group). A purely activity-based system would sort them by the issue they wanted to support (e.g., the church planting group). If you try to use both systems, though, it will become unclear where to put people. Do you put the United Methodist member interested in church planting in the "United Methodist" group or the "church planting" group? Naturally, each of these groups will want the person in their group. Even if the person can participate in both, his or her time and resources are going to be split between the two.

Sociologists refer to such a situation as niche overlap.[39] Niche overlap can occur with all types of religious and secular organizations. The more similar the organizations' activities, members, or customers, the more sizable the overlap will be. In this case, the niche or customer pool for an identity-based outreach organization overlaps with the market for an activity-based organization if it is offering the same activities as the latter (or if the identity-based organization is appealing to the same people who are interested in the activity-based organization). Parachurch organizations overlap with each other as well, as do denominations. Two men's ministries will be competing for members just like they might be competing with a denomination's men's ministry.

Visualizing how the niches of parachurch organizations map onto those of churches and denominations can help summarize the relationship. This is illustrated in figure 3-3. The niches of denominations are designated by the horizontal box with the thick border. These generalist organizations encompass a wide range of activities but surround one particular identity group. The niches of parachurch organizations are shown with the vertical boxes with the thinner line. Given the specialist nature of these organizations, their niches only encompass one or possibly two of the activities but cut across different groups.[40] The people and congregations contained within these imaginary boxes are going to be pulled in numerous different directions as different outreach organizations vie for their support.

A similar figure could be created illustrating the overlap between local congregations and parachurch organizations. However, because they provide different activities and have a different geographic scope, the niche overlap experienced by congregations is going to be different from that experienced by denominational agencies. Due to their own centralized and often international nature, denominational agencies are going to be more concerned about competition from similarly structured parachurch organizations, such as those engaged in relief and development, missionary work, and publishing agencies. While they may feel some of the effects of niche overlap with those centralized parachurch organizations, local churches are going to feel the overlap more with organizations having a local component, such as youth ministries.[41] They will be especially hostile toward organizations that come close to overlapping their core purpose of worship. This is an issue that will be raised again in this and later chapters.

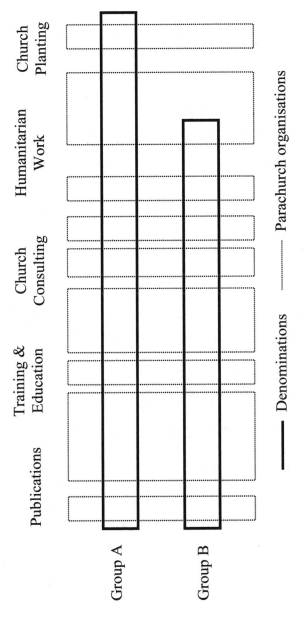

FIGURE 3.3. Denominational and Parachurch Niches.

From Jonathan McKee, "When 'Us vs. Them' Trumps Kingdom Mentality."[42]

When the para-church enters the picture, it seems as if churches often wonder:

1. Are they going to be in competition with us?
2. Are they coming because they think we can't do the job right?
3. Are they just going to take away from our program by drawing resources, people and funds toward their organization instead?

If you look at those questions they resemble the questions that churches often raise if another church is built in the same community. When a new church starts in an existing community with existing churches, some people switch to that new church. That new church, with its own gifting and its own style, will often meet a need in the community that is unique and maybe even void in the other churches. This can stir up bitterness and jealousy. I've heard comments from senior pastors like, *"The only reason that church is growing is because they've stolen from every other church in the area."*

Cooperation?

The issue of niche overlap raises two possible questions depending on one's demeanor toward the organization who overlaps your niche. First, "how do we better cooperate with those organizations that we currently share a niche with?" One answer to this question is to better coordinate activities so niche overlap is reduced and instead each niche is filled by only one organization. For instance, if there are activities or niches not covered by churches and denominations, then Christian nonprofits and other parachurch organizations can fill this space as a cooperative partner. Looking back at figure 3-3, we see that Denomination B does not actively engage in church planting. A specialized parachurch organization has filled this gap in the market. Because it is not overlapping the activities of the denomination, there could be a noncompetitive partnership between the two organizations. This gap-filling function is what some argue parachurch organizations should limit themselves to doing. As a former chairman of Christian Camping International put it:

If the parachurch is not the church but exists in behalf of the church, it should only exist so long as it is fulfilling [a] function . . . that the church is unable or unwilling to undertake.[43]

The absence of niche overlap is no guarantee of cooperation. Other conflicts could occur, such as arguments about theology or the authority of the parachurch organization versus the church or denomination. However, the likelihood of cooperation is higher without niche overlap than with it.

We know just from informal observations that, at the congregational level at least, there is a sizable amount of cooperative interaction with the parachurch sector. It is difficult to quantify because social science surveys often do not attempt to measure such exchanges. The National Congregations Study, a representative survey of congregations in the United States conducted in 1998, asked congregations whether they had "made use of any types of services offered by a denomination, another religious organization, or an outside consultant of any sort." Congregations were then asked to specify the source of this service or consultation.

Along with denominational offices, other congregations, and secular organizations, congregations were able to identify an "other religious firm, organization, or sole practitioner" as the provider of these services or consultations. We could use this response as representing parachurch suppliers. If we did, we would find that among all congregations, about 6% said that they had utilized a parachurch service or consultant. However, almost 70% of the congregations responded that they did not use any outside service at all, so this might be a little deceptive. If we look only among those who did use at least one outside service, almost one-fifth said that they had used at least one parachurch supplier. Because the question implied fairly formal services or consultations, it likely underestimates the overall use of external services and the use of parachurch suppliers, but it at least provides some way of assessing congregation-parachurch interactions.[44]

Using this same measure, we can also examine how use of parachurch suppliers varies by the denominational tradition of the congregation. If we simply look at the percentage of all congregations using a parachurch supplier, Presbyterian, Pentecostal, Baptist, and Lutheran congregations show the highest rates of parachurch interactions, while Catholic, Episcopal, and "other moderate or liberal" congregations show the lowest. However, the likelihood of using any external service varies across these traditions. For instance, only 21% of Pentecostal congregations reported using an outside supplier of any type compared to 46% of Lutheran congregations.

TABLE 3.3. Use of Parachurch Suppliers for Congregational Services or Consultations.

	Among All Christian Congregations ($N = 1,163$)	Among Christian Congregations Utilizing External Services/ Consultants ($N = 354$)
Use of parachurch suppliers for congregational services/ consultations (%)	6	21

Source: National Congregations Study (1998); parachurch suppliers defined as "other religious firms, organizations or sole practitioners" excluding denominational offices and other congregations.

TABLE 3.4. Use of Parachurch Suppliers for Congregational Services or Consultations by Denominational Tradition.

	Pentecostal	Nonspecific Christian	Baptist	Presbyterian or Reformed	Episcopal	Lutheran	Methodist	Other Conservative, Evangelical, Sectarian Protestant	Catholic	Other Moderate, Liberal Protestant
Percent using any external services/consultants	21	14	31	45	36	46	44	11	32	43
Percent using parachurch services/consultants	8	4	9	11	8	8	6	2	3	3
Percent using external services using parachurch services	36	29	28	23	20	18	14	13	8	7

Source: National Congregations Study (1998); parachurch suppliers are defined as "other religious firms, organizations or sole practitioners" excluding denominational offices and other congregations.

If we take this into account, then Pentecostal, Baptist, and congregations with no specific tradition become the traditions most likely to utilize parachurch suppliers.

Nancy Ammerman conducted a more recent examination of church-parachurch cooperation when it comes to acquiring educational publications for children, youth, and adults. Not surprisingly, she found that nondenominational congregations were the most likely to rely entirely on resources coming from outside denominational sources. Catholics were the least likely to look beyond denominational boundaries. Mainline congregations were equally or more likely to use resources from outside their denomination as evangelical congregations, but this did not always mean that they were going to the parachurch sector, at least as typically conceived. Instead, they were using scouting, community sports, and other resources that are not explicitly or exclusively part of the Christian parachurch sector. Evangelical congregations, on the other hand, were most likely to acquire resources from national parachurch organizations like Young Life and Child Evangelism Fellowship. They were also much more likely to give money to parachurch mission agencies.

However, among Protestants, Ammerman found that factors other than theological tradition may have more to do with the willingness of a congregation to cooperate with the parachurch sector. Urban and suburban churches were more likely than rural churches to utilize the parachurch sector, as were larger churches. Newer congregations and those that contain large numbers of individuals that are not lifelong members of the denomination (i.e., "switchers") were the most likely to go outside of denominational boundaries to acquire resources. In other words, in congregations where organizational and individual ties between church and denomination are weakest is where the parachurch is most likely to find a role.[45]

Or Competition?

Getting all congregations, denominations, and parachurch organizations to perfectly coordinate their activities is highly unlikely. So the next question one might ask is, "how do I effectively compete with those other organizations that I currently share a niche with?" This is particularly a concern for congregations and denominations as many seem to feel like they are currently on the losing side of this competition.

Emphasizing Identity

Niche overlap can be made irrelevant if one organization can convince potential supporters (i.e., donors, volunteers, members, customers) to ignore all other options. For corporations and many other organizations, this is difficult to do. Although many businesses will tout the advantages of their product over their competitors, few can legitimately tell customers that they simply cannot patronize those competitors. Religious organizations, however, have a special advantage. The nature of religious beliefs can provide or withhold legitimacy from outsiders. If a church or denomination is able to define outside organizations as theologically illegitimate, then an overlap in activities becomes less of an issue. In other words, a religious group is an identity group, so emphasizing that identity can help fight off organizations outside of that identity.

We have already seen examples of such efforts. Arguments about parachurch organizations being unbiblical or contrary to a denomination's tradition are all attempts to alleviate the effects of niche overlap by reemphasizing group identity as the primary basis of outreach.[46] The success of such a strategy will differ by the group and activity in question. Those that are more theologically or culturally unique will be more able to make such claims. Ammerman found that Catholics and highly sectarian groups (e.g., Jehovah's Witnesses) seem more successful in making such claims as they are least likely to go outside of denominational structures for educational resources.[47] There are some activities that even a theologically or culturally exclusive church or denomination cannot claim as unique. For instance, members may accept that the denomination offers unique religious education products, but they may not believe that there is something inherently unique about the denomination's programs for humanitarian relief. In cases where a group has no foundation for making such a claim or where members do not accept the claim, denominations will likely lose some of their resources to Christian nonprofits and other parachurch specialists.

Utilizing Relationships

Another competitive advantage that churches, and denominations through their churches, have over many parachurch organizations is their personal connections with individuals. The relationship between an individual and their church is often more intimate than the individual's relationship with a national nonprofit, such as a missionary support or humanitarian agency. Ministers and other church members know you. They were there to celebrate weddings and births and mourn deaths. You have formed friendships with other members, and you see each other in the neighborhood, at school, and while shopping. These connections alone provide churches a foundation for support that many large national parachurch organizations cannot rely on since their connection to their contributors is often more utilitarian and contractual than personal and emotional. Therefore, when it comes to worship and fellowship, where community and intimacy are major selling points, churches have a distinct advantage over large parachurch organizations.

It is for this reason that churches are particularly threatened by those parachurch organizations that build local support structures, like Campus Crusade for Christ or Young Life, which are composed of networks of many local cells or groups.[48] While parachurch missionary, publishing, and humanitarian organizations might be the bane of denominational agencies, these national-local hybrid fellowship organizations are the major thorn in the side of churches. Their local component provides them the opportunity to form the same intimate social ties on which churches thrive. They begin to provide the same social and psychological benefits that make churches more appealing when it comes to activities like worship and fellowship.

The parachurch organization would say that, like ivy, they are growing around local churches and making them stronger and more beautiful. But many churches might instead see them as slowly destroying the building's walls. If these parachurch organizations are able to build the same social capital within their local groups, then this would eliminate one of the central bases of support for the local church and indirectly for the denomination. If a person begins to feel more socially connected with his parachurch men's group, then he might just decide that he will stop going to the church.

The Parachurch Strategy

So far we have just explored the potential strategies of churches and denominations in competing with the parachurch sector, but the latter has its own cards to play. Indeed, beyond appeals to theology and local relationships, churches and denominations are at somewhat of a disadvantage when it comes to competing with nonprofits and other parachurch organizations. Some of this is due to their generalist strategy when it comes to activities, and some of it is due to how they are operated and organized. When an organization is focused on one specific goal, evaluating and marketing becomes easier. If the goal is publishing bibles, then the organization can present clear quantitative data on its impact and effectiveness. Such statistics are attractive to donors and even participants because they provide a manifest, even if not accurate, feeling of success. Comparatively, what can a church or denomination provide in the way of data? Should they rely on growth of members? Which of their many ministries should they measure? Churches and even denominations are not set up to provide the same quantitative evaluations because their main goals are much less tangible.

This hints at the subtle crux of the problem for churches and denominations when it comes to competing with parachurch organizations. Churches and many denominations are not built around the same highly rationalized business model that most parachurch organizations utilize.

> . . . the parachurch agency may be run like a business . . . People who don't do the job can be dismissed. Decisions can be quickly made. Their promotions are slick and results obvious. Pragmatic people like this.[49]

Indeed, few churches would want this "McDonaldized" model.[50] But the organic nature of churches also handicaps them. Unlike parachurch organizations, churches cannot simply fire members or recruit highly trained professional managers. They must work with what they have to accomplish what they can. The purely voluntary nature of a church, with all of its ensuing struggles, compromises, and fellowship, is what many would argue is the beauty of churches. An Amish barn raising would be less inspiring if it was done by subcontractors. Nonetheless, when it comes to many of the overlapping activities, the bureaucratic model allows parachurch organizations to produce more goods and services faster, more efficiently, and more predictably.

Furthermore, organizations specializing in an activity often make more attractive options for donors than generalists because they appear to provide more value for the money. Let us assume that an individual views financial support of foreign missionaries as the best outlet for their religious philanthropy. They know that their church and/or denomination has a program that funnels money to missionaries, but they also know that these organizations fund many other programs. If this individual gives $100 to these generalists, they cannot be sure of how much, if any, of this will go directly to the program they are most interested in supporting. Some of it may go to the building fund, staff salaries, publishing, and so on. The donor lacks a sense of direct connection to the intended outcome of his or her donation.[51] A specialist, on the other hand, provides a way for the donor to feel that they are getting the maximum amount of bang for their buck when it comes to their preferred form of philanthropy. If you like Bible translation, there is a nonprofit just for that. If you like religious radio, there is a nonprofit for that. If you like church planting, there is a nonprofit devoted just to that activity. Instead of a few dollars making it to this specific program in a generalist, a specialist allows almost all of your money to go toward that activity.

Church-Parachurch Fluidity

Before moving on, it is worth pointing out another feature of the church-parachurch relationship. In the previous chapter, we saw historical exchanges that have been

made between church and parachurch organizations. This chapter saw the competitive dynamics that can occur between the two populations due to their overlapping niches. Both these issues assumed or implied that church and parachurch are
distinct and static categories. This is not necessarily the case. What happens if
church becomes parachurch or parachurch becomes church?

History provides a number of examples of just how porous the boundary
between church and parachurch can be. For instance, most people associate Sunday
school with traditional churches. This is, after all, where Sunday schools almost
always take place today. However, Sunday schools began in the late 18th century,
first in England and soon after in the United States, as charity schools that were
independent of congregations. In fact, many churches "frowned" upon the Sunday
school movement.[52] They were usually founded and supported by individuals and
voluntary religious societies. Unlike today, they were not targeted toward members
of congregations but were meant to educate poor children in both secular and religious matters. The schools were held on Sundays because it was the only day the
people the schools were targeted toward had off from work. During the 1830s,
Sunday schools became increasingly limited to religious instruction and targeted
toward members of individual congregations. This corresponded to the schools
being incorporated into local congregations and becoming closer to their present
form.[53] Over time, they became organized around identity instead of activity.

There are other similar examples of the "parachurch" becoming the "church."
The denomination we know today as the Christian and Missionary Alliance began
as a much less structured missionary movement. Its founder, Dr. Albert Simpson,
"was reluctant to establish churches, preferring to call together Christians with a
vision to evangelize the world but who remained in their local churches."[54] Eventually, though, these missionaries settled into various communities and started to
look a lot like churches, and those churches started to look a lot like a denomination. This fact was made official in 1974 when the group declared itself to be what
everyone else already knew . . . a denomination.

We can see this same flexibility between church and parachurch today,
although in the moment, it is perceived more as ambiguity. For example, certain
types of Christian nonprofits straddle the church-parachurch boundary. If you
think about large television ministries, they often look like churches in that they are
focused on providing worship services, albeit to an electronic membership. However, many are organized as nonprofits and their ministries extend far beyond their
weekly worship broadcast. The same can be said of large megachurches that are not
organized as a parachurch nonprofit but whose activities go far beyond that of
most local churches.

The flexibility and uncertainty of church and parachurch categories plays a
very interesting role in the operation of contemporary Christian nonprofits as it

has implications for their status in the eyes of the Internal Revenue Service. This is a topic that will be explored in chapter 7, but before getting there, let us explore the Christian nonprofit population in more detail as we have only explored in abstract form up to this point. The next chapter will provide a survey of the wide range of activities conducted by Christian nonprofits and will profile a range of organizations within each of those activity subsectors.

4

Parachurch Profiles

From Christian Cowboys to Donating Cows

Parachurch organizations have grown dominant in missions and evangelism, in all forms of communication (print and broadcast), in service to the poor, in political and social advocacy, and even in defending doctrinal orthodoxy.

— Tim Stafford, "When Christians Fight Christians"

Upon hearing that I was doing research on Christian nonprofits, many people would pause and then ask, "what are Christian nonprofits?" It is not that they were unaware of nonprofit organizations or the possibility that some of them might be Christian in nature. They had just never realized their number and their scope or that they might represent some larger type of parachurch phenomenon. I would typically respond by providing a couple organizations as examples because I found that even if people were not aware of Christian nonprofits on the whole, they were very aware of at least some individual Christian nonprofits. Although I had about 2,000 potential examples to provide, I found that I almost always said, "like Habitat for Humanity or Focus on the Family." These happened to be effective in ending the line of questioning as most people have heard of at least one of these organizations. Both are large and highly visible, and together, they appeal to a wide range of theological, social, and political tastes. Many written accounts of the parachurch sector utilize a similar strategy of offering a handful of "big names" as illustrations of the entire population.

However, it occurred to me that while useful in that social situation, these high-profile examples were not as useful in representing the population of Christian nonprofits. Instead of being representative, these were exceptions rather than the norm when it came to Christian nonprofits. First, most organizations in the Christian nonprofit population are much smaller than either Habitat for Humanity or Focus on the Family. Very few are as politically active as Focus on the Family, and very few receive government funding like Habitat. Most are more explicitly religious than Habitat (it is noteworthy that the third question usually asked in the above dialogue was, "Habitat for Humanity is religious?"). Most are engaged in more traditionally religious activities, such as preaching, distributing Bibles, or training pastors, than either Habitat or Focus on the Family.

Nine Sectors

The population of Christian nonprofits is so diverse that it would be impossible to provide an accurate picture with just two organizations. Their missions range from translating the Bible to producing Christian films, from training pastors to organizing short-term mission trips for youth, and from providing legal support to providing dental clinics. In much of this book, the stories of these organizations are hidden behind aggregated statistics and abstract discussions of organizational dynamics. In an attempt to provide some sense of the diversity in organizational missions, histories, and operations, this chapter will look at nine major sectors within the Christian nonprofit population.[1] I provide an overview of each sector and a few example organizations of different sizes within each sector. While all the organizations in any particular sector share major characteristics, it is important to realize that each sector contains its own internal diversity. Similarly, some organizations have multiple missions and therefore overlap sectors in varying degrees. They have been categorized by their primary activity based on their expenses. In short, these sectors are useful conceptual tools, and we will see in later chapters that there are significant differences between the sectors, but we should also be aware that their boundaries can be fuzzy in places.

Although more detail will be provided below, I will briefly describe each sector here. The first is the *Charismatic Evangelism* sector. These organizations are highly focused on worship and conversion. Common activities include mass revivals, dramatic and musical performances, and itinerant speaking. The last activity is often focused around one individual who serves as the focus of the nonprofit's services and activities. The *Relief & Development* sector consists of nonprofits working toward short-term relief of emergencies and long-term economic development. They are charities in the common understanding of the word. *Education & Training* nonprofits are a diverse group, but they are all engaged in activities that try to improve the quality and functioning of the larger "church." This can include church consulting, training new pastors, or lay religious education. The *Publishing & Resources* sector includes nonprofits whose primary purpose is to translate, publish, and/or distribute printed and other forms of media. The activities in the *Radio & Television* sector are fairly self-descriptive, but as we will see, this does not necessarily equal televangelists. *Missions & Missionary* nonprofits tend to be internationally focused. Common activities include church planting, long-term missionary support, and the organization of short-term mission trips. Organizations in the *Fellowship & Enrichment* sector are often focused on serving particular social groups, such as mothers, prisoners, men, or specific occupations. They attempt to provide outlets for building community and nurturing faith among these groups. The *Activism & Advocacy* sector contains some of the most politically charged Christian nonprofits. These organizations work toward particular social and legal issues inspired by their faith. The sector also includes nonprofits trying to reform particular religious groups. Finally, the *Fund-Raising, Grant-Making, & Other* sector provides financial support for a wide range of activities, often stretching across the previous sectors.

Each sector contains anywhere from 5 to 20% of all the nonprofits examined. However, some of the smallest sectors in terms of number of organizations are the largest in total revenue (or vice versa).[2] Possibly, only the Relief & Development sector does not seem explicitly religious on its surface, although many of them also engage in evangelism and other explicitly religious activities. This observation should not come as a surprise since we are, after all, looking at *Christian* nonprofits. But it is important to acknowledge that few of these organizations are just superficially or nominally Christian. Much of the research on religiously affiliated nonprofits has focused on their predominantly secular activities, such as their role in providing social services.[3] This can blur not only the content but also the nature of the Christian nonprofit population.

In describing the activities of individual nonprofits, I rely heavily on the organizations' own narratives or descriptions. It is important to not be oblivious to the fact that nonprofits, like any organization, present an image that may not always represent some objective reality. After all, nonprofit Web sites, brochures, newsletters, and other materials are typically aimed at motivating viewers to participate in or contribute to the organization. This does not mean that these materials are meaningless, but it is to say that the profiles given below are not meant as an endorsement of any organization or a confirmation of their image or activities. Indeed, I also provide the occasional third-party criticism and attempt to provide some analysis of how and why there is variation in how these organizations and sectors present themselves to the outside world.

TABLE 4.1. Snapshot of Charismatic Evangelism Sector.

Activities		Size	Financials	
Itinerant speaking and preaching		387 organizations	Median revenue: $366,525	
Crusades and revivals		20% of population	Aggregate revenue: $329,621,952	
Dramatic/musical performances				
Sector Profiles				
Name	Ruling Year	Location	Web Site	Revenue
Mike Hagen Strength Team	2002	Missoula, MT	www.strengthteam.com	$347,742
Jentezen Franklin Ministries	2003	Gainesville, GA	www.jentezenfranklin.org	$614,366
Teen Mania Ministries	1987	Garden Valley, TX	www.teenmania.org	$26,565,575

Exploring the Sectors

Charismatic Evangelism

We begin our exploration of Christian nonprofits with the largest group of organizations. Nonprofits in the Charismatic Evangelism sector could be considered the most traditional type of religious organization within the nonprofit sector. If we were to think of parachurch organizations as existing on a continuum ranging from intimately tied to churches to entirely separate from them, nonprofits in this sector would be on the former part of the scale. Indeed, the activities of these nonprofits often occur in churches.

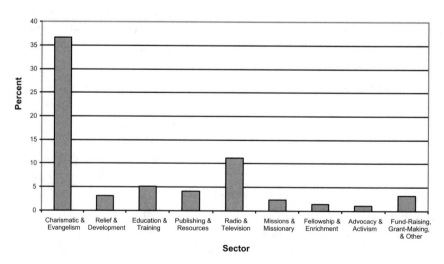

FIGURE 4.1. Percentage of Organizations Named after Executive.

Many of the Charismatic Evangelism nonprofits are simply engaged in preaching and resemble churches minus the buildings and members. These nonprofits can be seen as descendants of the great itinerant preachers of the 18th and 19th centuries, such as George Whitefield and Peter Cartwright.[4] Just as those men were known for their charisma, these nonprofits also tend to be personality-driven organizations, dependent on one or two charismatic individuals. Thirty-seven percent of the nonprofits in this sector are named after the founder or central figure of their organization (e.g., Al Menconi Ministries, Barry Wood Evangelistic Association). No other sector has even half as many leader-named organizations. The next highest is Radio & Television, with 11% of the nonprofits named after a leader. This likely makes these organizations relatively fragile as the entire organization rests on the personality, health, and interest of one person.[5]

Because itinerant preaching requires little capital and, on its own, generates relatively little revenue, organizations in this sector tend to be smaller than those in any other sector. Those that are larger tend not to go from church to church but are instead focused on mass revivals, crusades, festivals, or other large-scale events. These events require more infrastructure and capital (e.g., audio/video equipment,

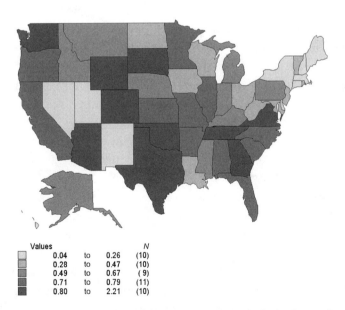

FIGURE 4.2. Density of Christian Nonprofits by State. The map shows the number of Christian nonprofits per 100,000 people in each state. While the District of Columbia has the highest rate at 3.3 organizations, Colorado leads the list of states at 2.2 organizations per 100,000 people. These are followed by Oklahoma (1.54), Tennessee (1.5), Virginia (1.2), Georgia (1.2), and Texas (1.0).

stadium/arena rentals, multiple performers, staff) and provide more opportunities for revenue generation (e.g., ticket sales, souvenirs, CD/DVD sales). Although the Billy Graham Evangelistic Association falls primarily in the Radio & Television sector, its namesake is the father of the mass crusade. Billy Graham, his son, and his grandson continue the tradition by conducting multiple festivals around the world every year. Organizations in the Charismatic Evangelism sector are disproportionately based in the South. While 43% of organizations in other sectors have their home offices in the South, 62% of the organizations in the Evangelism sector are based there. The South has the highest rate of evangelical adherence, so it is not entirely surprising that evangelical itinerant preachers originate and thrive there.

Sector Profiles

Mike Hagen is a former professional football player who can bench-press over 500 pounds. Although impressive, this would be a fairly irrelevant piece of information except for the fact that it plays a major role in the activities of the nonprofit he founded, called the Mike Hagen Strength Team. Hagen, along with a team of other professional athletes, travels the country performing various feats of strength in churches, schools, and other venues. The organization's Web site features pictures of steel bars, bricks, and other props being bent, broken, and generally abused. In between this, the Strength Team provides religious and inspirational messages. As the mission statement of the organizations puts it, "[i]n a sight and sound generation, The Strength Team provides a means for audiences of all ages to be captivated by a powerful, visual demonstration. The feats of strength grab the attention of the audience, but the message is what changes hearts. The Strength Team preaches and declares the uncompromised message of salvation through Jesus Christ, His Death, burial and resurrection as the finished work to equip the believer for a life of victory." Hagen's story represents a common pattern among entrepreneurs, spiritual or otherwise, in that he drew upon his previous personal and professional experiences when designing his organization's mission and activities. If a person has skills or knowledge in a specific area, such as athletics, he or she will often use that expertise as the foundation for his or her organization.[6]

Although he might not be able to bench-press 500 pounds like Mike Hagen, Jentezen Franklin's nonprofit is the more typical style of itinerant preaching found in the Charismatic Evangelism sector. The organization's mission statement states that "through his experience as a pastor, teacher, musician and author, Jentezen Franklin continues in the pursuit of helping people encounter God through inspired worship and relevant application of the Word of God in our daily lives." Franklin is the pastor of a "traditional" church in Georgia, but his nonprofit exists to extend his efforts into itinerant speaking at other churches and venues. As with other similar organizations,

Jentezen Franklin Ministries features other products and services based on Franklin's personality, such as books, audio materials, and student conferences.

Because many nonprofits in this sector are essentially selling a personality, there is an unknown element to them in the eyes of potential buyers. They are not just selling some tangible good or service—they are selling a person. Therefore, many organizations in this sector offer testimonials that help build up a reputation for evangelists who represent their main product. For example, Hagen's Web site has a section of recommendation letters, many of which note the "integrity" or "genuineness and passion" of him and his co-evangelists.[7] Franklin's Web site contains a section of testimonials from people he has interacted with, each speaking to the personal benefits they have received from his teachings.

The activities and marketing and organizational structure of Mike Hagen's Strength Team and Jentezen Franklin Ministries are both primarily centered

---

From Lauren Sandler, *Righteous*, discussing an event conducted by Teen Mania Ministries.[8]

Desperate to crack Heather's depression, her mother bought her tickets for an event called Acquire the Fire at the Richmond Coliseum that promised loud bands, a state-of-the-art light show, engaging theatrical performances, and a mass of teenagers gathered to focus on something other than boys and beer. Mildly intrigued and dying for distraction, Heather splashed water on her face and drove into town with her sister to check out the show.

Once inside the stadium, what Heather saw overwhelmed her: ten thousand teens rocking out to catchy power pop, their hands raised to the domed roof, their eyes closed, their faces ebullient. . . . The lyrics on the giant prompters framing the stage proclaimed what they were there for: the magnificent, unifying, unconditional love of Jesus Christ . . .

Anyone who has attended Acquire the Fire knows what's happening to America just by simple math: [Ron] Luce is filling stadiums where the Detroit Lions and Washington Redskins have a hard time selling out seats . . .

This is not the story of a youth movement gathering on the horizon. It's already here. And it's growing every day.

---

around one person, which is a common strategy in the Charismatic Evangelism sector. However, this can often limit the ability of these nonprofits to grow just for the simple fact that so much rests on the shoulders of one or two people. But some organizations in this sector, such as Teen Mania Ministries, are able to overcome this barrier. Teen Mania has the largest revenue of the Charismatic Evangelism sector. As with most organizations its size, Teen Mania Ministries has multiple

TABLE 4.2. Snapshot of Relief & Development Sector.

Activities	Size	Financials
Home building Well drilling Child sponsorship Distribution of food, medicine, clothing, and other essentials	229 organizations 12% of population	Median revenue: $1,044,876 Aggregate revenue: $5,905,474,074

Sector Profiles

Name	Ruling Year	Location	Web Site	Revenue
FARMS International	1967	Knife River, MN	www.farmsinternational.com	$240,540
Warm Blankets Orphan Care	2001	Rolling Meadows, IL	www.warmblankets.org	$1,075,889
Feed the Children	1979	Oklahoma City, OK	www.feedthechildren.org	$958,778,536

programs, but its primary and most well-known activity is the organization of large events for youth. These Acquire the Fire festivals and larger BattleCry stadium events are held in cities across North America and feature a blend of speakers, music, and dramatic presentations. According to the organization, 32 of these events were held in 2004 and were attended by more than 193,000 individuals. Depending on the city and event, admission tickets range from $40 to $100.

The organization was founded by Ron Luce who, after various delinquent behaviors as a teen, found Christ at age 16 and wanted "to dedicate his life to reaching young people." Luce claims ties to a number of other Christian nonprofits, including Focus on the Family and the Trinity Broadcasting Network. Luce and Teen Mania have been listed as consultants to President Bush's National Drug Control Strategy, and Luce served on the White House Advisory Commission on Drug-Free Communities.[9]

Relief and Development

The Relief & Development sector contains some of the most well-known Christian nonprofits. Some of this is due to the generally nondivisive missions of these organizations. Indeed, many individuals who do not consider themselves religious have participated in a Habitat for Humanity project or sponsored a child in a developing nation through a Christian nonprofit. Many of these organizations supplement the humanitarian nature of their mission with a more inclusive message to appeal to a wider population of donors. For example, in the self-descriptions of organizational purpose and activities provided on their Internal Revenue Service tax returns, only 55% of these nonprofits include at least one religious keyword, while 78% of organizations in the other sectors contain a religious term. When Relief & Development organizations do use religious keywords, they are somewhat more likely to be inclusive words, such as "spiritual" instead of "biblical" or "Jesus Christ."

Organizations in the Relief & Development sector are the second largest in the Christian nonprofit population, with median revenue of just over $1 million. It contains three organizations with over half a billion in 2004 revenue. The large size of these organizations is partly a product of their wider appeal and also the higher capital requirements to conduct humanitarian efforts, especially since 88% of these organizations are working overseas in at least some capacity. Thirty-nine of the 229 Relief & Development organizations (17%) received government funding in 2004, making it the sector with the highest rate of public funding. This raises questions concerning the relationship between church and state or, more accurately, parachurch and state. I address this topic more in chapter 7.

Sector Profiles

Activities in the Relief & Development sector are divided into three major categories. The first contains organizations involved in long-term economic development projects, such as home building, well drilling, agricultural projects, job training, and small-business loans. A second type of nonprofit in this sector is focused on child sponsorship, orphanage, or adoption programs, although the last activity is smaller than the former two. A third focuses on more short-term relief of suffering due to disaster or long-term conditions.

FARMS International falls into the first category. As their mission statement puts it, "FARMS International is a Christian ministry that serves the church by equipping families in poverty with the means for self-support. Working through the local church, FARMS provides loans, technical support for income generating projects and spiritual training for families. The result? Families find a biblical path out of poverty!" The organization is currently working in nine nations, including Bangladesh, Ecuador, and Thailand. The FARMS strategy is fairly unique in that they provide loans for families in these nations to begin income-generating ventures, such as small-business or agricultural projects. The loan recipients are then expected to tithe their profits back to the organization and the community. These profits are then used by the FARMS to provide more loans and by the community to build churches and other religious programs. In short, it is meant to be at least partially self-sustaining as loans are made, repaid, and made again.

Warm Blankets Orphan Care is in the child-focused category. Although Warm Blankets does work in several nations, including India, Uganda, and Thailand, their main focus is on Cambodia where they have built more than 70 orphan homes. Unlike large institutional orphanages, Warm Blankets constructs smaller group homes housing approximately 40 children that are run by widows who become the surrogate parents of the children. Each orphan home shares a building with a church. The organization offers opportunities for donors to sponsor a house and also organizes mission trips to assist orphans.

On the large end of the Relief & Development sector, there is Feed the Children. With close to a billion dollars in revenue, Feed the Children is the largest Christian nonprofit not only in the Relief & Development sector but also in the Christian nonprofit population as a whole in 2004. In fact, it is one of the largest U.S. non-profits overall.[10] In the United States, Feed the Children distributes surplus food and supplies from corporations and other donors to other agencies that then provide the materials to shelters, churches, and food banks. Internationally, Feed the Children works in more than 118 countries to provide food, clothing, medicine, and other goods to children, families, and organizations. Feed the Children is also a major responder to disasters and other emergencies. The organization was founded by Larry and Frances Jones. The inspiration for the organization came after Mr. Jones visited and observed the poverty in Haiti and realized that grain and food simply sitting in storage in the United States could be redistributed to the benefit of all involved. Many know the Joneses and their organization through their television appeals for support. Although generally highly regarded, as demonstrated by its large revenue, Feed the Children does receive some criticism for its use of television fund-raising and the Jones' six-figure salaries. As one watchdog group states it, "Feed the Children means 'feed the children,' not buy expensive television time."[11] However, the same rating agency gives Feed the Children high marks on organizational transparency and efficiency.

Because most Relief & Development nonprofits operate internationally and for the benefit for people who are not the donors to the organization, a major challenge is to make their work seem less abstract and distant. Therefore, many of the advertising materials of organizations like FARMS, Warm Blankets, and Feed the Children prominently feature images of the people and places they assist along with detailed stories and updates from the organizations' projects. There is variation in how this is executed, though. While clearly there is a fund-raising element, FARMS presents pictures of the people and projects they are funding and narratives of their progress in a way that appears informational. This could reflect their more long-term developmental strategy. On the other hand, some organizations use these tools to make a more explicit appeal for support. For example, Feed the Children's Web site offers videos and pictures of children in desperate conditions to motivate viewers to donate. Warm Blankets offers similar dramatic images and stories. Some have argued that these types of appeals cross a line and become a "shameless appeal to sympathy," but given organizations like Feed the Children's success, it seems to be effective in motivating individuals to give to these causes.[12]

TABLE 4.3. Snapshot of Education & Training Sector.

Activities	Size	Financials
Pastor training	259 organizations	Median revenue: $533,126
Church consulting	13% of population	Aggregate revenue: $342,654,549
"Leadership" or "equipping"		
education for various lay audiences		

Sector Profiles				
Name	Ruling Year	Location	Web Site	Revenue
Leadership Transformations	2003	Lexington, MA	www.leadership-tranformations.org	$221,578
AFMIN USA (Africa Ministries Network)	1994	Colorado Springs, CO	www.afmin.org	$716,495
Purpose Driven Ministries	1993	Lake Forest, CA	www.purpose-driven.com	$20,857,606

Education & Training

Although Christian nonprofits in the Education & Training sector all provide some form of religious and spiritual training, they differ in their target audiences, which roughly fall into three categories. First, there are organizations looking to train pastors, often indigenous or native pastors in foreign countries. Second, there are those that provide consulting and continuing education for churches and church leaders. This consulting is often related to church growth, transitions in leadership, or ministry development. Finally, there are nonprofits providing religious education for lay individuals, often labeled as "equipping" individuals for a Christian life. The latter two segments of this sector tend to be more domestic in scope than the first.

One might observe that many of these activities are exactly what we would expect denominational offices to provide for leaders, congregations, and lay members. As noted in chapter 2, Christian nonprofits and the larger parachurch population are partially taking advantage of a growth in congregations without denominational affiliations. But they are also creating a competing market for these services for individuals and congregations with a denominational affiliation. It is easy to see why some, at least in denominational offices, view the rise of Christian nonprofits and the parachurch population with some trepidation. This is especially true in the case of religious education and training. A denomination probably does not care if an individual or a congregation wants to support a nonprofit Relief & Development organization, but organizations in this sector seeking to train and shape religious leadership strike at the very heart of denominational services and identities.

Sector Profiles

An author of several books on church health, the Rev. Dr. Stephen Macchia founded Leadership Transformations. The organization falls within the second category in the Education & Training sector of nonprofits providing consulting and continuing education for churches and church leaders. Its mission statement states that its "vision is to see Christian leaders and teams transformed by a lifestyle of spiritual formation and discernment, resulting in depth of spiritual insight and vitality in God's service. Our mission is to encourage the spiritual formation of leaders and equip leadership teams to discern God's unique will for their life and ministry." The organization offers several different assessment programs for congregations based on Macchia's principles of church health. One of these utilizes online surveys of church members, which are used to provide reports and suggestions to the church's leadership. It also offers retreats and training seminars for leaders.

AFMIN USA was the result of a merger between two organizations called Equip Ministries and Karel Sander's African Ministries. AFMIN, like many of the internationally focused organizations in this sector, trains native pastors to evangelize the population as an alternative to using foreign missionaries. This strategy is partly due to the perceived benefits of having native representatives of Christianity but also due to the logistical difficulties in some nations of using foreign missionaries. As the Web site of AFMIN puts it:

> Recent terrorist attacks on the USA have virtually closed the opportunities for American and Western missionaries to evangelize Muslims. African church leaders equipped for effective Muslim evangelization by *AFMIN* not only fill that gap, but also form a significant part of the overall strategy to reach Islam with the Gospel of Jesus Christ.

The organization currently works in 15 African nations. AFMIN's main program is a 1-week course for native pastors in advanced pastoral training. These courses cover a variety of topics, including "How to Interpret the Bible," "African Church History," and "Biblical Counseling."

Purpose Driven Ministries, the largest representative in the Education & Training sector, may be as well known for its founder and president as it is for the nonprofit's actual activities. It is led by Rick Warren, pastor of Saddleback Church with more than 20,000 attendees each week and author of *The Purpose Driven Life*, a book that has sold more than 25 million copies. Warren has become an influential leader and celebrity. Indeed, his message has become the slogan for a social movement within the Christian community with individuals and churches around the world adopting the Purpose Driven slogan. Purpose Driven Ministries has several outreaches, but its main purpose is to train churches and leaders to have effective (i.e., "Purpose Driven") ministries, whether they are youth ministries, small groups, recovery ministries, or any other aspect

of church life. The organization offers conferences, seminars, books, educational cur-
riculums, and multimedia training tools. Purpose Driven Ministries has grown rapidly.
In 2000, the organization received just over $300,000 in gross receipts. In 2001, this
became more than $2 million and in 2002 more than $25 million. The close relationship
between Purpose Driven Ministries and Saddleback Church, the former is called a ministry of the latter on its Web site, is another illustration of the sometimes fuzzy boundary
between churches and parachurch. As noted in the previous chapter and seen in these
profiles, many nonprofits have their beginning within churches and are launched as
independent organizations when they outgrow the church in size or scope.

Although these organizations vary in many ways, it is hard to escape a common
theme in how they describe themselves. We have already seen that nonprofits in the
same sector frequently adopt similar strategies when it comes to demonstrating effectiveness or expertise. In the Education & Training sector, this strategy seems to center
around presenting a highly technical form of competency. Flowcharts, multistep
"models" or "systems," and creative acronyms (e.g., CHAT = Church Health Assessment Tool; SHAPE = spiritual gifts, heart, abilities, personality, and experiences) are
common in the presentations of each, all of which produce the feeling of scientific pre-
cision. Words like "strategic," "effectiveness," and "assessment" are commonplace.
Purpose Driven offers a "matrix" for locating your church on different dimensions.
Leadership Transformations seeks to help with the "attentiveness quotient." Even
AFMIN, which is more international and less focused on traditional church consulting,
writes about their "multiple track model of training for multiplication impact." It is
likely that the health metaphor that seems to be dominant in this sector helps fuel this

TABLE 4.4. Snapshot of Publishing & Resources Sector.

Activities	Size	Financials
Translation and distribution of scripture (e.g., bibles, tracts), magazine, and general book publishing	253 organizations	Median revenue: $603,892
Study guides and other print/multimedia resources	13% of population	Aggregate revenue: $670,928,185

Sector Profiles				
Name	Ruling Year	Location	Web Site	Revenue
Deaf Video Communi- cations of America	1984	Carol Stream, IL	www.deafvideo.com	$256,472
Reach the Children Foundation (a.k.a. Book of Hope USA)	1991	Pompano Beach, FL	www.bookofhope.net	$4,723,786
American Bible Society	1931	New York, NY	www.bibles.com	$65,851,876

strategy. These nonprofits are playing the role of a doctor offering a diagnosis for a problem, such as an ailing church or leader. By presenting the nonprofit's services, or cure, as a complex solution to a complex problem, the organization helps assure the patient that it knows what it is doing. After all, you would not want someone performing surgery on you who seemed to have no better idea of what is going on than you.

Publishing & Resources

The Publishing & Resources sector consists of two primary subgroups. There are organizations that translate, publish, and distribute various forms of scripture, usually in the form of Bibles and religious tracts (although many also produce multimedia resources, such as audiotapes and videos). These nonprofits are descendants of some of the earliest parachurch organizations that distributed religious literature in the 18th and 19th centuries, as discussed in chapter 1. Some of them, such as the American Tract Society and the American Bible Society, *are* the organizations that distributed literature in those centuries. The other group of organizations within this sector closely resembles commercial publishers. They produce nonscripture books, magazines, newspapers, and other print or multimedia resources of Christian nature. Outside of the reform and renewal organizations in the Advocacy & Activism sector (discussed later), the Publishing sector contains the largest number of nonprofits claiming a specific denominational or religious tradition. Twelve percent identify as Baptist, Catholic, or some other Christian tradition. Examples include Baptists Today, Lutheran Heritage Foundation, and the New Oxford Review (Catholic).

Sector Profiles

Deaf Video Communications of America is not a typical publisher in the sense that they do not produce print materials. Their mission statement reads, "The Apostle Paul asked, *'How shall they believe if they have not heard?'* Our prayer is that the Deaf will hear the Gospel of Jesus Christ in their own language—sign language." As this and their name makes clear, their resources are designed for deaf individuals. The organization produces and distributes videos addressing a wide range of topics, such as "God's Rules for Marriage" and "Personal Evangelism." Churches, individuals, and others can request a video loan and the organization will mail them the tape for use up to 6 weeks without any charge. Deaf Video Communications can also produce videos at the request of individuals or organizations.

The Reach the Children Foundation, also known as Book of Hope, represents a more traditional nonprofit in this sector. The organization was founded by the Reverend Bob Hoskins, who previously was the president of a different Christian publisher. Book of Hope's main activity involves the production and distribution of a modified child-friendly book based on the four Gospels. The original *Book of Hope* was distributed to children in El Salvador, but now multiple versions designed for different target audiences are distributed worldwide. The organization states that they have distributed more than 415 million books in 125 different countries. Book of Hope also offers mission trips for individuals or groups to distribute the books and has also produced an animated film to accompany the books.

The American Bible Society's newsletter, the American Bible Society Record, "is the second oldest continuously published periodical in the United States." Although in the eyes of the federal government the American Bible Society became an official non-profit in 1931, the organization is actually much older. It was founded in 1816 in New York City and began by distributing Bibles to sailors on the USS John Adams and to local Bible societies in New York. Its international work began in 1823 with a grant of $1,000 to a missionary translating the Bible in India. The organization has had many notable presidents, including a Supreme Court Chief Justice, a New York City mayor, and a U.S. Senator. The American Bible Society's first translation project was a Delaware Indian version of three Epistles of John. It claims a number of other firsts among Bible societies in its history, including the first Bibles placed in hotels and the first distribution of Bibles to the military. Today, its work is still very much the same. It works through affiliated Bible societies in other nations to distribute scriptures. Domestically, the organization produces various programs and resources aimed at getting specific groups (e.g., urban youth, inmates) and the general public involved in reading the Bible. Recently, the organization has gotten attention for its multimedia presentations of scripture and its efforts to make the language in scripture more contemporary. It is common for the American Bible Society to run an annual deficit, but this is not a significant problem due to its over half-a-billion-dollar endowment as it can make money on its assets even while losing money on its operations.[13]

Unlike the previous sectors we have looked at which have to work hard to sell products or services that are abstract, intangible, or distant, nonprofits in this sector are offering goods that are easier to relate to and understand. As a result, they present themselves in a much more straightforward manner. Many of these nonprofits' Web sites do not differ greatly from any commercial bookstore (e.g., Amazon.com). Books and resources are categorized by type or content, prices are clearly listed, users add them to their "shopping cart," and then "check out." If they are unhappy with their purchase, they simply contact "customer service" or send the product back for a refund.

Radio & Television

On average, the organizations in the Radio & Television sector are the largest among the Christian nonprofit population with a median revenue more than $1 million in 2004. It also may have the most self-explanatory title. However, there may be

TABLE 4.5. Snapshot of Radio & Television Sector.

Activities		Size	Financials	
Radio broadcasting		135 organizations	Median revenue: $1,092,963	
Television broadcasting		7% of population	Aggregate revenue: $1,148,133,508	
Sector Profiles				
Name	Ruling Year	Location	Web Site	Revenue
Hand of Hope Outreach International (a.k.a. Prison Television Network)	2004	Palm Harbor, FL	www.ptnoutreach.org	$264,693
HomeWord	1985	San Juan Capistrano, CA	www.homeword.com	$3,118,100
Christian Broadcasting Network	1961	Virginia Beach, VA	www.cbn.com	$186,482,060

some misconceptions about the organizations within it. It is true that many of the organizations in this sector are engaged in televangelism. Outside of the Charismatic Evangelism sector, the Radio & Television group contains the highest percentage (11%) of organizations named after an executive within the organization, who is usually the person appearing on the radio or television (see figure 4-1). However, we should not see these organizations as significantly different in mission from many in the Charismatic Evangelism sector except for the fact that they use modern means of distributing their messages and are often larger in audience and revenues. Furthermore, it would be inaccurate to say that the entire sector is composed of televangelists. Some of the nonprofits in this group are missionary focused and use radio or television to reach people in other nations and languages. Some are educationally focused, providing religious training or personal development opportunities through their programs. As the following profiles will show, the self-explanatory nature of the sector's name should not be equated with homogeneity.

Sector Profiles

Hand of Hope Outreach, known as Prison Television Network, says in its mission statement that "PTN is a television network designed and programmed specifically to help meet the spiritual and educational needs of the growing prison population." It does this by providing satellite dishes to prisons that offer Christian programming. Each satellite dish costs about $600 to install. The network shows general educational programs, such as GED preparation and literacy programs, but the main purpose is to provide programs that will "bring inmates to Jesus." The organization has agreements with other Christian nonprofits and church ministries to provide religious programming.

HomeWord's resources and programs are aimed at an entirely different population than that of Hand of Hope. Many know HomeWord by its previous name of YouthBuilders. The organization adopted the new name in 2004 to reflect its growth beyond a focus on youth. HomeWord is led by Dr. Jim Burns, who is the voice of the organization's radio programs, the author of many books, and a contributor of columns in religious magazines. HomeWord provides a variety of resources to train families "to make wise decisions and lead positive, vibrant, Christian lifestyles." These include seminars, books, videos, and study guides. However, the primary activity of HomeWord is the production of a 30-minute daily radio program and 1-minute radio commentaries that are broadcast across the United States. These radio programs accounted for more than 75% of the organization's program expenses in 2004.

One of the best-known organizations in all the Christian nonprofit sectors is the Christian Broadcasting Network. CBN began as one of the first Christian television stations in the nation. It was founded by Pat Robertson and began with a small broadcasting range around Portsmouth, Virginia. Today, its programs are broadcast across the United States on local stations and national cable and satellite networks. Its flagship program, the 700 Club, is hosted by Robertson and features "a mix of news and commentary, interviews, feature stories, and Christian ministry." The name of the program comes from a telethon held in the early days of the network in which Robertson stated that the $7,000 operating budget of the station could be covered by 700 individuals providing $10 each. The Christian Broadcasting Network has ties to other nonprofits founded by Robertson, including the relief and development organization Operation Blessing. The organization has drawn criticism for some of its programming, particularly concerning some commentaries by Robertson on the 700 Club program.[14]

The advertising style of HomeWord and CBN demonstrates this sector's similarity to the Charismatic Evangelism sector. Each, at least partially, relies on the personality and credentials of their host(s) as a primary product. Burns and Robertson are featured prominently in their advertising materials. As with many organizations in the Charismatic Evangelism sector, this strategy raises important questions for Radio & Television nonprofits concerning transitions when central personalities are no longer around.[15] On the other hand, the Prison Television Network is a good an example of how not all organizations in this sector fit into the typical televangelist mold. It is much closer to the Publishing & Resources sector in how it conducts its operations and advertising.

Missions & Missionary

Like the descendants of the 18th-century tract and Bible societies in the Publishing & Resources sector, nonprofits in the Missions & Missionary sector claim their roots in the mission societies of the same period. Many of the activities in this sector have not changed significantly since those first mission societies. Church planting and

TABLE 4.6. Snapshot of Missions & Missionary Sector.

Activities		Size	Financials	
Church planting		312 organizations	Median revenue: $523,077	
Long-term missionary support		16% of population	Aggregate revenue: $449,299,186	
Short-term mission trip planning and coordination				
Sector Profiles				
Name	Ruling Year	Location	Web Site	Revenue
South American Call	2000	McDonald, TN	www.southamericancall.org	$294,910
Construction for Worldwide Evangelism	1993	Tampa, FL	www.cweforthegospelsake.org	$698,623
MIO Frontiers	1982	Phoenix, AZ	www.frontiers.org	$15,483,626

financial support of missionaries in the field are common. Short-term mission agencies are also contained in this sector. These organizations essentially serve as travel agents who coordinate trips, often for youth or church groups, to provide work and/or evangelism teams to an area for a week or two.

Many nonprofits in this sector are hybrids of the Charismatic Evangelism and the Relief & Development sectors. They are more explicitly focused on evangelism than the organizations in the Relief & Development sector, yet they frequently supplement their evangelism with humanitarian activities that are common in that sector. This synthesis of activities is likely a product of the fact that most of these organizations are working in less developed parts of the world, where the physical or material needs are pressing. As shown in table 4-7, more than 80% of the Missions & Missionary organizations mentioned having an international reach in their statements of purpose and activities on their tax returns, second only to the Relief & Development sector.

Sector Profiles

South American Call was founded and is led by the Reverend Joe Mercer. Mercer's interest in South America, specifically Ecuador, was sparked by a missionary who made several presentations to his Tennessee church in the 1990s. He slowly began to increase his involvement by taking groups to build churches and minister to children. Eventually, Mercer left his church and created South American Call as a full-time effort to build churches, provide medical help, and organize crusades and other missionary activities in Ecuador and later in Peru. Today, South American Call organizes mission trips utilizing a riverboat to reach villages along the tributaries of the Amazon.

TABLE 4.7. International Activities by Sector.

	Charismatic Evangelism	Relief & Development	Education & Training	Publishing & Resources	Radio & Television	Missions & Missionary	Fellowship & Enrichment	Advocacy & Activism	Fund-Raising, Grant-Making, & Other
No international activities mentioned	57	12	48	57	64	17	76	76	37
International activities mentioned	43	88	52	43	36	83	24	24	63
Canada*	4	1	2	3	23	4	3	9	2
Latin America (including Mexico)	20	27	19	11	21	30	6	13	17
Asia	24	24	22	18	27	22	8	17	25
Europe (including Russia)	17	13	22	17	27	18	8	13	23
Middle East	5	6	6	8	8	4	3	13	5
Africa	16	21	25	11	15	15	11	13	15
Australia-New Zealand	2	1	2	3	10	0	3	9	0
Unspecific international activities	48	43	42	58	40	43	78	70	37

Note: Regional percentages are calculated only from those organizations reporting international activities. Organizations could mention activities in multiple regions, so regional totals might not sum to 100%.

Construction for Worldwide Evangelism's mission statement says that it aims "[t]o assist the local church in fulfilling the Great Commission by providing and facilitating spiritually effective mission opportunities throughout the world." The organization has partnered with volunteers from the United States and missionaries in the field to build more than 40 churches since its founding. Most of its projects have been in the Caribbean and South and Central America. General and skilled volunteers (e.g., carpenter, concrete finisher) pay a fee to go on a trip and assist in the construction. These fees compose about half of the organization's revenue, with direct donations composing the other half. The organization also offers medical mission trips.

The last featured organization in this sector, Frontiers, was founded by Dr. Greg Livingstone, who is the author of *Planting Churches in Muslim Cities: A Team Approach.* Following the theme of that book, Frontiers' primary goal is to witness to Muslims. This usually occurs in predominantly Muslim nations in Africa, the Middle East, and Asia. Frontiers offers a variety of opportunities for both short- and long-term missionaries. It offers short trips where individuals can assist long-term missionaries, provide humanitarian aid, and evangelize the local population. Frontiers also recruits, trains, sends, and supports long-term missionaries who plant churches and provide other services to local populations. The organization has doubled its revenue in the last several years. From 1998 to 2000, the organization's revenue was steady at just over $10 million. Between then and 2006, this revenue had increased to more than $22 million. It is difficult to know the exact source of this growth, although it seems likely that some of it is related to world events. The terrorist attacks of September 11 and the wars in Afghanistan and Iraq have focused attention, including the attention of Christian donors, on the Muslim world.

The presentation style of these three nonprofits is in many ways similar to those we saw in the Relief & Development sector. Both sectors attempt to make their activities seem more real by providing many pictures of the people and places

TABLE 4.8. Snapshot of Fellowship & Enrichment Sector.

Activities		Size	Financials	
Counseling		147 organizations	Median revenue: $585,410	
Rehabilitation		8% of population	Aggregate revenue: $655,161,229	
Professional or social support				
Sector Profiles				
Name	Ruling Year	Location	Web Site	Revenue
Covenant Keepers	1987	Tulsa, OK	www.covenantkeepers-inc.org	$293,980
Christian Legal Society	1966	Springfield, VA	www.clsnet.org	$1,945,268
Young Life	1942	Colorado Springs, CO	www.younglife.org	$169,147,946

they are helping. However, the emphasis between the two sectors is much different. Although Missions & Missionary nonprofits are not oblivious to the material hardships of those they are helping, their main selling point is that these individuals have not been ministered to or are not aware of Christianity. This is in contrast to Relief & Development organizations that emphasize more physical needs. This difference in strategy has consequences. Many people who might not typically contribute to a Christian nonprofit might contribute to a Relief & Development organization that happens to be Christian. Indeed, they may not even know the nonprofit is Christian. However, the evangelism focus of Missions & Missionary nonprofits makes it less likely that such an individual would contribute to these organizations, even though they are engaged in many of the same activities. This partially explains why the Relief & Development sector is so much larger than the Missions & Missionary.

Fellowship & Enrichment

Nonprofits in the Fellowship & Enrichment sector are eclectic in their target audiences. Virtually, every demographic, social, and professional group is represented. Families, couples, working women, mothers, fathers, businessmen, athletes, soldiers, lawyers, surfers, and cheerleaders all have their own organization to provide support and personal development. The sector also includes organizations active in rehabilitation and counseling. This subgroup tends to overlap with the missions of the Advocacy & Activism sector, which is evidenced by the lobbying expenses of a handful of Fellowship & Enrichment organizations.

Often, these nonprofits have a more federated or franchised structure by which members interact in small local groups or chapters that may meet at regional or national conventions. Eighteen percent of the nonprofits in this sector claimed at least some revenue through "Membership dues or assessments." The next highest sector on this measure is the Advocacy & Activism group (10%). While some of these dues are from individual members, they are often from local branches of the organization paying a franchise fee to the national organization. The central organization provides resources and advertising, publishes newsletters, and organizes larger meetings. For example, Mothers of Preschoolers International (MOPS) requires a "charter fee" of $275 for a local group to acquire the MOPS branding and an annual renewal fee of $125. MOPS provides the training materials, logo, and other support for the group. Along with the Advocacy & Activism sector, this is the most domestically oriented group (see table 4-2). Next to the Relief & Development sector, the Fellowship & Enrichment sector is most likely to receive government funding. Four percent (6 of the 141 organizations) received government funding in 2004.

From Jeffrey L. Sheler, *Believers*. The Fellowship of Christian Cowboys claimed just under $250,000 in total revenue for 2004.[16]

I was anxious to see what happens when the Sermon on the Mount meets the Marlboro Man. And so, on a brilliantly sunny Saturday morning, I headed east out of town on a gently winding ribbon of blacktop highway to link up with Jerry Wyatt, a former rodeo rider who runs the national headquarters of the Fellowship of Christian Cowboys.

By pure happenstance I had timed my visit to coincide with the first annual Fellowship of Christian Cowboys Golf Tournament. It wasn't exactly the slice of Wild West Americana I had anticipated, and I felt a little tinge of disappointment. But Wyatt assured me this would be no ordinary golf outing. There would be no fancy clubhouse, no golf carts, no manicured greens. In fact, no golf course. "We're burying a bunch of five-gallon buckets in a cow pasture," he explained. "It should be a real challenge. We're just gonna hit some balls around, and then have a barbecue and a little preaching service. I think you'll enjoy it. You'll meet some good people."

As we crossed the parking lot near the grove Wyatt described his frequent travels for the fellowship and his behind-the-scenes work helping to organize programs at rodeos and at youth Bible camps all over the country. "It's a pretty neat deal to be around kids and cowboys," he said. "I sure do enjoy it. I know there must be a lot of people more qualified than I am to do this job, but they weren't available. So I'm just here, trying to serve God as best as I know how."

Sector Profiles

Covenant Keepers was founded by Marilyn Conrad, an ordained minister and author of two books on marriage and divorce. It is one of the many nonprofits in this sector providing enrichment and counseling for couples and families. Covenant Keepers' position is that "marriages can be healed if only one person in the marriage will apply scriptural principles to the situation." The organization is part of a larger Covenant Marriage Movement, which is a network of marriage ministries located in and out of traditional church structures. Covenant Keepers follows the federated structure mentioned above. It claims more than 50 Covenant Keeper groups across the United States and in several other nations. The central organization produces a newsletter and curriculum for the groups. It also organizes an annual conference.

Unlike Covenant Keepers, the Christian Legal Society represents the portion of this sector providing professional and social development outside of the context of rehabilitation or counseling. Its mission statement states that "CLS is a national non-denominational membership organization of attorneys, judges, law professors, and law students, working in association with others, to follow Jesus' command 'to do justice with the love of God' (Luke 11:42; Matthew 23:23)." The society is an organization with more than 4,000 members who are primarily lawyers, judges, and law students. Despite its somewhat different motivations from more psychologically focused organizations, the Christian Legal Society and other professional societies operate in much the same way. The central organization publishes a magazine and member directories, organizes an annual conference, and provides other support for members. There are local and campus chapters for attorneys and law students, respectively. The organization was founded by two lawyers, Paul Barnard and Henry Luke Brinks, who had both attended Wheaton College. The first director's meeting was held in 1962. The society also provides legal counsel and court briefs through its Center for Law and Religious Freedom. This aspect of their mission puts the society partially in the Activism & Advocacy sector below. In 2004, however, its collective expenses on fellowship activities (e.g., conferences, local chapter support) were greater than its expenses on litigation.

The final featured organization in the Fellowship & Enrichment sector is Young Life, a well-known Christian nonprofit serving youth. Young Life's numerous ministries include youth groups based in schools across the United States and in other nations, 23 summer camp locations, ministries for disabled youth, and clubs on college campuses and military bases. The organization began as the local youth ministry of Jim Rayburn while he was a seminary student in Texas. Rayburn created a club for a local high school that met weekly, and Young Life was created to plant this model to other schools. Over time, Young Life diversified its activities from the primarily suburban high school clubs to include rural, urban, international, and other specialized ministries.

TABLE 4.9. Snapshot of Advocacy & Activism Sector.

Activities	Size	Financials
Advancing social or political issues	97 organizations	Median revenue: $646,913
Denominational renewal advocacy	5% of population	Aggregate revenue: $359,334,205

Sector Profiles				
Name	Ruling Year	Location	Web Site	Revenue
Christians for Biblical Equality	1989	Minneapolis, MN	www.cbeinternational.org	$421,474
Thomas More Law Center	1999	Ann Arbor, MI	www.thomasmore.org	$2,516,085
Focus on the Family	1977	Colorado Springs, CO	www.focusonthefamily.org	$136,611,180

Because Young Life's activities tend to overlap with what many local congregations try to provide in their youth ministries, some argue that it, along with other similar organizations in this sector, actually competes and takes resources away from the local church. Young Life is clearly aware of these concerns since it states on its Web site that its "goal is not to compete with these programs, but to complement what they do." Similar statements appear on many of the Web sites of local Young Life clubs. Whether or not Young Life really does compete with local churches, this is an illustration of the tensions that can result from the overlapping goals and activities of the traditional church and the Christian nonprofit sector.

Advocacy & Activism

Although the Advocacy & Activism sector is the smallest group in the Christian nonprofit world, the organizations within it are some of the most well known among Christians and non-Christians alike. The very nature of activism does not foster organizational wallflowers. These organizations want or, more accurately, *need* to be seen and heard. The sector consists of two major subgroups. The first contains organizations whose advocacy is directed toward larger social and political issues, such as abortion, marriage and family policies, and schooling. The second group's

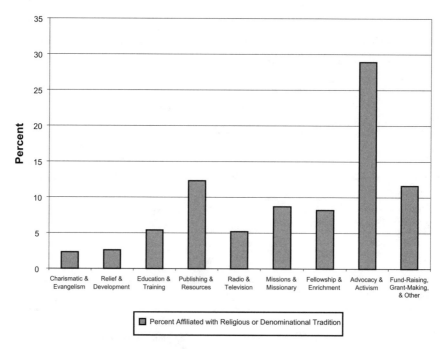

FIGURE 4.3. Percent Affiliated with Religious or Denominational Tradition.

advocacy is directed toward particular religious groups, typically in an effort to get a denomination or group to return to traditional beliefs and/or practices.

The uniqueness of this sector is seen in several characteristics. Just under 30% of this sector claims some specific religious tradition (e.g., Baptist, Catholic). This is over double the amount in any other sector and represents the presence of denominational reform organizations. Six percent of the organizations in this sector reported lobbying expenses to influence either the government or the general population on legislation. Only one other sector (Fellowship & Enrichment) has even half as many organizations with lobbying expenses. In 2004, much of this legislative effort was directed toward marriage initiatives (i.e., gay marriage). Not coincidentally, 7% of the nonprofits in this sector have their home offices in Washington, DC. Another 12% have their home offices in nearby Virginia. No other sector has more than 2% located in the District of Columbia and 7% in Virginia.

Sector Profiles

Christians for Biblical Equality is an unusual organization in the Advocacy & Activism sector on a number of counts. Its mission statement says that it "equips believers by affirming the biblical truth about equality and justice. Thus, all believers, without regard to gender, ethnicity, and class, are free and encouraged to use their God-given gifts in ministries, communities, and families." First, Christians for Biblical Equality straddles the line between externally focused social activism and internally focused religious activism. On the one hand, the organization is working to provide a Christian basis for gender equality in society. But they are also trying to reform churches' and denominations' view of men and women. The organization produces resources for congregations on gender equality and church diversity. It also organizes conferences and workshops and maintains a list of "Egalitarian Churches." It may also be considered by some to be a somewhat more liberal or progressive organization than other nonprofits in this sector. However, there is a limit to the accuracy of that perception. Christians for Biblical Equality began from a group that withdrew from the Evangelical Women's Caucus after the latter passed a resolution supporting homosexuality during its 1986 conference in Fresno, CA.[17] Despite their progressive stance on gender equality, the group that would become Christians for Biblical Equality viewed this decision as "unbiblical" and stated that they believe "in the family, celibate singleness, and faithful heterosexual marriage as God's design."

Representing the more litigious element of the sector is the Thomas More Law Center. The organization is named after an Englishman who would become a Catholic saint after being beheaded for refusing to recognize King Henry VIII as the head of the church in England. It primarily provides legal support in the form of attorneys and consultation for individuals and groups involved in three broad types of cases. The "Defending Religious Freedom" aspect of the center focuses on issues like school prayer, religious displays such as Ten Commandment plaques and Christmas symbols, and school vouchers. Its "Family Values" work focuses on "challenging special rights for homosexuals," pornography, and homeschooling issues. Its "Sanctity of Human Life" issues revolve around abortion, euthanasia, and cloning. The center was founded by Tom Monaghan, founder of Domino's Pizza and a prominent Catholic activist and philanthropist (although the center claims no explicit Catholic focus), and Richard Thompson, a former Oakland district attorney. Thompson serves as the president and chief counsel for the center. Although less than 10 years old, the center has been involved in many high-profile court cases.[18]

Finally, we take a look at Focus on the Family, the largest representative in this sector. A fair argument could be made for Focus on the Family to be placed in several of the sectors described here. Its ministries include radio programs, publications, and personal development resources, making it active in the Radio & Television, the Publications & Resources, and the Fellowship & Enrichment sectors. However, many of those activities are intertwined with its social and political mission. Note that its Web site refers to its "constituency," a term usually used in the context of political organizations. Focus on the Family states that its "Public Policy" program is "educating the Christian community on public policy and legislative matters that are critical in the battle to preserve the Judeo-Christian foundation" of the United States. It spent more than $10 million on this program in 2004, but this does not include large amount of spillover this program has into the organization's media and publication programs.

Focus on the Family was created by James Dobson, a child psychologist. Dobson began with a 15-minute radio broadcast in 1977. As the leader of Focus on the Family, Dobson became an influential player in the political world.[19] His view of legislation and elections is a topic of concern for many Christians and, in turn, politicians.[20] However, the line between Dobson's personal views and the official organizational views of Focus on the Family is often blurred. To expand the political power of Focus on the Family, a new organization called Focus on the Family Action was created in 2004. With a 501(c)(4) designation, this spin-off is able to conduct more explicit political activities than its 501(c)(3) parent organization. Dobson stepped down from his official leadership position in Focus on the Family in 2009, beginning what could be a difficult transition process for the organization.[21]

Fund-Raising, Grant-Making, & Other

The organizations in this sector, as with any "other" category, are difficult to categorize. However, the largest group within this sector is easier to describe

TABLE 4.10. Snapshot of Fund-Raising, Grant-Making, & Other Sector.

Activities		Size	Financials	
Unspecific financial support of other organizations and individuals		95 organizations	Median revenue: $681,383	
Other		5% of population	Aggregate revenue: $485,393,774	
Other activities				

Sector Profiles					
Name	Ruling Year	Location	Web Site		Revenue
Society for the Increase of Ministry	1973	West Hartford, CT	www.simministry.org		$258,553
African Christian Schools Foundation	1960	Nashville, TN	www.africanchristianschools.org		$616,529
National Christian Charitable Foundation	2001	Atlanta, GA	www.nationalchristian.com		$213,021,311

because it essentially comprised grant-making organizations. These nonprofits accept donations or raise money in other ways and distribute these funds to other ministries or individuals (e.g., students, missionaries). In this respect, they are functionally the same as private foundations. The only difference is that they accept donations from many sources instead relying on an individual or a family for funding, making them a public charity.

Sector Profiles

The Society for the Increase of Ministry identifies with the mission of the Episcopal Church but is an independent grant-making organization. Its sole activity is to provide scholarships to seminary students attending an Episcopal institution. The organization has a long history. It was created in 1857 by faculty at Trinity College in Hartford, Connecticut, along with local clergy. The organization provides around $200,000 in scholarships each year. Although there is variation across years, about half of this comes from donations and half from assets in its $4,000,000 endowment.

Like the previous profile, African Christian Schools Foundation exists to provide financial support to both Christian schools and students. Unlike the previous profile, it works internationally in Nigeria, Swaziland, and other African nations. Both overlap the Education & Training sector, but they are placed in this category because their work is primarily focused on the raising and distribution of funds. The organization traces its roots to a correspondence Bible course based in a Nashville church in the 1940s. This led to a contact in Nigeria that blossomed into a larger ministry to support Christian education in Nigeria and, later, in other African nations. Over its history, the foundation has shifted from a direct control model to more of a "partnership" model by which it provides financial and technical support for local efforts.

The National Christian Charitable Foundation serves as a type of clearinghouse for Christian philanthropists and charities. It offers various services for individuals, such as asset liquidation, charitable trusts and annuities, and personalized management and advice concerning charitable giving. The organization compares its services to a "brokerage account—but instead of investing in companies by buying stocks and mutual funds, you're investing in God's Kingdom by giving to the ministries and causes closest to your heart." The foundation also provides services for churches or other organizations to create a fund that accepts various types of donations (e.g., money, property, stocks) and then manage it like an endowment. In 2004, the foundation distributed grants ranging from $100 to millions to individual churches, local and national Christian nonprofits, schools, and secular organizations like the American Cancer Society. The foundation works with and through a network of Local Christian Foundations that help organize donors at the local level.

Themes

While focusing on statistics risks losing the individual stories contained in those numbers, the danger of referencing only individual stories is the potential to lose the larger patterns. Despite heterogeneity within and across sectors, there are a number of themes that run throughout them. For example, there are several standard routes by which Christian nonprofits seem to be generated. Several of the organizations profiled began as the ministry of a local church but outgrew the boundaries of the church walls. They either became too large in staff and/or money to stay a church ministry or grew beyond their original mission. Other nonprofits were parachurch from day one. These organizations are often the result of one or two religious entrepreneurs. Some of these individuals come from secular areas (e.g., former athletes, lawyers, businesspeople) to synthesize their faith and life into a new organizational form. Others come from traditional routes, such as a seminary or church, but decide to leave those structures to pursue another path. Some Christian nonprofits originate from within existing nonprofits. A leader may leave to form a new nonprofit, or the nonprofit decides to spin off a new organization. Similarly, the organizational and sector profiles highlight differences in the structure of Christian nonprofits. Some organizations, especially those in the Charismatic Evangelism sector, are driven by one or two individuals. These nonprofits are frequently named after these individuals and prominently advertise their credentials or reputation. This will clearly have an effect on the decision-making process within the organization since this person inherently has a great deal of power.

TABLE 4.11. Percentage of Ruling Dates by Sectors.

	Charismatic Evangelism	Relief & Development	Education & Training	Publishing & Resources	Radio & Television	Missions & Missionary	Fellowship & Enrichment	Advocacy & Activism	Fund-Raising, Grant-Making, & Other
Before 1950	0.8	0.9	0.8	7.2	4.5	2.6	1.4	2.1	2.1
1951–1960	0.8	2.2	2.3	4.8	6.0	4.2	4.1	2.1	5.3
1961–1970	3.6	4.8	5.8	11.6	7.5	4.5	6.8	5.2	8.5
1971–1980	11.4	9.6	13.6	14.3	22.4	10.6	14.3	19.8	11.7
1981–1990	27.8	29.8	20.5	22.7	25.4	21.6	24.5	25.0	22.3
1991–2004	55.6	52.6	57.0	39.4	34.3	56.5	49.0	45.8	50.0
Total (%)	100	100	100	100	100	100	100	100	100

Others, such as those in the Relief & Development sector, are highly professionalized and bureaucratized.

Each sector also differs in its individual history. We can get some feel for this
by comparing the organizations' ruling dates or the date in which they registered as
nonprofits with the Internal Revenue Service.[22] Table 4-11 shows that the Publishing
& Resources and Radio & Television sectors have some of the oldest nonprofits
when measured by when they received their tax-exempt status. Seven percent of
the Publishing & Resources organizations existed before 1950, while 4% of the
Radio & Television nonprofits date back that far. This compares to only 1 or 2% for
the other sectors.

The pattern for the Charismatic Evangelism and Relief & Development sectors
shows that many of these nonprofits are fairly young. This does not necessarily
mean that nonprofits in these sectors were nonexistent before this time; rather,
these patterns are a product of both sector age *and* sector stability. If a sector is
particularly unstable, then it may appear to be young even though there have been
many nonprofits in the sector throughout the years. For example, if the life span of
a Charismatic Evangelism nonprofit is only a few years, we clearly would not
observe many old organizations still existing today even if there were many in the
1950s, 1960s, and so forth. Given that many of the Charismatic Evangelism organizations are smaller and dependent on one individual, it would be reasonable to think that
it is characterized by a high rate of turnover, not a young sector age. This is particularly
true considering that itinerant preaching and revivals are some of the oldest forms of
religious outreach. The Relief & Development sector, however, may truly be a younger
type of Christian nonprofit. There are some factors that cut across these
sectors' histories. For instance, when you look at the Advocacy & Activism sector,
you will see that many of the nonprofits in this sector were created between 1970
and 1980. Indeed, while all the sectors saw significant growth during this period, the
Advocacy & Activism sector saw the greatest growth. Given the cultural turmoil of
the 1960s and early 1970s, it makes sense that the Christian nonprofit world would
respond with their own perspective during this time. Many of the well-known organizations in the sector were created in this period, including Focus on the Family
and the American Family Association.

We can also think about these different sectors in terms of the worship and
outreach typology presented in the previous chapter. Religious outreach is categorized into four outcomes or goals: conversion, charity, community, and communication. This was in addition to the worship behaviors. Most of these activity sectors
tend to be somewhere between the four outreach goals. Relief & Development
organizations, for instance, are mainly oriented toward charity. Missions & Missionary
nonprofits are more in-between the conversion and charity goals but are oriented

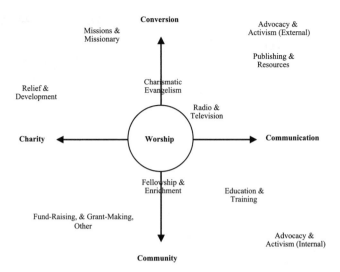

FIGURE 4.4. Placement of Christian Nonprofit Sectors on Worship-Outreach Dimensions.

more toward the former. Organizations in the Publishing & Resources sector are often conversion focused (e.g., producing religious tracts and Bible translations), but many also provide intragroup resources, such as Bible study resources and worship materials. The Advocacy & Activism sector is difficult to place on this map, though, because it consists of a very internally focused subgroup (i.e., those looking to renew or reform a particular denomination or tradition) along with a very externally focused subgroup (i.e., pursuing social and political activism). The latter could actually be considered to be somewhere between the conversion and communication axes as these organizations are trying to communicate a certain theological position in an attempt to convert others politically or socially. The more internally focused group, though, is better placed between the community and communication axes as they are trying to communicate a position to better their own community.

You can also think about each of these activity sectors being closer or further away from worship, which is at the core of religious behavior. Fellowship & Enrichment nonprofits are closest to the community-building types of outreach. However, they can sometimes come close to overlapping activities of worship (e.g., Bible study groups). The same can be said for many Radio & Television ministries. Clearly, they are attempting to communicate the Christian message to a wider audience, but they are essentially providing worship services on television. This means that people can, and some likely do, substitute such media for their worship within an actual church.[23] Comparatively, the sectors such as Advocacy & Activism and Relief & Development are typically very distant from worship. This obviously has implications for these organizations' relationship to local congregations who specialize in worship. They might be less likely to run into conflict with churches, although they would still likely run into conflict with denominational agencies. The next chapter will continue to looking at these trends running across and between these different activity sectors, but will do so in the context of how Christian nonprofits acquire and utilize the money they depend on to operate.

5

The Balance Sheet

A Financial Portrait of the Parachurch Sector

In barbarous times, when men were in the dark, it was believed that the success of the gospel was according to the outpourings of the Holy Spirit, but in the age of light and improvement, it is estimated according to the pourings out of the purse.

—John Leland, 1826

According to the 2007 *Yearbook of American and Canadian Churches*, the Southern Baptist Convention received the most money for all Protestant denominations at over $10.5 billion.[1] It has more than 40,000 individual congregations in the United States. Comparatively, if we were to consider the over 1,900 Christian nonprofit organizations examined in this book as congregations within a collective parachurch denomination, they would easily constitute one of the wealthiest denominations in the United States in both total and per church income as they took in more than $10 billion in 2006. Even if we considered them individually, the largest nonprofits in this group receive more annual income than many major denominations.

Where does all of this money come from? How is it raised? How is it spent? And how do answers to these questions differ across and within the sectors presented in the previous chapter? The acquisition and use of money can be a sensitive issue for all organizations. However, with nonprofits, the issue can be particularly challenging. On the one hand, money is obviously vital to the operations and success of a nonprofit. But if they appear to be *too* concerned with raising money, or if they seem to waste

TABLE 5.1. Largest Christian Nonprofits' Revenue Compared to Select Denominations.

Name of Denomination or Nonprofit	Number of Churches or Nonprofits	Total Contributions or Total Revenue
Southern Baptist Convention	43,669	$10,721,544,568
Largest Nonprofits Collectively	1,941	$10,366,955,673
United Methodist Church	34,660	$5,541,540,536
Feed the Children, Inc.	1	$958,778,536
World Vision	1	$803,810,000
Church of the Nazarene	5,225	$765,434,742
Food for the Poor	1	$643,350,124
American Baptist Churches in the United States	5,740	$332,030,013
MAP International	1	$258,540,948

Source: 2007 *Yearbook of American and Canadian Churches*; IRS-990 forms (2004).

or abuse the money given to them, then the opinion of donors can quickly sour along with their financial support. In other words, nonprofits must care about money just as much as for-profit organizations without appearing like they care. How these organizations handle money is not just a matter of being able to financially support their operations but also a matter of maintaining a sense of legitimacy to those operations.

The delicate balance between meeting the financial needs of an organization and maintaining a sense of legitimacy is not limited to the parachurch population. Congregations and denominations face many of the same challenges. It might seem obvious that congregations need to raise money just like any parachurch organization, but it is often easy to forget the financial demands of running a church in the face of its focus on worship and fellowship. In interviews with congregations, Christian Smith, Michael Emerson, and Patricia Snell observed a clear ambivalence about fund-raising. Comments like "I wish we could be more open about [money], but people are touchy" were common among pastors, and the parishioners expressed a similar uneasiness.[2]

While a complicated topic in both congregations and parachurch organizations, there are some clear qualitative differences in the dynamics underlying fund-raising for each. One critical difference lies in the reasoning underlying the appeals. Congregations can often be more commanding in their requests for contributions by framing giving as a theological requirement or duty. Indeed, in some cases, financial support is formally defined and expected as a duty of membership. Christian nonprofits, on the other hand, often must make a more concerted effort at selling some service or good on its own merits. This is not to say that they cannot use theological arguments in their pitch. There are also social and psychological advantages for congregations when it comes to appealing for money. Most churches have a regular membership. This is important because it means that members have likely developed deep social ties in the church. They have friends there, they like the pastor, and their children like the youth minister. Few nonprofits have anywhere near the amount of face-to-face contact or long-term relationships with their donors as churches have with their members, nor do they have as strong of a theological argument for requesting funds. This makes it much easier for an individual to simply stop giving money. If a donor only receives contact from a nonprofit once a year through a newsletter, there are little social or psychological repercussions for deciding to withhold a contribution. To put it bluntly, you do not have to look anyone in the eye the next week if you do not send money to the nonprofit. On the other hand, you *will* have to see your friends and pastor at the church. If you stop attending church altogether you will likely lose those friendships, so there is motivation not only for continuing to be a member but also for being a contributing member. Social ties make churches incredibly persuasive when it comes to appealing for support. Marketers and fund-raisers like to say that "people give to people, not causes." Abstract ideas or causes lack the human face that moves donors to action. It is not an accident that many nonprofits provide pictures and stories of individuals (e.g., children being sponsored) they are helping instead of relying on arguments about "global economic stratification" to persuade donors.

Sociologists would explain all of this as a difference in the monitoring and sanctioning capabilities of congregations and parachurch organizations.[3] Because most nonprofits have little ability to monitor donors or to provide any consequences for not contributing, they are relatively weak when it comes to enforcing commitment among contributors. Of course, it is important to note that some nonprofits, such as those that operate through many local groups or auxiliaries, are able to cultivate relationships similar to those of congregations. The differences between these nonprofits and congregations in fund-raising are less pronounced than those that raise funds at a purely centralized level. The dynamics are also similar when comparing denominations and parachurch organizations. Contemporary parachurch organizations are often accused of using slick advertising and sophisticated techniques adopted from the corporate world in their fund-raising efforts, which is said to diminish the spiritual nature of their activities.[4] What is often lost in these critiques is that denominational organizations pioneered such tactics. We saw in chapter 2 how denominations began to form their various regional and national offices and agencies in the last half of the 19th century. These centralized structures would take over the activities previously conducted by the independent religious societies. However, to raise the money needed to support these agencies, denominations turned to emerging techniques in corporate advertising and finance. Denominational offices launched strategic fund-raising campaigns that today would make any nonprofit CEO proud. Congregations would be classified by how much money they sent to the denomination. Stingy congregations would be shamed into giving more by having their name listed in the lower categories, while generous congregations would receive awards or titles. Episcopalians hired a New York advertising agency to assist with their fund-raising. Methodists began a program by which individual congregations would sponsor a missionary so that they would feel a personal connection and therefore give more. This sponsorship technique is a model utilized today by many nonprofits, secular and religious. All of these methods were successful in building up the denominations, but as Ben Primer noted, they "paid a price . . . in the form of a diminished sense of the Church's traditional religious goals." While pursuing the material needs of the denomination, the image of the organization had suffered.[5]

Parachurch Revenue Sources

A public charity is popularly conceived of as an organization that pleads for donations through mailings, telethons, phone calls, and various other fund-raising events, such as dinner banquets and charity walks/runs. These appeals are usually for free money. That is, the organization hopes that you will provide a donation to support their cause without personally asking for anything in return. Sometimes, the donor receives a small item of appreciation such as a bumper sticker, coffee mug, or the always popular tote bag, but, for the most part, the exchange is one sided.

      This classic image is accurate for many nonprofits, but others have an entirely different strategy for raising money. These organizations, often called commercial nonprofits, raise money by charging fees for services or selling products to their donors. They then use this income to produce more goods or offer more services. In many ways, then, these organizations do not superficially differ from businesses in their operations except they might charge less for similar services and do not use revenue to benefit owners or shareholders. Instead, all of the money raised is channeled back into the nonprofit's operations. Despite these differences, the similarities in operations and often products and services can lead to competition between for-profit businesses and commercial nonprofit organizations. For example, many Christian nonprofits in the Publishing & Resources sector face direct competition not only from other nonprofit publishers but also from for-profit publishers. The books distributed by the nonprofit publishers are often the same type of books one can find in Barnes & Noble or some other retailer. One can think back to the discussion of "niche overlap" in chapter 3 to hypothesize which Christian nonprofit sectors have more or less overlap with activities of other types of organizations, such as for-profit organizations and government agencies. Along with the Publishing sector, the Radio & Television sector also likely has a high level of overlap with for-profit organizations, especially since mainstream networks and movie studios have begun to produce programs with Christian themes.[6]

Christian nonprofits operate predominantly on donations, but there is variation across the different sectors in the balance between donations and commercial revenue. Comprising only 9% of its total revenue, the Relief & Development sector is the least reliant on commercial activities. Selling products or services could actually undermine the image of Relief & Development nonprofits. On the other hand, Publishing & Resources and Fellowship & Enrichment sectors have the highest mean proportion of revenue coming from commercial activities with about 30% coming from sales and fees. These sectors can charge for products (e.g., books) and services (e.g., seminars) without losing much in the way of credibility because people are accustomed to such transactions in their everyday life.

The proportion of commercial revenue is likely underestimated across all of the sectors because many nonprofits may give a donor a book or some other item in return for money or recommend a donation in exchange for some item or service. When exactly such exchanges become commercial and not donative is

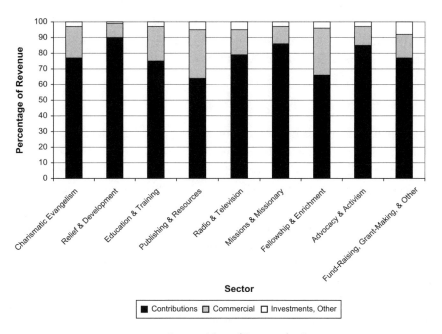

FIGURE 5.1. Composition of Revenue by Sector.

a fuzzy issue, but most organizations would probably prefer to classify them as the latter since "donation" has a better sound to it than "sale" in the nonprofit world. Commercial revenue is seen as everything from a guilty pleasure to "sacrilegious" among nonprofit managers. Regardless of any misgivings on the part of organizational leaders, commercial activities have become an increasingly significant source of revenue for all nonprofits. This might be because donors are often unaware of where and how nonprofits get their money, so there is little risk in terms of public image when an organization engages in commercial activity. Even when they are aware of a nonprofit's commercial activities, the public do not seem to care as long as the activities appear relevant to the organization's mission.[7]

Donation Revenue Sources

While the idealized image of a nonprofit may be of the donative type as opposed to commercial type, we also have idealized ideas about the source and nature of the donations received by those nonprofits. That is, we often assume that the donations received by a nonprofit are from individuals who provide small donations. After all, this represents most of our personal experiences with the nonprofit world. You may receive a mailing or phone call from a nonprofit that asks for a $20 donation, or perhaps you have a favorite charity that you make a small donation to every year. This image is accurate to a certain extent. About three-fourths of all charitable giving comes from individuals.[8] However, while personal monetary donations given directly to the nonprofit are prominent, contributions can also come from a variety of other sources and in different forms.

Direct versus Indirect Support

Direct public support is defined as money and goods (e.g., donated cars, food, clothing) given from individuals or other organizations to the nonprofit. This is in contrast to indirect public support, which is cash or noncash support received through an intermediary organization. For example, there are collective fund-raising agencies like the United Way and the Combined Federal Campaign that receive direct support and then transfer this to member agencies. When received by those third-party agencies, this contribution counts as indirect public support. More common among Christian nonprofits is indirect support from affiliated parent or subordinate organizations. For instance, Christianity Today International received grants in 2004 from the Christianity Today Foundation, a related fund-raising nonprofit that is primarily focused on supporting the activities for the former organization.

Government Contributions

A third source of noncommercial revenue comes from government contributions. While there are parts of the nonprofit world that rely predominantly on government funding, it is quite rare among the Christian nonprofits examined in this book. Only 56, or less than 3% of the 1,941 organizations identified, received government contributions in 2004. It is possible that if we were examining smaller local Christian organizations focused on social services (e.g., shelters, food banks), that public funding would be more prominent, since their activities lend themselves more to receiving government funds. We will explore this topic more in chapter 7.

Close to 70% of the government-funded organizations are in the Relief & Development sector, which makes sense given that these nonprofits are providing services that the government would clearly be interested in supporting as a way of outsourcing its own relief and development efforts. Another 11% of the publicly funded Christian nonprofits are in the Fellowship & Enrichment sector. Much of the government support in this sector goes toward prisoner rehabilitation and youth programs, including abstinence education.

Membership Dues

The final category of donation-based income comes from membership dues. This is admittedly an ambiguous revenue source that straddles the line between donations and commercial activity. Members often have a more stable relationship with the nonprofit than random donors. However, membership dues are often separate from the commercial activities of the organization, which can include income coming from conference fees and publications above and beyond the dues. As discussed in the previous chapter, "members" are often not individuals but local chapters of a national organization. Organizational scholars refer to this as a federated structure.[9] Revenue from membership dues is most common in the Fellowship & Enrichment sector, but even there it only accounts for an average of 10% of the organizations' total donation revenue and even less of its overall revenue.

Overall, the overwhelming majority of Christian nonprofits' donative revenue comes from direct public support. The Relief & Development and Fellowship & Enrichment sectors rely slightly less on direct public support given their government and membership funding sources, respectively. Remember that this category includes contributions from corporations and other organizations along with noncash donations. For instance, within the Relief & Development sector, more than 17% of the total donations are in noncash form, usually food, medicines, clothing,

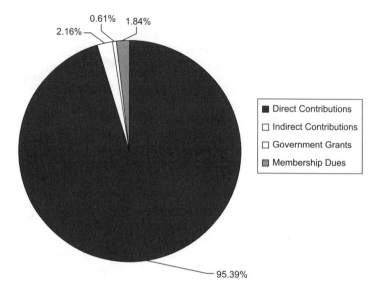

FIGURE 5.2. Composition of Contribution Revenue.

and so forth. It is difficult, though, to decompose this large direct public support category further because the organizations are not required to separate out contributions coming from isolated individuals, corporations, or other actors. There is no doubt that small monetary donations from isolated individuals constitute a large part of this category, but it is not the only revenue stream included within this category.

Commercial Revenue Sources

There are three primary sources of commercial revenue. The first and largest category is revenue generated through program services. This is revenue that nonprofits acquire by charging fees in exchange for some service of the organization. Usually, these services form the basis of the nonprofit's exempt purpose and can include things like speaking fees, conference and seminar registrations, consulting fees, and low-cost medical and legal services. In short, if the nonprofit generates money through its primary activities, then this is included in the program service revenue category.

In addition to program service revenue, another significant source of commercial income comes from the sale of products or inventory. For instance, much of the commercial activity across the Christian nonprofit population consists of selling books, audiotapes/CDs, videos/DVDs, devotional materials, and similar resources.

The subject matter of the materials varies when looking across the different sectors. Books coming out of the Charismatic Evangelism sector are often focused on the teachings of the organization's leader and feature him or her on the cover. Materials coming out of the Education & Training sector are less personality driven and include things like Bible study guides or ministry manuals.

A third commercial revenue source, although much smaller than the previous two, comes from special events. These events do not provide any service, at least not a service related to the organization's nonprofit purpose, but raise money through the sale of goods, admissions, or some other exchange. For instance, a fund-raising golf tournament or dinner banquet sponsored by the nonprofit would be a type of special event.

Looking across the sectors, the variation in commercial revenue sources is clear. All of the sectors produce at least half of their commercial revenue through program services, but the proportion ranges from 50% for the Publishing & Resources sector to almost 80% in the Fellowship & Enrichment sector. Much of this can be explained through the nature of these sectors' activities. Producing books and print materials naturally leads to the sale of such materials in the Publishing sector, while the conferences, seminars, retreats, and other common

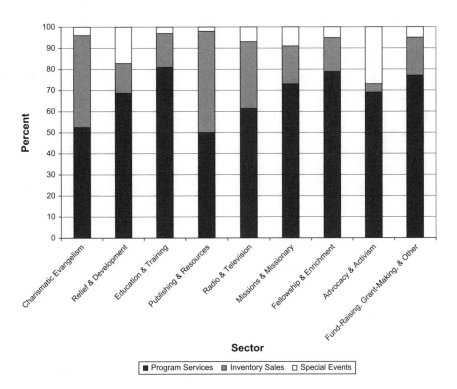

FIGURE 5.3. Composition of Commercial Revenue.

activities within the Fellowship sector naturally generate program service revenue. Special event revenue is relatively rare but is most common within the Relief & Development and the Advocacy & Activism sectors where it comprises about 12 and 28% of the commercial revenue, respectively.

Consequences of Revenue Source

Whether a nonprofit relies on donations or commercial revenue can have an important impact on its operations. The relationship between a contributor and a nonprofit is much different in donative and commercial organizations. With a pure donation, the organization likely contacts the donor and is able to persuade the individual to contribute. While this may occur with commercial nonprofits as well, it is much more likely that the individual does not need to be persuaded outside of some simple advertising. If the person has a preexisting need or desire for the good or service, then they may be quite willing to donate in exchange for the service. Donative nonprofits must continuously persuade individuals with each appeal. On the contrary, individuals may continuously patronize a commercial nonprofit if its products and/or services proved satisfactory in the past. In short, the donor-recipient relationship is much more tenuous in the donative context than the commercial one. Donative nonprofits are at the mercy of whims of donors who have little directly to gain from an exchange, while commercial nonprofits can create a relationship based on the donor's desire for the products and services of the organization.[10]

We can see these dynamics in the financial data of the Christian nonprofits we have been examining. Table 5-2 looks at the financial stability of two groups of nonprofits: those that are predominantly donative versus those that are primarily commercial. "Predominantly" is defined here by those that have 80% or more of their revenue coming from either donations or commercial activities. Notice, first,

TABLE 5.2. Mean Change and Variation in Revenue by Revenue Source.

	Between 1 and 2 Years Ago	Between 2 and 3 Years Ago	Between 3 and 4 Years
Mean percent change			
Donative	+7	+12	+11
Commercial	+15	+11	+13
Standard deviation			
Donative	0.70	0.59	0.78
Commercial	0.38	0.47	0.34

that the average percent change in revenue from year to year is about the same in the two groups—typically a little over 10% growth in revenue year over year. These overall percentages, however, hide differences within each group. When we look at the standard deviation, which is a measure of how widely spread out the percentages are for each group, we see that variation in growth or decline for donative nonprofits is much greater than that in commercial organizations. While overall growth is similar in the two groups, there is much more instability among those relying on donations.[11]

Revenue instability can make the logistics and operations of donative organizations challenging. If revenue increases greatly one year, does this mean that the organization should hire more staff or rent more office space? The volatile nature of donations makes such decisions difficult. What if donations decrease the following year? An economic recession or some other unknown could drastically cut donations. A natural disaster or some other fluke event could shower attention and support on the nonprofit, but this attention can just as easily fade with the next event. Commercially focused nonprofits can grow much more predictably since the unknowns are fewer and less damaging in their consequences. Their customers have some dependence on their goods or services, so they will be less willing to just eliminate their support for the organization. Of course, this does not mean that current customers will always continue their support or that random occurrences cannot affect commercial nonprofits, but overall, there is more stability in commercial revenue than donations.[12]

Expenses

We have looked at the revenue sources of Christian nonprofits and how these vary across sectors and examined some of the consequences of different revenue sources. The topic of revenue naturally leads to questions concerning expenses. Regardless of how they receive their money, how do Christian nonprofits spend it all? How and where nonprofits get money can be a sensitive issue among donors and watchdog groups, but the spending of funds is the usual cause of controversy. A perception of inefficiency or abuse is a fast way for an organization to lose support. As we will see later in this chapter, a favorite way to assess nonprofits, Christian and otherwise, is to compute various efficiency ratios based on expenses. Those that spend more than a certain percentage of their revenue on fund-raising or on similar expenses are declared inefficient. We will take a look at these evaluations along with their pros and cons, but for now, let us look at the expenses themselves and how they are related to the sectors and other factors we have been examining.

Nonprofit expenses are categorized into three broad areas. The first and usually largest type of expense is for program services. The second largest type of expense is for overhead costs, such as office supplies and employee salaries. The third and usually smallest expense category goes toward fund-raising expenses. All of this might seem fairly straightforward, but partitioning expenses can get a little tricky at times because the same activity can often fall under any of the three categories. Consider a nonprofit that spends $1,000 to print newsletters. Now, if the newsletter is part of their promised activities to keep the organization's members connected and informed, then all or some of this expense would fall under the category of program services. If the newsletter is a direct appeal for money, though, then it falls in the fund-raising category of expenses. Then again, if the newsletter is for internal use among employees (e.g., "there are three birthdays in the office this month . . ."), then it becomes a general management and overhead expense. There is pressure for nonprofits to have very low expense percentages in the fund-raising and overhead costs. The reasoning is that donors do not like to give money to an organization that simply exists to ask for more money, nor do they like to just pay for office supplies. They want to see their money doing something. Some have argued that this desire is unrealistic at times as some donors expect a nonprofit to spend virtually nothing on overhead. However, some research has questioned how much these percentages actually affect donations. One study found that low overhead costs have no benefit when it comes to donations, while high fund-raising costs increase donations.[13]

Across all Christian nonprofits, an average of 80% of expenses are directed toward program services, 16% toward management and general operating expenses,

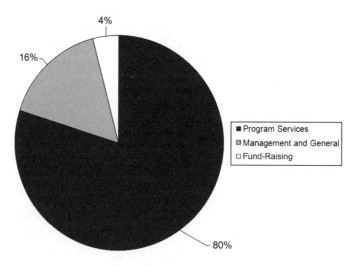

FIGURE 5.4. Overall Composition of Expenses.

and 4% toward fund-raising. These numbers are in line with other types of non-profits. For instance, the average management and general expense ratio is 18% across other types of nonprofits.[14] There are some notable differences across the activity sectors. The Advocacy & Activism sector averages twice as much as the average on fund-raising at 8% of total expenses. The Relief & Development sector is the most efficient when it comes to overhead expenses, spending just under 10% on overhead.

But what exactly are these expenses going toward, whether they are of the fund-raising, program services, or management variety? On their financial returns nonprofits must provide some itemization of their expenses. The form provides twenty categories of expenses for the organization to report on along with lines for "other" expenses not covered by the provided categories. In practice, organizations tend to put a large number of their expenses in this "other" category, making it difficult to systematically examine those expenses. This is true for all nonprofits, not just Christian ones. It is likely a product of two forces. First, there are many expenses that genuinely do not fit into the predefined categories provided by the Internal Revenue Service. Second, putting expenses in the "other" category makes it more difficult to compute efficiency measures and other assessments of the organization, so there likely is some intentional dumping of expenses into this category. However, we can still take a look at those preset categories to get some idea of where organizations' money is going.

We can see some clear differences across sectors that result from the unique activities of each. For instance, when it comes to cash and noncash donations to other organizations and individuals, the Relief & Development, Missions & Missionary, and Fund-Raising & Grant-Making sectors lead the way. There are likely differences in the type of grants, however. The Relief & Development sector's grant-making probably consists of food, medicine, clothing, and cash to the needy, whether due to long-term development goals or short-term emergencies and disasters. The grants in the Missions & Missionary sector are typically for missionaries in the field to support their work. The Fund-Raising & Grant-Making sector primarily makes grants to other nonprofits and churches. There does seem to be some correlation between the amount of money spent on grants and allocations and the amount spent on salaries or wages as the Relief & Development, Missions & Missionary, and Fund-Raising & Grant-Making sectors are also the lowest when it comes to expenses on compensation. It is not particularly labor intensive to simply transfer money or goods to other people or individuals, so it is not entirely surprising that the more organizations' activities are based in grant making, the less it spends on the payroll.[15] The Fellowship & Enrichment sector appears to require the most in the way of paid employees, as close to half of its expenses goes toward salaries. The Advocacy & Activism sector along with the Education & Training

TABLE 5-3. Expense Composition by Sector.

	Charismatic Evangelism	Relief & Development	Education & Training	Publishing & Resources	Radio & Television	Missions & Missionary	Fellowship & Enrichment	Advocacy & Activism	Fund-Raising, Grant-Making, Other
Program services (%)	78.5	85.4	77.8	77.6	77.1	83.5	75.7	74.1	80.2
Management and general (%)	18.4	9.7	16.7	18.1	15.9	13.2	19.6	17.4	12.6
Fund-raising (%)	2.2	4.7	4.8	3.4	5.8	2.8	4.5	8.1	5.0

Note: Not shown is a "payments to affiliates" category, which is less than 1% for all sectors except the fund-raising.

TABLE 5.4. Detailed Expense Composition by Sector.

	Charismatic Evangelism	Relief & Development	Education & Training	Publishing & Resources	Radio & Television	Missions & Missionary	Fellowship & Enrichment	Advocacy & Activism	Fund-Raising, Grant-Making, Other
Grants, assistance to others	4	30	7	6	4	19	2	6	42
Salaries, pensions, wages	36	19	39	35	31	23	45	39	19
Fund-raising, legal, accounting fees	1	1	1	1	1	1	1	2	1
Supplies, occupancy, equipment, telephone	8	5	7	8	9	5	9	8	4
Postage and publications	4	2	4	15	5	2	5	12	3
Travel, conferences, meetings	10	5	9	4	3	9	9	7	5
Interest and depreciation	4	2	2	4	6	2	3	2	2
Other expenses	32	36	30	26	40	39	26	22	23
Total* (%)	100	100	100	100	100	100	100	100	100

Note: Numbers may not add up exactly to 100% due to rounding.

sector are also wage intensive with almost 40% of their expenses taken up by compensation of employees.

Across all sectors, the smallest type of expense is toward professional consultants, whether legal, financial, or fund-raising. Although it only represents 2% of its expenses, it is not surprising that the Advocacy & Activism sector spends the most on such consultants. As noted earlier, these organizations spend twice as much as any other sector on fund-raising and their activities often involve issues where legal counsel would be useful.

There is relatively little variation in expenses toward the most basic overhead costs such as rent for office space, supplies, and telephone charges, although Fund-Raising & Grant-Making organizations spend the least in this area at 4% of the sector's expenses. The Radio & Television and the Fellowship & Enrichment sectors have the highest expenses in this area at 9% of their total. The cost of broadcasting equipment and studios is likely the source of the Radio & Television sector's high rate, while the Fellowship & Enrichment sector's rate may be the result of supporting various branch offices and its more labor-intensive operations.

The cost of printing, publications, and postage sees a wider range of variation across the different sectors. The Publishing & Resources sector spends the most in this area, representing 15% of its expenses. In fact, it might be surprising that this is not a higher proportion of these organizations' expenses. The Advocacy & Activism sector spends the second most on printing and mailing. These organizations use newsletters and other mailings to keep their constituents informed concerning their various social, religious, or political issues to their constituents to either encourage direct action or ask for support for the organization's actions.

Travel and conference costs are lowest for Radio & Television nonprofits, followed by the Publishing & Resources sector. Neither of these sectors have a clear reason to travel, particularly the Radio & Television organizations. Publishers may travel somewhat more to book exhibits. The Charismatic Evangelism sector spends the most in this area, which makes sense given the itinerant preaching and speaking that is common among these organizations. The Missions & Missionary, Education & Training, and Fellowship & Enrichment sectors all spend a little less than 10% on travel and conference expenses.

A Comparison

How do these revenue and expense numbers for parachurch nonprofits compare to congregations? At first glance, the revenue breakdown for congregations is quite similar to that of Christian nonprofits, at least in the fact that most revenue comes from direct contributions. It does not come as a surprise that 81% of congregations' revenue comes from the contributions of its members, whether through collections or preplanned giving.[16] A remaining 14% comes from sources like tuition, rental fees, and other income from programs or services, while the last 5% comes from denominations, charities, and other organizations. Although superficially similar, these revenue numbers are probably hiding some differences. For instance, parachurch organizations likely receive more contributions from organizational sources (e.g., congregations, denominations, corporations, foundations) than do congregations.[17]

When it comes to expenses, there are more obvious differences between congregations and nonprofits. Christian nonprofits, along with all nonprofits, place great emphasis on how little they spend on basic administration and overhead while operating the organization.[18] The idea is to show donors that the maximum amount of their contribution is going to the actual goals of the nonprofit and not just toward building and maintaining a bureaucracy. This is often described as how efficient the nonprofit is—a topic we will return to in a moment. We saw above that the average for management and general expenses is 16% for Christian nonprofits. On the other hand, congregations spend most of their revenue toward simply keeping the congregation in operation. For example, 44% of congregations' revenue goes toward salaries, 27% toward property maintenance or construction, and 12% toward other overhead costs. This represents 83% of the congregation's total revenue. The last 17% is sent to the congregation's denomination, nondenominational agencies, and/or a savings account.[19] There are some difficulties in directly comparing these numbers. Undoubtedly, some of these congregational expenses could and probably should be counted as program service revenue and not as overhead costs. For instance, much of a pastor's salary funds his or her activities in worship, education, and other official congregational services, not his or her activities as an administrator. However, research has supported the idea that congregations spend much of their funds toward simply maintaining the basic operation of the congregation and that this has increased over time.[20]

This might get at a fundamental difference between church and parachurch. The primary purpose of a congregation is to exist. An effective congregation is one that survives and offers a place for a community of people to worship. There is no real need or purpose for its expenses to go beyond maintaining its presence, although clearly many congregations do go beyond this primary purpose. On the contrary, it is not enough for a parachurch organization to just exist. No one is seeking out the parachurch's office building for the sake of the office building itself. The money being given to it, therefore, must extend beyond that building for the organization to have a purpose. It is worth mentioning that this is yet another area where parachurch organizations and denominations show a similar dynamic. After all, if congregations saw that their contributions to the denomination went almost entirely to maintenance of the denominational offices, then they would feel quite similar to a parachurch donor in the same position. It is not surprising, then, that at least some denominational agencies have adopted the same financial standards as parachurch organizations or belong to the same associations, like the Evangelical Council for Financial Accountability. When it comes to both denominations and parachurch organizations, contributors want some evidence that their money is being used efficiently and effectively. However, demonstrating either of these qualities is not as easy as it might seem.

Efficiency and Effectiveness

Scholars make a clear distinction between organizational efficiency and effectiveness. Technically,

> efficiency refers to an input-output ratio or comparison, whereas effectiveness refers to an absolute level of either input acquisition or outcome attainment.

We can put this more concretely through an example. Let us consider two organizations whose mission is to build churches. The first builds 10 churches with $1,000,000, while the second builds 10 churches with $750,000. Maybe the first organization spent more on fund-raising, salaries, or some other overhead expense. These two organizations were equally effective but the first was less efficient. Or consider two organizations that both raised $10,000, but one spent $1,000 to raise this money and the other spent $5,000. The fund-raising was equally effective in its outcome, but the latter was much less efficient. In short, effectiveness is an issue of whether an organization actually accomplishes its goals, while efficiency is an issue of how it accomplished those goals.[21]

It would seem easy, then, to assess organizations on these standards of efficiency and effectiveness. Unfortunately, things are rarely as clear-cut as they first appear. First, assessing effectiveness can become much more complicated depending on the type of goals an organization is pursuing. Measures of effectiveness can be easily quantified when the goals of an organization are of a clear and visible nature, or what you might call a "hard goal." This is easy in factories and other manufacturing settings. If the stated goal is to produce widgets, then effectiveness can be measured through the number of widgets produced per hour.[22]

The above example of a church-building organization provides a clear quantifiable measure, assuming that the actual building of churches was the only goal. But what if church building was really only a method to accomplish other goals? What if they really cared about whether people attended the church or whether it led people to convert or whether it improved the spiritual lives of individuals in the neighborhood? Effectiveness becomes less quantifiable for nonprofit organizations that often have more value-based goals that are not easily measured through such objective criteria. A factory may have easily quantifiable criteria for measuring goal success, but it is more difficult to determine equivalent outputs for an organization that focuses on building individuals' character or other "soft goals."[23]

Although many Christian nonprofits see their goals as partially or wholly unquantifiable, they often attempt to provide measures of effectiveness in their annual reports. Below are the most common types of measures in each sector.

Sector	Common Measures of Effectiveness
Charismatic Evangelism	Number of people spoken or presented to; number of "commitments" made
Relief & Development	Number of houses built, wells drilled, money distributed, children sponsored
Education & Training	Number of pastors trained, seminars provided
Publishing & Resources	Number of books, tracts, magazines, etc., published/distributed/translated
Radio & Television	Size of listening/viewing audience; geographic range
Missions & Missionary	Number of missionaries supported, trips taken
Fellowship & Enrichment	Number of services (conferences, publications, etc.) offered to members or clients
Activism & Advocacy	Size of mailing lists/constituents, rallies organized, legislative outcomes
Fund-Raising, Grant-Making, & Other	Amount of money distributed, other

If it is difficult to measure these soft goals in secular nonprofits, one can imagine the potential challenge for religious nonprofits. A report by the Independent Sector found that religious congregations were most likely to believe that their "accomplishments are intangible." It is reasonable to assume that many religious nonprofits feel the same. It is common for religious nonprofits to speak of being "holistic" in their goals. For example, most Christian relief and development organizations state that their goal is meet the physical *and* spiritual needs of those they help. The physical aspect of this goal may be clearly quantifiable (e.g., amount of food distributed), but the spiritual is more difficult.[24]

In lieu of such quantifiable effectiveness measures, especially those that allow comparisons across different types of organizations, efficiency measures often become the way nonprofits are judged. These types of measures are used prominently in popular charity evaluation tools and services, such as Charity Navigator (www.charitynavigator.org) and the American Institute of Philanthropy (www.charitywatch.org). Ratings services such as these are very clear that they are evaluating each nonprofit's organizational efficiency and not necessarily the "quality of the programs and services a charity provides." However, the language that is often used in these evaluations ("outperforms", "underperforms") and the grading scales ("4 stars") can muddle this fact. The visibility and ease of access of such ratings can also make them have a disproportionate influence on potential donors.[25]

Efficiency measures have taken a prominent role in the evaluation of Christian nonprofits as well. MinistryWatch.org is a Web site maintained by a nonprofit organization called Wall Watchers. It provides financial profiles of more than five hundred Christian nonprofit organizations. The site provides efficiency ratings based on virtually the same measures used by other charity rating services. Ministry Watch also provides similar disclaimers about the meaning of the information they provide:

> The ratings do not consider program outcome measurements. Although program outcome measurements may be relevant to donors, they are not reported in a standard format that facilitates comparison of ministries with very different missions.

Despite these disclaimers, the rating system provided by Ministry Watch is likely taken by many potential donors as an important indicator of organizational effectiveness. Many of the nonprofits profiled by Ministry Watch are clearly concerned about this potential confusion as they have posted critiques of the rating system. For example, in response to Ministry Watch's ratings of their organization, American Leprosy Missions Inc. provides the following:

> There are many watchdog groups out there who are all trying to rate charities with letter grades, stars, points and percentages. But they all miss the bottom line: How effective are the organization's program

TABLE 5.5. Sample Efficiency Measures Used by CharityNavigator.org.

Measure	Definition	Scoring
Administrative expenses	Percentage of total budget spent on administrative expenses (e.g., salaries)	Lower scores are better (excellent = less than 15%)
Fund-raising expenses	Percentage of total budget spent on fund-raising efforts	Lower scores are better (excellent = less than 10%)
Fund-raising efficiency	Ratio of fund-raising budget to amount raised ($ spent/$ raised)	Lower scores are better (excellent = less than $10/$1)
Program service expenses	Percentage of total budget spent on nonprofit programs and services	Higher scores are better (excellent = above 75%)

efforts? These are never measured because it is a time consuming process. It is easy to sit in an office somewhere with an annual report, an audit and a tax return and crank out some kind of analysis. It takes getting out of the office to measure programs. To date no watchdog group has taken on that task which is to the detriment of their efforts.

Christian nonprofits, it seems, are acutely aware of the difference between efficiency and effectiveness and the potential consequences resulting from their confusion. There is also a spiritual element of giving that some Christian nonprofits feel these ratings do not take into account. In a response to Ministry Watch's rating of their organization, the Executive Director of Romanian Missionary Society argued that . . .

> missionary work is motivated by vision and the way God moves upon the hearts of people to give. Your study is an insult to God's guidance and influences people to consider ministry on the same basis as they would a business investment. People like that lose money very often, but anything that is given to the Lord's work is totally retained as treasury in heaven, and they get the blessings on earth for having sent it ahead. In my experience, people who support the work of the Lord are very wise people. I recommend you rethink your motivations for such a "service" you are trying to provide without the consent of those who may be harmed by your presence in this arena.

This does not mean that efficiency is unimportant, only that it should not be confused for characteristics that are likely more important, namely effectiveness.[26] Most donors would be happy to give money to an organization that is somewhat less efficient (e.g., higher expenses on salaries or fund-raising) if it was known to be more effective in producing its desired outcomes. Efficiency measures are probably most effective in identifying the extreme cases of organizational wrongdoing where nonprofits clearly are spending exorbitant amounts on salaries or other fraudulent purposes. Unfortunately, efficiency measures tend to take the place of effectiveness measures because the latter are more difficult and expensive to produce.

This discussion of efficiency versus effectiveness is to make two points. First, when we look back over the tables presented in this chapter, we should be cautious about drawing unfair conclusions about the financial data included in them. For instance, when looking at table 5-3, should we conclude that since they spend the least on management and fund-raising that Relief & Development organizations are the most admirable, honest, or even the most effective sector? I would argue not. Many sector differences and even differences within sectors may be due to the demands and requirements of particular activities. A certain activity may simply require more skilled labor than another, meaning more expenses must go toward overhead. Even if we could make the argument that one sector or one organization is more efficient, does this really matter if they are not truly accomplishing what they intended? That is, if they are ineffective? There is much of interest in these numbers, but much that must be taken with perspective.

A discussion of efficiency and effectiveness also provides an opportunity to revisit the comparison of traditional religious organizations with Christian non-profits, a comparison that is necessarily raised throughout these chapters. When we look back at chapter 3, one can see that many of the criticisms of the Christian nonprofit population result from its focus on efficiency. Or maybe more accurately, some of the frustration of churches can be traced to their feeling that they are ultimately more effective even if they are not more efficient than Christian nonprofits. Most churches would likely admit that their generalist nature and lack of professionalization lead to fairly inefficient use of labor and resources, but they would also argue that they are incredibly effective at accomplishing their goals and therefore their inefficiency is irrelevant. However, given the intangible and more long-term goals of churches (e.g., spiritual development, fellowship), it is very difficult for them to provide clear-cut evidence of their effectiveness. So churches are left with comparisons of efficiency, which is a comparison that Christian nonprofits will undoubtedly win.

6

Leadership and Accountability

Executives, Boards, and Watchdogs

When you give, it qualifies you to receive God's abundance. . . . If God gives to you before you give to him, God himself will become a liar. . . . If you're not prospering, it's because you're not giving.

> —John Hagee, President of Global Evangelism Television,
> a Christian nonprofit

I know the reason that he earns what he earns is because God has blessed him. It is powerful to preach the word of God. And because he does, he is going to receive everything he needs and more.

> —Supporter defending Hagee's $1.25 million compensation package

You receive a donation request by a Christian humanitarian agency in the mail. The appeal inspires you to write a check for $50 to help the organization dig a well, clothe a child, provide medical care, or do whatever it is they promise to do. About a week goes by and you notice that the check has been deducted from your bank account. At that point, your donation has gone out "there," but it is not entirely clear to you where exactly "there" is. You were obviously confident enough in the organization's credentials to write the check in the first place. But you still might wonder . . . is my money going to where I thought it would go?

That slight twinge of worry you feel represents both the greatest promise and the greatest peril in the nonprofit world. Most donors are motivated to give to nonprofits precisely because they are helping others. However, individuals face a dilemma when they provide support to an organization but are not the primary recipients of the organization's goods or services. Namely, how do they know their money is buying what it was supposed to buy when they are not ever going to see the end result of their purchase? If you walk into a store and pay for a good or service that you can see or use, it is easy to recognize if it did or did not live up to its billing. If you are not satisfied, you can seek immediate recourse either through reimbursement or by simply discontinuing your patronage of the store. But the donor to a nonprofit is in a more difficult situation. What are you supposed to do? Fly across the world to make sure the organization is building the homes it promised you in its pamphlet? Unless you are giving millions to an organization, it is probably not worth your time and effort to personally police the activities of a nonprofit. But that does not mean that you do not care how your money is used. If you thought that it was not going to help the intended population, then you would not have made the donation. And if you thought the donation was just going into the pockets of the organization's leaders, then you definitely would have kept your money.

The Nonprofit Promise

The very idea of a *nonprofit* organization is meant to ease the concerns of donors. Corporations and other for-profit businesses are designed to earn money for the benefit of a select few, namely stockholders or owners. Such organizations cannot make a serious appeal for a donation because potential donors have no guarantee whether the organization really needs the money or if the owners simply want a new summer home. And even if the organization really did need the money for its survival, the business would still do everything possible to make sure the maximum part of the donation is turned into a profit for the owners. In short, the pursuit of profit eliminates the foundation of trust that is a prerequisite for receiving donations. The classification of an organization as nonprofit and the rules surrounding that classification are meant to eliminate those basic concerns. There are no owners or shareholders. The revenue of a nonprofit organization cannot benefit individual leaders, so there is no motivation for leaders to skimp on their use of donations in an effort to save the rest. Of course, as with so many other great ideas, all of this should be prefaced by the *in theory* disclaimer. For the most part, all of this is true. Nonprofits are quite successful at keeping donors happy, as people are more likely to trust nonprofits than they are to trust businesses or local, state, and federal governments.[1]

Still, there is a great deal of wiggle room when it comes to how nonprofits use their resources. We saw some of this variation in the previous chapter. Many of these differences are simply due to the varying demands of different sectors. Some activities are just more labor intensive or require more travel or need more outside consultants. But other differences may not be as easily explained. How can a donor be confident that their money is not being used inefficiently or improperly? Beyond the basic promise of being a not-for-profit, what systems are in place to oversee the operations of Christian nonprofits, and are those accountability systems effective? This chapter explores the internal and external accountability structures, their prevalence and nature in Christian nonprofits, and their role in shaping outcomes like the compensation of leaders.

Internal Accountability

The most obvious place to look for accountability is with the nonprofit itself or, more specifically, with the leadership of the nonprofit. There are two potential leadership groups in a nonprofit, although organizations will vary in size and nature of each group.

The Executives

First, there is the executive leadership group that is typically headed by a person with a title like CEO or executive director. Often, this person is the entire executive group, although larger or more professionalized nonprofits may have various divisional presidents, vice presidents, chief financial officers, and other secondary executives. Whether this group consists of 1 person or 10, the executives are the individuals who oversee the day-to-day operations of the organization and are usually employed by the nonprofit. If something were to go wrong with a nonprofit or if questions were raised about its practices, it is typically the executive(s) who would be blamed.

Nonprofits often go through two phases of executive leadership. The first is when the organization is led by its founder. Research has suggested that executive-founders tend to operate differently than executives that are not founders. For instance, founders are often creative and innovative but not necessarily great managers of bureaucracies. They tend to make ad hoc and reactive decisions instead of relying on policies and long-term plans. They reward loyalty and personal relationships over expertise or performance. This lack of refined management skills can often prevent an organization from growing. Founders tend to take less input from others in the organization and resist efforts to take power away from them. We will see some evidence of these dynamics in Christian nonprofits below. It is easy to have some sympathy for founder's position. After all, the nonprofit is the founder's creation, so it is natural for him or her have an interest in it that goes deeper than any other person. However, many people speak of a "founder's syndrome" that can actually harm the organization precisely due to the emotional and possessive nature of an executive-founder.[2] There is also the challenge of what a nonprofit does after the founder retires or dies, a transition process that some organizations are not prepared for and as a result leads to some organizations' end.

Those organizations that survive the postfounder transition usually enter the second phase of executive leadership where they become headed by a more professional managerial type of executive.[3] Regardless of whether they are a founder or not, executives have a personal stake in the organization because if the nonprofit fails or is accused of wrongdoing, their employment status and reputation could be harmed. Despite this, many scholars and nonprofits argue that executives alone should not be the sole form of leadership. This is partially due to a fear of intentional misbehavior (e.g., stealing money) on the part of the executive. Even without such malevolent actions, though, many organizations utilize a second set of leaders to make sure the organization is on the right track.

The Board

This second leadership group is the governing board, often called the board of directors or trustees. Almost all nonprofits have at least one person who could be considered part of the executive leadership group because, well, someone has to be running the organization. On the other hand, not every nonprofit will have a governing board. In a moment, we will look at some factors that lead a Christian nonprofit to have or not have a governing board. Board members are usually not employed or compensated by the organization and are recruited to serve based on their expertise, fund-raising ability, and other talents and resources. The board's main role is to meet periodically to review the major decisions and direction of the nonprofit.[4]

The 10 primary tasks of a nonprofit board are as follows:

1. Determine the organization's mission and purpose.
2. Select the chief executive.
3. Provide proper financial oversight.
4. Ensure adequate resources.
5. Ensure legal and ethical integrity and maintain accountability.
6. Ensure effective organizational planning.
7. Recruit and orient new board members and assess board performance.
8. Enhance the organization's public standing.
9. Determine, monitor, and strengthen the organization's programs and services.
10. Support the chief executive and assess his or her performance.[5]

The board has a complex task. On the one hand, they are supposed to provide advice and support to the executive leaders and often raise funds for the organization. On the other hand, they are also meant to supervise and oversee the executives. A strong board can even terminate a leader who is seen as ineffective or guilty of wrongdoing. They are the boss of the bosses. Because of their supervisory role, one large step nonprofits can take in the effort to provide internal accountability is to have a governing board, typically called a board of directors or trustees, which monitors the organization's finances and behavior. For instance, the Evangelical Council for Financial Accountability (ECFA) requires its members to have a board of at least five members and other charity evaluators often consider the presence of a board in their ratings. Whether these boards actually have a real effect on how the organization operates is a different issue, but the perception that they do has significant symbolic value when it comes to public relations. Part of the problem in assessing the effectiveness of boards is that their most important traits are difficult to gauge based on easily obtained information. For example, are the board members related to the executive? How often does the board meet? Does the board actually have the power to make binding decisions?

Measuring Leadership

Nonprofits are required to list their officers, directors, trustees, and key employees in one section of their tax return. This list represents both the executive and the board components of the nonprofits' leadership structure. The organizations we are examining list an average of eight such leaders. However, it is often difficult to tell where the executive group stops and the governing board starts. For example, the executive director may also be a board member. Making things even more complicated is that sometimes executives and board members may have the same title. There may be an executive president and a board president. From a practical standpoint, this makes assessing both the quantitative and the qualitative nature of these two leadership groups somewhat complicated.[6]

Let us assume, though, that among these leaders, the executives tend to be paid while the board members, or at least the nonexecutive board members, tend to be unpaid. With such a definition, we see that average number of executives varies somewhat across the different sectors. The Missions & Missionary and Fund-Raising & Grant-Making sectors have smallest executive groups on average, while the Radio & Television and Fellowship & Enrichment sectors have the largest. A stronger effect is seen across different revenue categories, with those less than $500,000 averaging 1.26 executives and those more than $10 million averaging 4.37. Keeping in mind that it tends to have some of the largest organizations, the relatively small executive groups found in the Relief & Development sector are notable. Looking at

TABLE 6.1. Mean Size of Leadership Groups by Sector.

	Charismatic Evangelism	Relief & Development	Education & Training	Publishing & Resources	Radio & Television	Missions & Missionary	Fellowship & Enrichment	Advocacy & Activism	Fund-Raising, Grant-Making, Other
Executives	1.61	1.55	1.68	1.69	2.42	1.44	2.15	1.95	1.47
Board members	4.29	8.23	6.73	5.52	5.72	6.19	9.06	7.64	6.71
Total size of leadership group	5.9	9.78	8.41	7.21	8.14	7.63	11.21	9.59	8.18
Board members per executive	2.7	5.3	4.0	3.3	2.4	4.3	4.2	3.9	4.6

Note: Executives defined as paid individuals listed in Part V ("Officers, Directors, Trustees, and Key Employees") of the 990 form. Board members defined as unpaid individuals. The total leadership group is the sum of all individuals listed in Part V.

TABLE 6.2. Mean Executive Group Size by Total Revenue.

Total Revenue	Number of Executives
$200,000–$500,000	1.26
$500,001–$1,000,000	1.39
$1,000,001–$2,500,000	1.83
$2,500,001–$10,000,000	2.65
More than $10,000,000	4.37

Note: Executives defined as paid individuals listed in Part V ("Officers, Directors, Trustees, and Key Employees") of the 990 form.

the ratio of executives to board members, we see that organizations in the Charismatic Evangelism and Radio & Television sectors have the lowest number of board members per executive. The Relief & Development sector has the highest ratio, followed by the Fund-Raising & Grant-Making sector.

Despite its symbolic value, only 53% of these Christian nonprofits have a board of at least five members, the standard established by the ECFA. If we lower the standard to three members, then 75% can be considered to have a governing board.[7] There are some significant differences across the activity sectors, though. As seen in figure 6-1, more than 70% of Relief & Development organizations have at least five board members. On the other hand, only 33% of Charismatic Evangelism organizations have a board this size. It is important to keep in mind that it is difficult to know much about the power or independence of these boards. Just because they exist does not mean that they are entirely strong. For example, we do not know if they consist of family members of the executives or have other preexisting relationships with the organization. Nor do we know how much say the board has in the organization's decision making. There are many reasons to believe, though, that the sectors that are less likely to have a board based on the standard we have been using are also less likely to have an independent or a strong board. For example, informal examinations show some evidence that nonprofits in the Charismatic Evangelism and Radio & Television sectors often have boards that contain the executive's family members or other less than entirely independent individuals.

We discussed earlier the role that revenue source has on the willingness for an organization to voluntarily subject itself to external regulation, such as through the ECFA. It seems reasonable to think that this would have a role in internal regulation as well. If a nonprofit relies on donations, then having symbols of internal regulation and accountability can help reassure potential contributors. A nonprofit relying on commercial revenue would have less incentive to prove it has taken measures to provide internal accountability. So are Christian

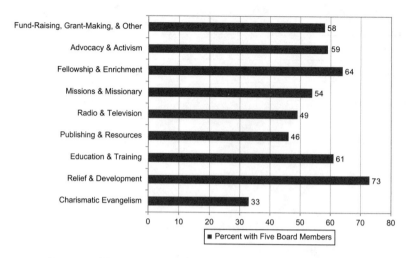

FIGURE 6.1. Presence of Governing Board by Activity Sector.
Note: Governing board defined as five unpaid individuals listed in Part V ("Officers, Directors, Trustees, and Key Employees") of the 990 form.

nonprofits relying on donations more likely to utilize this symbol of accountability? The presence of a governing board does seem influenced by revenue source. Twenty-eight percent of commercial nonprofits in the smallest revenue category have a governing board compared to 45% of noncommercial nonprofits. This gap holds through all the revenue categories. Commercial organizations know that their "contributors" are less likely to monitor or even care about accountability, so they are less likely to provide the symbols of internal governance as a way to reassure them just like they are less likely to provide symbols of external governance.

TABLE 6.3. Presence of Governing Board by Revenue Source and Total Revenue.

Total Revenue	Percent with a Governing Board of At Least Five Members	
	Not Predominantly Commercial (%)	Predominantly Commercial (%)
$200,000–$500,000	45.1	27.9
$500,001–$1,000,000	56.4	43.6
$1,000,001–$2,500,000	61.1	48.0
$2,500,001–$10,000,000	62.7	39.3
More than $10,000,000	79.6	57.1

Note: Governing board defined by five unpaid individuals listed on Part V ("Officers, Directors, Trustees, and Key Employees") of the 990 form. Predominantly commercial defined by 80% or more of total revenue coming from commercial activities.

Executive Power and Boards

Because boards are meant to at least partially supervise the executives, you might imagine that a struggle between the two could occur. Indeed, one might ask why executives would ever let a governing board exist in the first place. Executives and organizations can live without a board, and they likely did before the board was created. There is symbolic value to having a board when it comes to donor relations, so that creates some motivation for executives to create their own boss. But some executives may balk at the idea of a board looking over their shoulder regardless of any symbolic benefit. This possibility was hinted at earlier in reference to founder-executives. So in addition to looking at revenue total and source, we might also want to look at the executive leaders themselves as a reason that nonprofits do or do not have governing boards.

A distinction can be made between what you might call mom-and-pop nonprofits and highly professionalized nonprofits. A similar and an often overlapping distinction could be made between organizations where leadership power is concentrated in one or two individuals and those where power is diffused through many people, committees, and organizational bylaws. This distinction ultimately comes down to who makes the important decisions and how those decisions are perceived by others in the organization. Are the organization's decisions the product of one person's vision or whims, and does everyone else accept those decisions at face value? Or are the decisions a product of rules and procedures that are out of the hands of any one individual, and are people able to appeal those decisions through a process recognized by all involved? Sociologists refer to the former as charismatic authority and the latter as rational-legal or bureaucratic authority. If you have had some experiences in different denominations or churches, you have probably noticed these different types of authority types within those contexts. Some congregations, for example, are guided entirely by a powerful leader who makes all decisions, while others have committees and meetings to propose resolutions and vote on new rules and procedures. Churches or denominations that are charismatically based tend to be schism-prone, while schisms tend to be rarer in rational-legal groups.[8]

Without having the ability to observe the decision-making process in all Christian nonprofits, how can we get a feel for whether leadership is concentrated and charismatic or diffuse and bureaucratic? One possibility is to identify those organizations that are named after an executive. This typically means that the executive was the founder, but not all founders name their organizations after themselves, so these executive-named organizations represent a subset of founder-led organizations. All of the dynamics mentioned earlier concerning founder-executives are likely even stronger when the organization is named after the founder-executive.

TABLE 6.4. Presence of Governing Board by Whether the Nonprofit Is Named after a Founder-Executive.

Total Revenue	Percent with a Governing Board of At Least Five Members	
	Not Executive Named (%)	Executive Named (%)
$200,000–$500,000	48	23
$500,001–$1,000,000	59	29
$1,000,001–$2,500,000	62	47
$2,500,001–$10,000,000	62	46
More than $10,000,000	80	80

Note: Governing board defined by five unpaid individuals listed on Part V ("Officers, Directors, Trustees, and Key Employees") of the 990 form.

Consider an organization that is named after an executive. This inherently provides the executive a great deal of power. Referring to founder-executives, John Carver noted that "it is difficult not only to 'say no' to any plan of the founder, but even to subject it to rigorous scrutiny." This is even more the case when the organization is named after the founder-executive. It is difficult to fire or even disagree with John Doe if the organization is called John Doe Ministries. The sign on the building serves as a constant reminder of who is in charge. There is also a good chance the organization's very purpose is to promote the charismatic leader's personality as its primary product, which means that his or her opinion about the direction of the organization is the only opinion that matters. If the leader decides they do not want to do something, then that is the end of the debate.[9]

Does this have an influence on the willingness of an executive and hence the nonprofit to subject itself to oversight from a board? Does being the namesake of an organization make an executive less likely to turn over his or her organization for other people to judge and direct? When looking at the percentage of organizations with a governing board across revenue groups, there does seem to be an overall trend that the power concentration in executive-named organizations leads to a lower likelihood of having a governing board. Not coincidentally, a similar pattern exists when looking at the probability of joining external accountability organizations, such as the ECFA.[10]

External Accountability

Executives and governing boards serve as the primary internal accountants of nonprofits' behavior. However, there is no shortage of people and organizations outside of the nonprofits with the ability to serve as a police force.

The Internal Revenue Service

While the Securities and Exchange Commission is the primary governmental agency regulating the corporate world, the Internal Revenue Service (IRS) is its counterpart in the nonprofit world. The IRS would appear to be the largest threat to a nonprofit's operations and the strongest motivation to operate honestly and efficiently. After all, it can revoke the organization's tax-exempt status, which would immediately cripple many nonprofits. This would eliminate the material benefits of being a donor (e.g., tax deductions) and take away the legitimacy of the organization. That "foundation of trust" which serves as a prerequisite for asking for donations can be swiftly taken away by the IRS if it feels a nonprofit is no longer deserving of it.

The truth is, though, that as a watchdog, the IRS is not particularly powerful. The issue is a lack of resources. Of the more than 1 million nonprofits in the United States, the IRS "may" actually examine the tax returns of 1% of them. The number they actually punish for any wrongdoing is even less. In fact, in 2005, the IRS reviewed just 3,454 of the over eight hundred thousand 990 forms submitted. So despite the potential strength of the IRS to be an enforcer of good behavior, it has admitted that abuse is rampant and it can do little about it. It is well aware of its inability to effectively monitor the nonprofit sector and it has pleaded with legislators to help it with both increased resources and updated laws. There does seem to be movement to provide additional scrutiny to nonprofits, including a new 990 form that will provide more information concerning the nature of the organization's leadership instead of just financial measures of revenue and expenses. For instance, the new form would contain questions about the independence of board members, the presence of whistle-blower and paperwork destruction policies and who is in charge of producing the financial statements for the organization. It is not clear that this will provide the IRS with much more power unless it is accompanied by a larger staff and budget, but it could make it easier for others to scrutinize nonprofits. But who are those "others?"[11]

Watchdogs and Charity Raters

There are a number of nongovernmental organizations that look to police and evaluate nonprofits. Some of these were mentioned in the previous chapter. For instance, the Better Business Bureau and the National Charities Information Bureau teamed up to create the Wise Giving Alliance. From its Web site, the organization provides reports on select nonprofits' finances and operations.[12] It also reports whether there have been any complaints registered and judges the organization based on 20 criteria, such as whether they have a governing board and how much they spend on fund-raising. Other Web sites, such as CharityNavigator.org, provide similar reports. There are also sites that provide information on nonprofits but do not attempt to evaluate them. GuideStar.org and FoundationCenter.org, for example, provide donors with scanned copies of organization's 990 forms so they can do their own research before making a contribution.

While these ratings sites include some Christian nonprofits, there is one organization devoted to providing profiles and evaluations for just this population. Wall Watchers, itself a nonprofit, produces the MinistryWatch.org site that provides ratings on more than 500 ministries.[13] For the most part, these ratings are similar to all the other evaluation services. Efficiency scores are computed based on the financial measures, and transparency scores are assigned based on availability of records. A twist that is different from other rating services is Ministry Watch's discussion of organizations' theological viewpoint and legitimacy. For instance, Ministry Watch says the following concerning the large relief organization, World Vision:

> Although its board of directors is generally evangelical, many of its contributors are not. World Vision has at times promoted itself as a nonsectarian, humanitarian organization and has downplayed evangelical components . . .

> World Vision displays the love of God by meeting physical needs of people, but with limited Christian impact.[14]

It is difficult to think what a comparable criticism would be for a secular relief agency, which demonstrates the additional complexity of trying to evaluate Christian nonprofits from the perspective of donors. Effectiveness is not only a matter of what gets done or even the way in which it gets done but also its theological foundation and impact. An organization may be successful in many ways but may be unacceptable due to its theological worldview.

Ratings services such as the Ministry Watch and similar sites do not provide a direct form of enforcement of nonprofit behavior. They do not have any ability to leverage fines or sanction any wrongdoing. They can publicize the wrongdoing or inefficiencies they perceive and encourage others to punish the organizations. In this sense, they serve more of a whistle-blower role than that of law enforcement. This has advantages and disadvantages. The independence means that they can criticize other organizations without worrying about their relationship with that organization. But this also means that their critiques cannot be backed up with any real penalties. It is easy to criticize other people's children, but it is easier to punish one's own. There is another type of watchdog that does provide more direct enforcement of Christian nonprofits.

Evangelical Council for Financial Accountability

The ECFA constitutes a type of family among Christian organizations, including churches, nonprofits, and other ministries. The ECFA was created in 1979 in response to a number of scandals involving religious and secular nonprofits. Given his influence in contemporary American religion, we probably should not be surprised that Billy Graham was a key force behind the creation of the ECFA. In 1977, a newspaper in North Carolina reported that the Billy Graham Evangelistic Association had not reported the existence of a $23 million fund in its assets. Although the fund was found to be legal and utilized for missions and other Christian projects, Graham began to support steps for religious organizations to make their financial records more open.[15] This was accompanied by a growing threat of increased governmental scrutiny. In a speech to Christian leaders, a U.S. Senator suggested a "Christian Better Business Bureau" as a way to prevent government action. Two years later, the vice president of Graham's organization along with the president of World Vision announced the creation of the ECFA. Even today, the ECFA lists less "government intervention" as a benefit of its existence:

> The fact that so many organizations have voluntarily submitted
> themselves to ECFA's independent standards of accountability has
> clearly forestalled this threat. As a viable accreditation agency,
> ECFA helps preserve freedom from governmental intrusion for all
> ministries—including those who are not members of ECFA.[16]

In its first year and a half, 150 charter members were certified. Today, the ECFA has more than 2,000 members ranging from national nonprofits (i.e., the groups examined in this book) to local social service ministries to some denominational offices and congregations.[17] In addition to an annual fee, organizations must fulfill a number of requirements to be granted ECFA membership. These requirements include the presence of an evangelical doctrinal statement, an independent board of directors, an annual audit of finances that is public and independent, and rules concerning fund-raising practices.

Of the 1,941 organizations we have been looking in the previous chapters, a quarter of them ($N = 479$) belong to the ECFA. There are differences in the rate of membership across the various sectors. The Relief & Development sector has the highest rate at 42%. At 13%, organizations in the Charismatic Evangelism sector are the least likely to hold membership. Membership in ECFA is also strongly related to the budget of the organization. For instance, of those with total revenue from $200,000 to $500,000, only 11% hold ECFA members, while the rate increases to 39% for those with revenue of $1 million to $2.5 million and 55% for those with

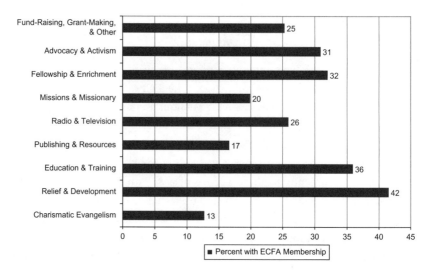

FIGURE 6.2. Membership in the Evangelical Council for Financial Accountability by Activity Sector.

total revenue above $10 million. However, even after taking into account revenue size, organizations in the Relief & Development, Education & Training, Fellowship & Enrichment, and Advocacy & Activism are still more likely to hold ECFA membership than those in the Charismatic Evangelism sector.[18]

Because the ECFA has a relationship with its member organizations, it actually has some power to enforce its rules and sanction transgressions of those rules. If a member is found to be in violation of the rules either through a complaint filed with ECFA or through one of its on-site reviews, the ECFA can require the organization to make corrections. If it does not or refuses to make the changes, then the ECFA can terminate the organization's membership. In practice, it rarely comes to this. From 2004 to 2007, the ECFA lists 90 former members. Of these, 73 voluntarily resigned, while 17 were terminated. The voluntary resignations include a variety of motivations that we cannot fully know. A look at the list shows that some of these organizations simply no longer exist. Others may have thought that the benefits of membership were not worth the annual fee or the cost of paying for an independent audit. Of the 17 involuntary terminations, 13 were simply because the organization did not submit a membership renewal, 1 failed to submit financial statements, 1 lacked a doctrinal statement, and 1 lacked a board of directors. Only one organization over those 4 years had its membership terminated due to financial wrongdoing. Over the past 20 years, an ECFA official estimated that only 1% of all former members left due to violations of its behavioral standards.[19] The rarity of such punishments would seem to speak either to the striking effectiveness of ECFA monitoring that sanctions do not need to be used in the first place or to a lack of real power behind that monitoring. A more likely reason might be the inherent bias within the membership of ECFA. Specifically, an organization that is looking to abuse its funds or take part in other wrongdoing is unlikely to join an organization that will be looking over its shoulder.

Donors

Later in this chapter we will assess the effect of ECFA membership on members' behavior. But implied in any benefit of membership or consequence of having a membership terminated is that potential contributors would react accordingly. In other words, while the ECFA may provide a more direct form of policing than charity raters, its punishments are ultimately still indirect. Having one's ECFA membership terminated does not itself harm the organization's health or ability to operate. This raises one of the easily forgotten but likely the most powerful force policing the behavior of Christian nonprofits: contributors to the nonprofits. The sanctioning ability of rating services, the ECFA, and even the IRS to some extent is channeled through the reaction of donors. While any of those actors publicize wrongdoing, terminate membership, or revoke nonprofit status, the ultimate question is whether donors stop providing funds.

However, the willingness and motivation for contributors to monitor the behavior of nonprofits likely varies with the type of contribution. We saw in the previous chapter that the source of a nonprofit's revenue, in terms of being from donations or commercial activities, has consequences for the financial stability of the organization. This is because the relationship between a donor and a nonprofit is much more tenuous than that of a customer and a nonprofit. Commercial nonprofits form an exchange relationship with its clients based on the clients' need for a service or product. Because they are not receiving anything that they desire or need, contributors to donative nonprofits can easily decide that they do not want to give anymore without suffering any personal loss.

In addition to its impact on financial stability, the different relationships that exist between contributors and nonprofits have consequences for the issues of accountability and organizational policing we are examining in this chapter. Consider a person who purchases a book from a nonprofit. The person has received something for their money, and they can immediately evaluate their level of satisfaction with exchange. They wanted a book, they thought the price was fair, and they are happy with the book . . . end of story. At that point, they do not really care what the organization does with the money. Because the exchange is complete, there is not much motivation to find the organization's tax returns, examine its board of directors, look at various charity evaluations, or take any

TABLE 6.5. Membership in ECFA by Revenue Source and Total Revenue.

Total Revenue	Percent Belonging to ECFA	
	Not Predominantly Commercial (%)	Predominantly Commercial (%)
$200,000–$500,000	12.1	0.0
$500,001–$1,000,000	26.4	2.6
$1,000,001–$2,500,000	40.3	28.0
$2,500,001–$10,000,000	50.6	25.0
More than $10,000,000	54.9	57.1

Note: Predominantly commercial defined by 80% or more of total revenue coming from commercial activities.

other steps to ensure accountability. On the other hand, a contributor to a donation-based nonprofit, however, receives nothing directly return for his or her money. Because of this, a donor has much more motivation to make sure their money gets where it is supposed to and does what it was intended to do. Ensuring that this is done provides the donor some of the satisfaction the customer receives from their directly received product or service. We would expect, then, that nonprofits that rely more on donations than commercial revenue would be more sensitive to the potential reactions of contributors than their commercial counterparts.

There is evidence of this sensitivity when we look at the ECFA membership rates of commercial nonprofits compared to donative nonprofits. Across all of the revenue categories, except for the largest group of organizations with more than $10 million in total revenue, commercial nonprofits are less likely to hold ECFA membership than donative organizations.[20] Since they know their contributors have less invested in the behavior of the organization, commercial nonprofits do not need to take as many steps to bolster their credibility and provide assurances to contributors. In short, the stamp of approval provided by ECFA membership is less crucial to these organizations.

Executive Compensation

We have examined some of the accountability structures that exist both inside and outside of Christian nonprofits. We also explored some of the factors that determine whether a nonprofit participates in any of them. Generally speaking, the larger the public profile of an organization, the more likely it is to prove it has taken steps to provide oversight. The public profile is a factor of organizational size and revenue source. On the contrary, the more concentrated the executive power within a nonprofit, the less likely those leader(s) are to give up that power to external watchdogs or internal governing boards. But do any of these accountability measures actually work? It is difficult to know exactly how to assess this question. The most obvious outcome of ineffective governance is an outright scandal resulting from blatant and extreme misbehavior on the part of the nonprofit. However, these scandals are relatively rare, and we only know about them after they are exposed, so it is difficult to use a "scandal/no scandal" outcome to analyze the Christian nonprofits in this book. We could, though, look at how these organizations use their resources toward one issue that has often been a flash point and the source of many of those scandals.

One of the most sensitive issues when it comes to the use of nonprofit resources is the compensation of organizational leaders. Many of the books and Web sites providing advice for nonprofits spend much of their time discussing the issue of executive compensation. Nonprofit watchdogs and research centers issue reports on executive compensation. While corporations and governments must answer questions about high salaries, the issue is even more delicate for nonprofit organizations. High salaries can give the impression that nonprofit leaders are doing the one thing they are not supposed to do . . . profit. The potential volatility surrounding compensation is partly a result of there being a perceived conflict of interest. Whether accurate or not, executives are seen as at least partially in control of their compensation. They are, after all, the decision makers in the organization.[21]

Salaries are also easy for donors to understand and interpret. Most organizational expenses, such as those for infrastructure or fund-raising, are abstract and could be justified with various appeals to organizational goals. It is common for nonprofits to be accused of being inefficient when it comes to these kinds of expenses, but this rarely leads to major controversy. These expenses are ultimately still going toward the larger mission of the nonprofit, and the organization probably did not intend to be inefficient. Donors, however, can personally relate to the salary issue. They know what they get paid in their job, and they at least have an instinct for what the organization's leaders should or should not get paid. Executive compensation is seen as an empty expense. It is not benefiting anyone but the executives, so the organization's nonprofit mission is not being advanced. It is often argued that executives are paid to help the organization and a high salary keeps them from leaving, but donors may not make the same connection or be convinced by it. In sum, while perceived inefficiencies with other expenses may annoy donors, the perception of excessive salaries can outrage them.

As the quotes that began this chapter illustrate, Christian nonprofits are not immune from compensation controversies. In fact, Christian nonprofits are probably held to an even higher standard than secular nonprofits due to their religious identity. This makes it all the more provocative when a religious leader or organization falls from grace by abusing donations or enjoying an overly worldly lifestyle. There are plenty of examples of scandals involving religious leaders, particularly televangelists, over the past 20 years (see Bakker, Jim). For whatever reason, these scandals seem to produce a more enduring memory among the public than similar issues in secular organizations. While televangelists are a small part of Christian nonprofit population, the taint of their negative publicity in the past seems to have cost all Christian organizations some of their ability to appeal to religious identity as a sign of credibility. But compensation controversies are not limited to televangelists. Religious schools, humanitarian organizations, fellowship groups, and other Christian nonprofit sectors have faced questions about compensation of leaders.[22]

When we look at leadership compensation by sector, there are some significant differences. Given the mention of televangelists, it is noteworthy that the Radio & Television sector pays the most on average to both the highest paid leader and the executive group as a whole. However, since all of the officers tend to be highly paid in this sector, the compensation is not concentrated to just one of the leaders. This seems to point to the possibility that leaders in these organizations command more money partially due to the professional and technical requirements of the television and radio industry. In other words, they are paid a higher salary given their training and the high salaries available in their for-profit competitors. Remember also that nonprofits in this sector tend to be some of the largest in terms of revenue, and total revenue is a strong predictor of leadership compensation. A leader cannot receive what the organization does not have to give. We will return to this point in a moment.

On the low end of the compensation scale is the Missions & Missionary sector. The highest paid leader in this sector tends to get just over $50,000, and the organizations spend an average of $82,000 on total leadership compensation. Both these numbers are the lowest of any sector. While not the highest compensation in absolute numbers, the Charismatic Evangelism sector does have the highest proportion of total compensation going to one person. Eighty-three percent of total compensation in these nonprofits goes to the highest paid leader. Given the prevalence of organizations named after the leader and the high concentration of power, this is not entirely surprising.

All of these numbers are slightly deceptive because we know that the sectors vary in total revenue and total revenue is a large predictor of compensation. It is one thing to pay a leader $100,000 if your total revenue is $100,000,000 and entirely different thing to pay a leader $100,000 if your total revenue is $500,000. It is possible to statistically adjust these compensation numbers for differences in sector and total revenue. This is basically like asking how the observed differences in

TABLE 6.6. Compensation of Executives by Activity Sector.

	Charismatic Evangelism	Relief & Development	Education & Training	Publishing & Resources	Radio & Television	Missions & Missionary	Fellowship & Enrichment	Advocacy & Activism	Fund-Raising, Grant-Making, Other
Percent compensating executives	83	72	84	77	76	68	82	88	56
Mean compensation of highest paid executive	$75,892	$80,430	$70,209	$66,613	$106,673	$50,899	$84,233	$84,365	$71,082
Mean compensation to all executives	$91,066	$128,893	$100,825	$108,908	$234,755	$82,430	$169,812	$140,471	$154,143
Percent to highest paid executives	83	62	70	61	45	62	50	60	46

Note: Compensation figures include salary, benefits, and expenses.

compensation would change if all sectors were given the same money to play around with. For instance, if a sector pays an above-average salary with below-average revenues, then we would expect this compensation to go up even more if they were given the average level of revenue. So statistically, we give the rich sectors less and the poor sectors more until they have the same amount and then examine what happens to the compensation levels.

Table 6-7 shows these revenue-adjusted compensation numbers for the highest paid officer by sector. When its large total revenue is taken into account, the Relief & Development sector actually pays a fairly small amount to its top leader. Even after considering its higher revenue, the Radio & Television sector is still one of the highest paying areas in the Christian nonprofit population. However, the highest paying sector after adjusting for revenue is the Charismatic Evangelism sector. This makes sense given its relatively high-unadjusted salary and below-average revenue. Once we boost these nonprofits up to the mean level of revenue, their salaries become even higher.

Now let us take a look at some of the leadership and accountability issues we have been discussing throughout this chapter. Does being an ECFA member or having a governing board help reduce the compensation given to leaders? There are clearly reasons to believe both would have an impact. The ECFA, for instance, states that board members should assess the "reasonableness of CEO compensation" and approve any compensation and benefits in advance. Table 6-8 presents results from a statistical analysis that adjusts for differences in revenue and sector, so we can just look at the impact due to differences in governance and accountability. Despite the policing abilities of the ECFA, there is no significant difference between members and nonmembers in the amount of compensation given to the top leader. Of course, ECFA members do not pay more than other Christian nonprofits, which could be taken as good news. But then again, one would probably expect membership to produce a noticeable effect on lowering compensation. Similarly, popular opinion would say that governing boards would lower salaries, but these data do not support such a conclusion.[23]

On the other hand, the measures of leadership power and revenue source we have been discussing in this chapter do have a significant impact on compensation. Leaders in predominantly commercial nonprofits receive over $15,000 more than leaders in organizations relying on donations. Given the discussion throughout this chapter, this finding is not entirely surprising. We have seen how the source of revenue affects nonprofit's sensitivity to the opinions of outsiders, especially contributors. Supporters of commercial nonprofits are less likely to monitor salaries and less likely to care that much even if they did.

An even stronger difference is seen when comparing Christian nonprofits that are named after one of the current executives versus those that are not named after

TABLE 6.7. Compensation of Highest Paid Officer by Sector Adjusted for Mean Revenue of Sector.

	Charismatic Evangelism	Relief & Development	Education & Training	Publishing & Resources	Radio & Television	Missions & Missionary	Fellowship & Enrichment	Advocacy & Activism	Fund-Raising, Grant-Making, Other
Revenue-adjusted highest paid officer*	$91,211	$53,738	$76,532	$67,966	$87,315	$53,533	$83,581	$81,154	$59,882

Note: Computed from a linear regression analysis controlling for sector and the log of total revenue.

TABLE 6.8. Impact of Governance and Power on Total Compensation of Highest Paid Executive.

Difference between	Impact on Highest Paid Executive
ECFA vs. non-ECFA Members	No significant difference
Governing board vs. no governing board	No significant difference
Predominantly commercial vs. noncommercial	+$14,785
Executive named vs. not executive named	+$25,348

Note: Linear regression examining organizations providing compensation controlling for sector and log of revenue. Compensation includes salary, benefits, and expenses. Governing board defined as five unpaid individuals listed in Part V of 990 form. Commercial defined as 80% or more of total revenue coming from commercial activities.

anyone or named after someone who is no longer in the organization. Leaders in organizations named after themselves receive over $24,000 more in compensation than those who are not the nonprofit's namesake. Many observers may interpret this finding as a sign of profiteering, or at least self-centeredness, on the part of these leaders. That interpretation may be true in some cases. After all, going around naming things after yourself is usually not a sign of modesty. But from a purely sociological stance, the higher payment given to these namesake leaders makes some sense. Organizations named after a leader are probably unusually reliant on the talents of that one person, such as their preaching abilities or writing skills. This makes the leader much more important to the organization than those in other nonprofits where they can be replaced with little interruption to the organization's programs. You could argue that the functional importance of these leaders allows them to command a higher salary.

On the whole, leadership power and revenue source seem more important in increasing compensation than governance and accountability structures seem in lowering it. This may seem to defy physics . . . salaries only go up, never down. But it might not be that inexplicable. It likely reflects standards and norms within respective sectors and size categories regarding appropriate compensation. Organizations tend to voluntarily, whether they are aware of it or not, fall in line with these standards. This would not be surprising because many nonprofits look to their peers for guidance on appropriate compensation.[24] This is a safe strategy since a leader cannot be accused of excessive compensation if his or her salary is the same as other leaders' (i.e., the "everyone else is doing it" defense). All nonprofits are restricted by these norms, so formal accountability structures (e.g., governing boards, ECFA membership) do not produce any additional reductions in compensation. However, unusual amounts of power or lack of interest on the part of donors (i.e., commercial revenue) provide leverage to executives to increase their salaries beyond the understood norms for their sector and revenue. So salaries can go above the baseline created by informal norms and peer comparisons but usually do not go below them. There is a floor but no ceiling.

While they do not directly decrease salaries, it is important to note that ECFA membership and governing boards are not necessarily meaningless. If we looked at two executive-named organizations, one that was in ECFA and one that was not, we would not expect a difference in compensation between the two since ECFA membership has no impact. However, as we saw earlier in this chapter, the fact is that executive-named organizations are less likely to be in ECFA or have a governing board in the first place. So, ECFA membership and governing boards indirectly provide some assurances that the nonprofit will stay close to the norms defined by their sector and size. If the executives wanted to go above those norms, then they never would have joined ECFA or created a governing board in the first place.

7

Parachurch and State

Tax Laws, Government Funding, and Nonprofit Lobbying

Because special tax rules apply to churches, it is important to distinguish churches from other religious organizations. Therefore, when this publication uses the term "religious organizations," it is not referring to churches . . .

—The IRS *Tax Guide for Churches and Religious Organizations*

As we have seen in the preceding chapters, Christian nonprofits have raised many questions about the relationships between consumers and suppliers within the religious market. But the growth of the parachurch sector has also presented new issues in the relationship between the religious market and the government. The relationship between church and state has long been of interest to politicians, academics, and church leaders and goers alike, so many of the questions raised by the parachurch sector are iterations of ongoing debates. Indeed, at their core, most conflicts between the religious and public sectors result from the First Amendment's mandate to simultaneously allow for the free exercise of religion while also forbidding any establishment of religion. These goals are often at odds when allowing for free exercise would lead to the preferential treatment of some religious group relative to another or relative to the general public. In short, how does the government balance its need to make and enforce laws without infringing or favoring religious practice or expression?

This question comes up in three specific areas when it comes to the parachurch and state relationship. Some of these questions have more to do with the "nonprofit" part of "Christian nonprofit," while others are produced by the religious nature of the organization. First, how does the government deal with religious organizations when it comes to exempting them from taxes? How and why is religion defined as a reason for receiving nonprofit status and does this exemption violate the establishment clause? How does the government regulate Christian or other religious nonprofits without violating the Free Exercise Clause? As we will see, the answers to these questions are often ambiguous, resulting in confusion and practical challenges for both the Christian nonprofits and the government.

The other two sources of tension in the parachurch and state relationship come from money. First, what issues are raised when the government provides funding for a Christian nonprofit not only for the government's no-establishment mandate but also for the nonprofit's identity? This is a question that has received a significant amount of attention in recent years as both Democratic and Republican administrations have pushed to enlist congregations and other religious organizations as more active partners in the provision of social services. However, much of this attention has focused on local social service ministries, not on the large national and international Christian nonprofits we have been examining in these chapters. We have already seen in chapter 5 how rare public funding is in this Christian nonprofit population, which is much more focused on the provision of religion than social services. This chapter will further examine this topic. A second question that has received less attention is what happens when the money flow is in the other direction. That is, what happens when Christian nonprofits use their funds to lobby the government in an attempt to pass legislation the nonprofit favors? Many people do not consider this issue because it is assumed that, by the rules that govern their tax-exempt status, nonprofits are forbidden from such lobbying. However, the reality is not quite as simple as this. This chapter explores all three of these parachurch and state questions, beginning with the treatment of church and parachurch in the tax code.

The Fine Line

We saw in chapter 2 that the relationship between church and parachurch organizations can be thought of as consisting of overlapping activities and resource pools. Because of this overlap, the boundaries between church and parachurch organizations often blend together. When a person looks to go on a mission trip, join a fellowship group, or help the needy, they will find options in both the church and the parachurch population. This is clearly the source of some tension between the two populations as it results in competition for the loyalty and support of individuals and congregations. Interestingly enough, though, the often blurry line between church and parachurch might best be seen in how the government, specifically the Internal Revenue Service (IRS), handles the distinction between the two. To appreciate the complexities of this situation, we must examine the history of how religious organizations are addressed in the tax code.

The exemption of certain organizations from paying taxes can be traced back to the Tariff Act of 1894 and the Corporation Excise Tax of 1909.[1] Both laws were essentially taxes on the profits of businesses. However, Congress felt it would be unnecessary and unwise to apply such taxes to organizations commonly thought of as charities, such as those that help the poor. First, they assumed, whether justifiably or not, that such organizations would never have profits above the donations they received, so a tax on profits was simply inapplicable. Second, charities were using their income toward "the relief of suffering, to the alleviation of our people, and to all things which commend themselves to every charitable and just impulse." Given such admirable goals, taxing their income just seemed, well, uncharitable. There was also a more practical reason for exempting charities. Since the money that goes to the charity goes toward activities the government wants to support anyways, exempting them from taxes simply cuts out the middleman. Although not quite expressed in explicit terms in those early days, this indirect subsidy or "quid pro quo" argument would eventually come to be one of the primary justifications for exempting organizations (i.e., nonprofits) from taxes.[2]

Interestingly, in addition to charitable and educational activities, Congress included religious purposes as a reason for tax exemption. The reasoning for this inclusion is not entirely clear. Some scholars have argued that religion had little to do with the inclusion of religious organizations as an exempt category. They say that religious organizations were exempted because of their role in public service, particularly in the relief of poverty, not because of their religious nature. There is some evidence for this in Congressional hearings preceding the 1909 law. In those hearings, legislators discussed the activities of churches, such as Trinity Church in New York City. They concluded that since "all of the avails of its business and its real estate . . . are distributed for benevolent purposes," churches should be exempt from taxes. In other words, it is the charitable activities of religious organizations that qualified them for tax exemption, not their religious nature.[3]

Tax Exemptions and the Constitution

While religious organizations were included in the first laws establishing tax exemptions, their exemption has not gone unchallenged. The primary argument for tax exemptions is that the government should provide an indirect subsidy in the form of tax exemptions for organizations providing services that the government has a direct interest in supporting, such as helping the poor or disaster relief. This argument has some problems when it comes to religion as it is unlikely that the government would provide religion in the absence of religious organizations. In fact, one could argue that the exemption of churches from taxes represents the government support of religion, which would violate the Establishment Clause of the First Amendment.

Indeed, this was exactly what a man named Frederick Walz believed. A lawyer himself, Walz challenged tax exemptions given to churches in the state of New York. Every state court in New York sided in favor of the exemptions, primarily based on the long history of such exemptions. Not easily discouraged, Walz pursued the case to the U.S. Supreme Court in 1970. However, the Supreme Court also argued in favor for the tax exemption of churches. The Court raised a number of points in support of its decision. The majority opinion stated that churches are seen as a "beneficial and stabilizing influence in community life" and they contribute to an overall level of pluralism in society, which is also seen as positive. In other words, by providing tax breaks, the government was encouraging these positive characteristics in society, much like they encourage third parties to provide help to the poor or provide relief after a natural disaster.

The Court also argued that the government was not really subsidizing churches, which would raise questions concerning a violation of the Establishment Clause, as much as it was staying out of religion altogether. In what came to be called the "no-excessive entanglement" principle, the Court argued that the government should do all that is possible not to become involved in the activities of religious groups:

> Obviously a direct money subsidy would be a relationship pregnant with involvement and, as with most governmental grant programs, could encompass sustained and detailed administrative relationships for enforcement of statutory or administrative standards, that is not the case . . .

> The government does not transfer part of its revenue to churches but simply abstains from demanding that the church support the state.

The excessive entanglement principle is not explicitly stated within the Constitution but can be tied into the idea of "Free Exercise." Also part of the First Amendment, the Free Exercise Clause states that "Congress shall pass no law . . . prohibiting the free exercise [of religion]." The Court felt that taxing churches could limit the exercise of religion by hampering them with too many administrative and financial obligations. Seemingly, this is the same logic behind the exempting churches from registering with the IRS and filing annual returns.

However, you could also argue that an organization's religious nature was its own distinct justification for tax exemption independent of any charitable activities it may or may not conduct. The 1894 and 1909 laws specified that organizations which have "charitable, religious, *or* educational" purposes qualify for tax exemption. The "or" in that statement gives the impression that religion alone was seen as being a legitimate reason for a tax exemption exclusive of a "charitable" or an "educational" nature. In short, if religious organizations were exempt because of their charitable activities, then why specify religion as a separate category?[4]

What is clear, though, is that the inclusion of religious organizations was not based on nuanced arguments concerning the separation of church and state or the Free Exercise Clause of the Constitution. While these arguments would come later, the original inclusion seemed to be based on a fairly unquestioned assumption that religious organizations were naturally in the same category as charitable and educational organizations. What is important to note, though, was that the law was applied equally to *all exempt* organizations, religious or secular, church or parachurch. The tax code did not distinguish between different types of organizations within the religion category. Churches, denominations, parachurch organizations, and all others were simply exempt from taxes due to their religious nature.

This began to change in the middle of the 20th century. In 1950, an important distinction was made in an otherwise routine piece of legislation. Referring to unrelated business income, the Revenue Act of 1950 stated that

> While churches and associations or conventions of churches . . . are
> exempt from the Supplement U tax, religious organizations are subject
> to such tax . . .[5]

The significance of this statement is subtle, but it represents the first time that the government separated churches out from other "religious organizations." Religion was no longer a homogenous category of exempt organizations. This distinction is maintained today as the IRS has established two broad categories when it comes to religion: churches and religious organizations. This terminology is a bit confusing since churches are obviously religious organizations. However, these categories are meant to distinguish between traditional churches, groups of churches (i.e., denominations), and church-based groups or auxiliaries (e.g., a church's men's group) from other nonprofits with a religious identity or mission that are not based within one of these church structures. In other words, intentionally or not, the tax code began to reflect the larger changes in the structure of American religion that were being driven by the growth of the parachurch sector.[6]

A Split in the Code

The separation of these two categories might not matter if it did not have real consequences for how an organization was treated by the government, but it does in fact have such consequences. In addition to the 1950 law that made the original distinction between churches and religious organizations and exempted the former from unrelated business income taxes, other practical distinctions would be made. The most significant implication resulted from the Tax Reform Act of 1969, which required all new nonprofits to obtain official recognition from the IRS and required all nonprofits to submit annual financial returns. These rules applied to religious organizations, or what we would call parachurch organizations, but churches, associations of churches, and church ministries were exempted from both these requirements. The different rules reflected a change in reasoning concerning the tax exemptions given to churches. While they were previously included with all nonprofits due to their public service role, churches were now seen as special due to the constitutional issues involved with regulating religion. It was now a matter of protecting the free exercise of religion, not a matter of their charitable nature.[7]

This has created a very unique, or what one writer called an "enviable," status for churches. Specifically, churches are the only type of nonprofit organization that receives an automatic and assumed tax exemption without any application or registration. This means that if you want to create a church, there is no need to contact the IRS to register or let them know you exist. The tax-exempt status of your church is assumed. This differs from any other nonprofit, religious or otherwise, which must submit an application to gain official tax-exempt status. Furthermore, churches, unlike almost all other nonprofits, are exempt from filing annual statements concerning their finances and other organizational information. The result of these exemptions is that the IRS is effectively prevented from conducting any audit on a church unless they receive some notice from a third party that there is reason to believe the church is violating nonprofit rules. In short, churches are shielded from almost all of the regulatory oversight and requirements that all other nonprofits are subject to.[8]

Somewhat paradoxically, the constitutional questions that provided this special status for churches do not seem to extend the same status to religious nonprofits that are not churches (i.e., parachurch organizations). This is curious, and the reasoning is not entirely clear. On the one hand, you might argue that what takes place within churches is religion in its purest form. That is, at its core, religion is about worship, and the special status of churches is meant to protect the most important part of religion. But this would seem to imply that what takes place outside of churches is somehow less religious and therefore less protected by the

Constitution. Despite what were probably good intentions, the two-tiered code for religion creates more questions than it solves. It also creates some logistical issues in its application.

Defining a Church

Because there are different rules for each, the question becomes how do we distinguish churches from other Christian nonprofits? The IRS does not have a definition of a church as much as it has various criteria it uses to guide its judgments. These criteria include:

- A distinct legal existence
- A recognized creed and form of worship
- A definite and distinct ecclesiastical government
- A formal code of doctrine and discipline
- A distinct religious history
- Membership not associated with any other church or denomination
- An organization of ordained ministers
- Ordained ministers selected after completing prescribed courses of study
- A literature of its own
- An established place of worship
- Regular congregations
- Regular religious services
- Sunday schools for the religious instruction of the young
- Schools for the preparation of its ministers

Making things complicated is the fact that these criteria are not all or nothing. There are many cases where some of these criteria would not apply to organizations that almost everyone would agree is a church. For example, the "distinct religious history" guideline would eliminate any new religious group. The "schools for the preparation of ministers" would eliminate Quakers and Jehovah's Witnesses.[9]

When an issue arises concerning the status of an organization as a church, the criteria are used in a fairly ad hoc manner. If an organization has a few features but not all of them, then they might be a church. Or they might not. But as we have seen, a group that claims church status is unlikely to run into problems unless some third party alerts the authorities since the IRS will never see their application for exempt status or their financial returns in the first place. If the IRS does investigate an organization claiming to be a church, the point of debate will most likely not be the church-ness of the organization as it will be its financial and political behavior. That is, is the church creating profits for its leaders or engaging in excessive lobbying? As one writer put it:

> ... when compared with the difficulties involved in defining religion and religious activities ... a private inurement [i.e. profiteering] investigation appears significantly less difficult than supporting a claim that a particular organization is not truly religious.[10]

Partly due to the difficulty in defining a church and the potential controversy created by telling someone that their church is not really a church, the IRS has been surprisingly flexible in the application of the church label. Consider the case of Young Life. You might be familiar with this youth-oriented organization whose activities range from providing summer camps for kids of all ages and backgrounds to organizing fellowship groups on high school and college campuses. It is an organization that brought in more than $150 million in 2004, is active across the United States and in 50 nations, and is probably not what most would consider a traditional church. Until 2005, Young Life did not consider itself to be a church, either. Before that point, it filed annual returns and had the status of any other nonprofit, religious or secular. However, in 2005, Young Life requested that the IRS consider changing its classification from parachurch nonprofit (i.e., religious organization) to church. To the surprise of many, the IRS obliged with this change. So looking back at the criteria above, how did the IRS come to this decision?

> In examining Young Life, the IRS viewed facts that were consistent with traditional church activities. For example, the fact that clubs typically hold weekly meetings (similar to church meetings) was important. ... Young Life is fully incorporated and has a distinct legal existence. It has a creed and form of worship recognized by its members. It has a formal doctrine as evidenced by its Statement of Faith and mission statement.

To be clear, the IRS probably did not view the entire Young Life organization as a single church. Instead, it fell under the latter part of the "church or association of churches" clause by which the individual Young Life clubs constitute individual churches and the national organization is the association. In other words, Young Life is the equivalent of a denomination. Although most people would not list Young Life if asked to name some denominations in the United States, you *might* be able to see how it could be considered denomination-like (at least if you were the IRS and did not have the stomach to debate why it is different from other denominations).[11]

The Symbolic Revocation

The special status of churches within the tax code raises some challenges for the IRS when it comes to enforcement of rules concerning financial conduct and political activity on the part of nonprofits claiming "church" status. The natural punishment for a nonprofit is to revoke their tax-exempt status. However, churches do not have to acquire recognition of their tax-exempt status in the first place, so how can something that was never given in the first place be taken away? The court case of *Branch Ministries v. Rossotti* established that the answer to this question is really, "it can't be."

Branch Ministries was a church that in 1992 placed advertisements in two newspapers urging Christians not to vote for Bill Clinton. The IRS revoked the church's tax exemption based on the rule that nonprofits cannot participate in political campaigns on behalf of or in opposition to any candidate. The church appealed stating that the revocation would force it to close due to "the inability of congregants to deduct their contributions from their taxes." The U.S. Court of Appeals for the District of Columbia ruled against the church, stating:

> In actual fact, even this burden is overstated. Because of the unique
> treatment churches receive under the Internal Revenue Code, the impact
> of the revocation is likely to be more symbolic than substantial. As the
> IRS confirmed at oral argument, if the Church does not intervene in
> future political campaigns, it may hold itself out as a 501(c)(3) organiza-
> tion and receive all the benefits of that status.

Branch Ministries had previously asked for and received official recognition from the IRS even though they had no need to do so. The Court ruled that the IRS was able to revoke that official recognition. However, given the automatic exemption for churches, nothing ultimately changed concerning its exempt status as it could simply assert the automatic exemption. The loss of an advanced letter of recognition would only become an issue if an individual donor was audited and they had to prove the charitable status of their donations. And given the automatic exemption for churches, the individual would likely not have much trouble establishing this point.

All of this raises another paradox about the two-tiered tax code for churches and other religious organizations. Part of the reasoning for exempting churches from registering and filing with the IRS is the fear that the government would begin to discriminate against some groups by saying they are not really a church or a religion. However, the understandable hesitancy of the IRS to make deter-minations regarding the church-ness or religiousness of an organization makes the entire religion issue practically irrelevant. The real issue is not the religious nature of an organization but whether it is truly nonprofit in the sense that there is no personal profiteering and the organization follows the other rules concerning nonprofit behavior. So assuming the IRS would not become bolder in its attempts to define religion, it is difficult to see how requiring churches to file annual returns or registering would risk the free exercise of religion.[12]

Churches, Nonprofits, and Nonprofit Churches

The result of the church-parachurch distinction is that there are two official categories as far as the IRS is concerned: churches and religious organizations. The latter is required to fulfill more rules than the former concerning registration and filing. However, this becomes slightly more complicated because the IRS allows organizations to both claim church status *and* fulfill the requirements of a religious organization. What this means is that, in practice, there are actually three different categories of religious organizations in the tax code: churches, religious organizations claiming church status, and religious organizations not claiming church status.

The first question to ask is if the organization simply looks like a traditional church or denomination? While it is difficult to define a church on paper, most of us feel like we have a working definition in our mind . . . a single building, pews, a pastor, weekly worship services, and so on. As noted already, churches have no requirement to register, but some do just for peace of mind or out of their own confusion about the tax code. Similarly, some churches will file annual returns just to be open about their finances, although this is probably a very small group. A 1998 survey found that about a quarter of congregations had a proxy exemption through their denomination, about 40% reported that they had their own letter of exemption, and another quarter had no official exemption recognition from the IRS. A significant portion simply did not know whether they had an official tax-exempt recognition.[13]

If most people would not view an organization as a church or an association of churches by traditional images of such, then the organization falls into the religious organization category. These organizations can then be broken down into two subcategories depending on whether the religious nonprofit claims to be a church. If it does, then just like churches, it is not required to gain official recognition from the IRS or file annual returns. Let us call this the "religious nonprofit church." The largest and most prominent organization falling into this category is likely the Salvation Army, which many people only know as a charity for disaster relief and

TABLE 7.1. Potential IRS Status of Religious Organizations.

	Looks like a Traditional Church?	Registered with IRS?	Files Annual Return?	Who
Church	Yes	Optional	Optional, not usually	Churches in your neighborhood; official denominational agencies
Nonprofit "church"	No	Optional	Optional	Salvation Army; Young Life (post-2005); select other parachurch organizations
Nonprofit	No	Yes	Yes	Most well-known parachurch organizations

social services. However, the Salvation Army sees itself as a church, claims that status, and does not file annual returns with the IRS. The notable absence of the Salvation Army has led some nonprofit evaluation services to offer a dedicated explanation on their Web sites explaining the absence of data on the organization. If the organization does not superficially look like a church and also does not see itself as or claim to be a church, then it is simply a religious organization and must gain tax-exempt recognition and file annual returns like all other secular non-profits. This category includes most of the parachurch organizations that you might imagine.[14]

You might be wondering whether the liberal application of the church label combined with the different requirements for filing financial statements invites organizations with less than honest intentions to take advantage of the system by claiming church status just to hide their finances. This is a long-standing concern among the courts and the IRS, and it has not been entirely unsubstantiated. In response to several highly dubious claims of church status in the 1980s, a court stated that . . .

. . . our tolerance for taxpayers who establish churches solely for tax avoidance purposes is reaching a breaking point. Not only do these taxpayers use the pretext of a church to avoid paying their fair share of taxes, even when their brazen schemes are uncovered many of them resort to the courts in a shameless attempt to vindicate themselves.[15]

Unfortunately, the shenanigans did not stop with that statement. Consider the Mike Murdock Evangelistic Association, which is a Christian nonprofit that files annual returns. In a series of investigative articles in 2003, the *Fort Worth Star-Telegram* reported that the large majority of the televangelist's funds did not go to helping the poor, as many might assume given Murdock's requests for money to help "break the back of poverty," but to overhead costs like salaries and travel. At the same time, the newspaper reported that Murdock lived a luxurious lifestyle with "Rolex watches, expensive sports cars and exotic animals."

The organization responded to this scrutiny in two ways. First, it actually started to spend more money on programs instead of salaries and other overhead costs. But more significantly, Murdock created a separate church organization that is, as we have seen, exempt from financial disclosure. This allowed expenses that were previously part of the nonprofit's balance sheet to be shifted to the church's. For instance, in 2003, the Mike Murdock Evangelistic Association (i.e., the nonprofit "religious organization," not the church) claimed revenue of $14.5 million. In 2006, it claimed just $500,000. While contributions may have taken a hit due to the negative publicity, it is likely that much of it was shifted to the church where it is closed to prying eyes. Helping to shed any doubts about this point, the newspaper interviewed the former general manager of the organization who stated that Murdock's intent behind the church's creation was to avoid financial disclosure.[16]

Despite the presence of clear mischief by some organizations, let us not assume that all religious nonprofits claiming to be a church even though they do not appear to be churches are simply hiding something. While there may be cases of manipulation, we should not let those exceptions distort the fact that the tax code's church-parachurch distinction is actually a substantive one that represents an element of inherent uncertainty and fluidity that exists between the two categories. We saw in chapter 4 that many parachurch organizations start off as church ministries before they branch out on their own. And as discussed in chapter 3, some churches and denominations begin as parachurch organizations or vice versa. Even if the tax code treated churches and other religious organizations exactly the same in terms of registration and oversight, we would still expect organizations to differ in how they perceived themselves. Some would still see their tax-exempt status as being due to their being a church and others because they are a Christian nonprofit.

We can actually use this "religious nonprofit church" category as a measure to explore some of this ambiguity and fluidity. Observed patterns of Christian nonprofits claiming church status are driven by two forces. First, there is the factor of how close the organization perceives itself to being a traditional church. Those organizations closest to acting, looking, and "feeling" like a traditional church, including actual congregations, are not going to ever register with the IRS or submit annual returns, so these are typically hidden from observation. At some point, the organization might become so different from a traditional church that even it will see claiming church status as too much of a stretch. However, between these

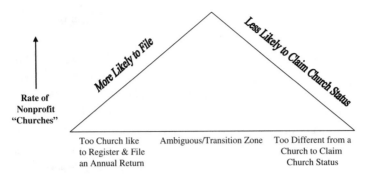

Rate of
Nonprofit
"Churches"

Too Church like   Ambiguous/Transition Zone   Too Different from a
to Register & File   Church to Claim
an Annual Return   Church Status

FIGURE 7.1. Dynamics of Church-Nonprofit Tax-Exempt Status.

two extremes is a transition zone where organizations might state that their reason for tax exemption is because they are a church, but they are also enough like parachurch organizations to feel some pressure to register with the IRS and file tax returns. This dynamic is illustrated in figure 7-1. Obviously not all organizations go through a transition process between church and parachurch. Some simply begin from the very beginning as a parachurch organization that never had any thought of considering itself as a church.

Of the almost 2,000 Christian nonprofits examined in this book, only 118 or 6% claimed that their reason for tax exemption was because they were a church. In short, a fairly small but not insignificant percentage of these Christian nonprofits exist within the ambiguous zone between church and parachurch. At just 1%, the Advocacy & Activism sector has the lowest rate of nonprofits claiming church status. This could be because organizations in this sector tend to be so similar to congregations that only the most parachurch-like Advocacy & Activism nonprofits even show up in IRS records. That is, all of the church-like organizations are filtered out so all we see are the clearly parachurch examples in this sector. However, given what we know about this sector, it seems more likely that this sector tends to be highly skewed toward the right-hand side of figure 7-1 where organizations are so unlike congregations that very few ever think to claim church status. On the contrary, just 3% of the organizations in the Fellowship & Enrichment sector claim church status, but I would argue that this is for the opposite reason. Organizations in this sector are in many ways very church like. They are often composed of small local cells that meet regularly to worship together. This is the very reason why Young Life was able to convince the IRS that they should be granted a church status, and it is the reason that organizations in this sector often draw the ire of local congregations (see chapter 3). There are likely many Fellowship & Enrichment organizations that never get to the point of filing annual returns because they perceive themselves as being very much a church, so the low rate of "nonprofit churches" in the sector is due to very different reasons than the low rate in the Advocacy & Activism sector.

Using the rates of organizations claiming church status, I have proposed an ordering of the different sectors based on the dynamics discussed above. With the highest rate of organizations claiming church status, the Missions & Missionary and the Radio & Television sectors exist in the murky area between church and nonprofit. On the one hand, many of these organizations are far enough from being like a church to where they are filing annual returns, but they are also close enough to be claiming church status. For instance, Radio & Television organizations are often broadcasting services of one or more churches. While they have a national profile, more viewers, and often larger revenues than the typical local church, these organizations are still very connected to the look and feel of traditional church activities.

To the left of the transition zone are those sectors where few organizations are seen claiming church status because many of the organizations are distributed on the left side of figure 7-1. In addition to the earlier mentioned Fellowship & Enrichment sector, this area includes organizations in the Charismatic Evangelism and Education & Training sectors. The Charismatic Evangelism sector is often focused on conducting worship services, even if through en masse and/or itinerant methods. They also frequently partner with traditional churches. Hence, the nonprofits that *do* file annual returns show a lower rate of claiming church status because many of the organizations in this sector never filed returns in the first place.

Beyond activities or sector, there are likely other factors that lead Christian nonprofits to lean toward or away from claiming church status. For example, it might become more difficult to see a nonprofit as a church when it begins to take in millions of dollars (although, clearly many megachurches do just that). Indeed, about 7% of those with total revenue of $200,000–$500,000 claim to be a church. This percentage goes down to about 3% when looking at those with revenue more than $10,000,000.

The issue of how the government defines and treats the distinction between church and parachurch organizations receives little attention but also has important legal, practical, and sociological implications. While relatively few Christian nonprofits even think about receiving government money or lobbying for legislation, all of them must define themselves as either a church or a parachurch religious organization in the eyes of the IRS and manage the consequences of that decision when it comes to the different rules that apply to each category. It will not be surprising if the government's distinction between church and parachurch becomes a point of debate in the future as the latter becomes an increasingly important player in the religious market and society as a whole.

TABLE 7.2. Claims of Church Status by Sector.

	Church like, Less Likely to File			Transition Zone, Church like but Likely to File			Not Church like, More Likely to File		
	Fellowship & Enrichment	Charismatic Evangelism	Education & Training	Missions & Missionary	Radio & Television	Publishing & Resources	Relief & Development	Fund-Raising & Grant-Making	Advocacy & Activism
Percent claiming church status	3	6	6	10	9	6	5	5	1

Funding and Lobbying

Having looked at how the government handles the church-parachurch distinction and how this is manifested in Christian nonprofits, let us now look at issues that many people are more familiar with. The issue of public funds going to religious groups has been a hot topic in the last decade. The impetus for much of this attention was George W. Bush's Faith-Based Initiative. Early in his presidency, Bush created a White House office meant to lead the effort to make funding available for religious groups providing social service programs. The executive order establishing the White House office stated the purpose of the Faith-Based Initiative:

> Faith-based and other community organizations are indispensable in meeting the needs of poor Americans and distressed neighborhoods. Government cannot be replaced by such organizations, but it can and should welcome them as partners. The paramount goal is compassionate results, and private and charitable community groups, including religious ones, should have the fullest opportunity permitted by law to compete on a level playing field, so long as they achieve valid public purposes, such as curbing crime, conquering addiction, strengthening families and neighborhoods, and overcoming poverty.[17]

The idea of public money going to religious organizations, even if it was for a soup kitchen or shelter, quickly raised questions concerning its consequences, particularly concerning its implications for the establishment clause of the Constitution. The media, scholars, and religious groups quickly jumped into debates about whether the program was constitutional and, even if it was legal, whether it was a good idea. Regardless of what side of this debate you are on, there are a couple of interesting points to make about it.

First, many people have come to associate the Faith-Based Initiative with the administration of George W. Bush. This is partially correct in that the name Faith-Based Initiative is what that administration called its program. He also made the program a major part of his election platform. Because of this, many people are surprised to hear that it actually originated in the welfare reform legislation of 1996. While the Personal Responsibility and Work Opportunity Reconciliation Act had many important features, one part of the act was known as the Charitable Choice provision. Charitable Choice required states to consider religious organizations when they contract with nonprofits to provide social services, without reference to their internal governance, use of religious art, scripture, or other symbols or the "definition, development, practice, and expression of its religious beliefs." In other words, the basic law behind the Faith-Based Initiative existed several years before the Bush presidency. The Bush administration simply added some organizational structure to the program by creating offices within various government agencies to facilitate the law.[18]

Also surprising to many is the fact that neither the Charitable Choice program nor the Faith-Based Initiative marked the start of religious organizations receiving government funding. Long before formal legislation, religious organizations were directly or indirectly receiving public funding for their shelters, child care services, relief programs, hospitals, colleges, and other social programs and agencies. As the political scientist Stephen Monsma observed,

> [the] "impregnable wall" . . . does not stop a host of religiously based nonprofit organizations—Catholic, Jewish, and Protestant—from receiving millions of public tax dollars. In 1993, 65 percent of Catholic Charities' revenues came from government sources, as did 75 percent of the Jewish Board of Family and Children's Services' revenues, and 92 percent of Lutheran Social Ministries' revenues.[19]

So those fighting against the prospect of government funding going to religious organizations due to the Faith-Based Initiative (or even its earlier Charitable Choice version) were a bit late to the party.

Given these points, you might be wondering why exactly the Faith-Based Initiative even exists. After all, neither the law nor the funding of religious organizations was new. The Bush administration argued that even if the law and the funding of religious organizations already existed, more needed to be done to overcome misconceptions and other barriers within the government that prevented cooperation with religious organizations. They argued that many federal agencies were confused about what they could and could not do when it came to interactions with religious nonprofits:

> Federal officials, and State and local officials participating in Federal formula grant programs, often seem stuck in a "no-aid," strict separationist framework that permitted Federal funding only of religiously affiliated organizations offering secular services in a secularized setting, and deny equal treatment to organizations with an obvious religious character.[20]

There likely was a great deal of confusion within the government concerning the church-state issue. But given the amount of debate that has and does exist among scholars, courts, and legislators concerning the same issue, it is difficult to fault government administrators for lacking clarity and consensus. There have been some obvious mixed signals concerning the relationship between religious organizations and the state. We saw some of this earlier in this chapter regarding the government's rationale for exempting religious organizations from taxes. In the central case concerning that issue, the Supreme Court ruled in favor of tax exemptions partially because *it was not a direct subsidy*. The Court stated that[21]

> Obviously a direct money subsidy would be a relationship pregnant with involvement and, as with most governmental grant programs, could encompass sustained and detailed administrative relationships for enforcement of statutory or administrative standards, but that is not the case [with an exemption].

In other words, tax exemptions prevented "excessive entanglement" between religion and government in addition to providing the assumed prosocial benefits of religion. So let us pretend that you are a government administrator reviewing an application from a religious organization for a grant to fund their alcohol treatment program. You are aware of the "no-excessive entanglement" principle, but you are also aware of the Charitable Choice/Faith-Based Initiative program . . . you might be a bit conflicted, too.

There is another paradox to be found in all of this. Part of Bush's motivation for the Faith-Based Initiative seems to have been the perception that more conservative religious groups were being filtered out of government funding due to agencies' interpretations of the law and/or outright discrimination:

> . . . reviewers of grant applications assume that Jefferson's "wall of separation" metaphor automatically disqualifies *all but the most secularized [religious] providers . . .*[22]

After Charitable Choice was passed, though, sociologists looked into this issue and found that more conservative religious groups were less likely to receive government funding not because they were being discriminated against but because they were less interested in receiving government funding. Why? Ironically, because such funding could create too much entanglement with the government. This should not have been such a surprise to anyone. Social scientists and theologians have long noted that the separation of church and state is a matter of "chance" for liberal groups but a "dogmatic axiom" and the "emanation of a religious idea" for conservative groups. Such groups fear, possibly accurately, that involvement with the state would mean a sacrifice of their religious identity and expression due to the regulations such a relationship would likely include.[23]

To be fair, the Faith-Based Initiative was not necessarily about dragging conservative religious organizations kicking and screaming into government funding ("you will take this money and you will like it!"). Instead, it was intended to alleviate the very concerns of religious organizations that were hesitant to apply for funding by specifying that they could stay religious while getting government funding.

[A] faith-based organization that applies for or participates in a social service program supported with Federal financial assistance may retain its independence and may continue to carry out its mission, including the definition, development, practice, and expression of its religious beliefs . . .

This sounds good, but it is not quite that simple. The organization can stay religious, but it must keep some key religious behaviors separate from the services funded by the government:

. . . provided that it does not use direct Federal financial assistance to support any inherently religious activities, such as worship, religious instruction, or proselytization.[24]

As you can imagine, this is a fine line to walk. Such partitioning of funds and activities can be cumbersome, and even if they could do it logistically, many of the most religious organizations would not want to make that sacrifice to their religious mission.

Christian Nonprofits and Government Funding

These issues raise a few guiding questions for us in our examination of the Christian nonprofits in these chapters. First, to what extent are they receiving public funds? Second, does receipt of government money differ by the "religiosity" of the nonprofit? Finally, is there evidence that receiving government funds reduces the religiosity of the organization? Interestingly, of the 2,000 largest national and internationally focused Christian nonprofits, *very few* receive government funding. Just under 3% or 56 of the 1,941 identified organizations received government funding in 2004. Collectively, though, these 56 organizations received $694,402,032 in public funding. The significance of that number depends on your perspective. On the one hand, over half a billion dollars is not pocket change to most of us. But then again, it is relatively a very small amount of the total government expenditures. It does, however, represent more than 6% of the total revenue of all these Christian nonprofits.

Most of this money goes to the Relief & Development sector. This is not too surprising since these organizations are performing a public service that the government is directly interested in subsidizing. If these Christian nonprofits, along with their secular peers, were not distributing food, clothing, and medicines and providing other relief and development services, then the government likely would have to do so in their place. It is also likely that these activities are more naturally separated from the religious activities restricted by public funding, such as worship services and proselytization. The largest recipients in the sector include World Vision with $284 million in government contributions and Food for the Poor with $107 million. Given that these two organizations received almost half of the total amount of government money, the distribution of money is obviously concentrated within a handful of nonprofits.[25]

Although much lower than the Relief & Development sector, the Fellowship & Enrichment sector has the second highest rate of government funding. Public-funded organizations in this sector include a ministry serving disabled individuals, two nonprofits aimed at prisoners (one of those toward youth/juveniles), two organizations working to prevent or treat drug and alcohol abuse among teenagers, and one that has multiple programs to support youth.

Religiosity and Government Funding

There are many differences between government-funded Christian nonprofits and their unfunded peers. First, the former tend to be larger. While only 6% of the 2,000 nonprofits examined here have total revenues more than $10 million, more than 50% of those receiving government funding receive this much money. They are also twice as likely to belong to the Evangelical Council for Financial Accountability. However, are government-funded Christian nonprofits different in their religious identity or at least how they express that identity? This is a question that has been of interest to religious organizations, social scientists, and policy makers.

To see whether the level or type of religiosity of an organization affects its likelihood of receiving public funds, we can examine the language used by each nonprofit to describe its purpose and mission on their tax returns. Table 7-4 compares the use of various religious terms by the government- and non-government-funded Christian nonprofits. The overall trend is that government-funded organizations are much less likely to use religious terms than non-government-funded organizations. While three out of four of the nonfunded nonprofits used at least one of the religious words, only half of the nonprofits receiving public funding did.

Given this overall finding, it is not surprising that when looking at the individual terms, the frequency of usage is consistently lower for publicly funded organizations. In fact, in only one case are publicly funded nonprofits more likely to use a religious term than their nonfunded counterparts and that is in the use of the term "spirit" or "spiritual." Nineteen percent of the government-funded organizations used this term compared to 10% of the nonfunded ones. This is a more inclusive religious term than many of the others, such as "Christ" or "evangelism," so it is interesting that publicly funded organizations use it more frequently.

TABLE 7.3. Government Funding of Christian Nonprofits.

	Charismatic Evangelism	Relief & Development	Education & Training	Publishing & Resources	Radio & Television	Missions & Missionary	Fellowship & Enrichment	Advocacy & Activism	Fund-Raising, Grant-Making, Other
Number of organizations (N)	1	38	3	1	0	3	6	2	2
Percent within sector (N/number of organizations in sector)	0.3	16.6	1.2	0.4	0.0	1.0	4.1	2.1	2.1
Percentage of government-funded organizations (N/56)	1.8	67.9	5.3	1.8	0.0	5.3	10.5	3.5	3.5

TABLE 7.4. Percent of Nonprofits Using Religious Descriptors by Government Funding Status.

	No Government Funding (N = 1,858)	Government Funding (N = 56)
Any religious term*	76	51
Bible/biblical*	23	4
Christ/Jesus Christ*	27	4
Christian	36	25
Church	35	25
Evangelism/evangelical/evangelize	21	12
Faith	7	5
God	10	4
Gospel*	24	9
Ministry/minister*	35	19
Religion/religious*	24	5
Spirit/spiritual*	10	19
Word*	6	0

*Difference is statistically significant at the .05 level (Fisher's exact test two sided).

All of this suggests a conservative-liberal gap in the public funding of Christian nonprofits, with the latter being the beneficiaries. But what is the source of this gap? It is possible that more inclusive or theologically liberal nonprofits are more likely to receive public funds. This could be due to differing levels of interest in applying for government funding, or liberal organizations may just be more successful in acquiring that funding for whatever reason (e.g., better resources, discrimination and agencies' confusion about laws). Either way, both these possibilities result from the application process. Technically, this is referred to as a selection effect. Another possibility results not from the application process but from the administration process. That is, maybe the applications are evenly distributed, and the rate of success is the same between liberal and conservative organizations. However, maybe exclusive or theologically conservative nonprofits become less religious or at least act less religious once they receive funding. This is called a causation effect. Of course, both these scenarios could be occurring, with more liberal nonprofits being more likely to be selected *and* conservative nonprofits becoming more liberal due to government funding.

Since we do not have data on applications for government funding here, it is difficult to know whether conservative organizations applied for funds at a lower rate than liberal organizations, although other research does suggest that this is the case.[26] We can, though, try to see if expressed religiosity changes due to funding. One way to do this is to see whether any of these Christian nonprofits received public funds for the first time in recent years. If we can identify those organizations, we can then see if and how the religiosity of their self-descriptions changed due to the acquisition of funding. This will at least give some idea whether the appearance of a conservative-liberal gap in funding is due to a causation effect. It turns out that 20 of the 56 publicly funded Christian nonprofits received these funds for the first time in 2004 or 2003. I went back and examined the self-descriptions provided on the tax returns for these organizations for the previous 2 years to see if there was any evidence of change. The majority used religious terms before receiving funding and used the same terms afterward. Five of the organizations did not use any of the religious terms before or after public funding. However, two of the nonprofits showed noticeable change in self-description when comparing pre- and postfunding narratives. Organization 1, a human rights advocacy organization, received government funding in 2004 but not in 2003. In its prefunding narrative, it described itself as a "Christian ministry" with a "scriptural" mandate. This was absent from their 2004 narrative, along with the word "spiritually" in a sentence that was otherwise exactly the same as their prefunding description. Organization 2's change is less clear and is seen 2 years before government funding. In 2002, they referred to their child sponsorship program as serving Christians, but in 2004, this specificity was absent. The 2004 narrative also added a "faith-based" label to the organization and dropped the 2002 references to "spiritual" goals.

What should we make of these findings? On the one hand, most of the organizations examined showed no change due to their new public funding. This alone does not provide much evidence that the conservative-liberal gap is due to the effect government funding has on restricting organizational religiosity (i.e., a causation effect). And as we saw earlier, government-funded organizations were less likely to use religious terms and more likely to use inclusive terms if they do. This, together with the lack of a causation effect, provides support for idea that more liberal or secularized Christian nonprofits have a higher likelihood of receiving funding due to a higher likelihood of applying for such funds and/or a higher likelihood of being chosen to receive such funds. In short, the inclusiveness

TABLE 7.5. Change in Use of Religious Descriptors among Christian Nonprofits First Receiving Government Funding in 2004 or 2003.

	N	%
No religious terms used before government funding	5	23.8
Religious terms used before government funding, no change after	13	61.9
Religious terms used before government funding, some change after	2	14.3
Total	20	100.0

or liberalness of Christian nonprofits getting public money was there before the money, not *because* of the money. But I do not want to gloss over the two exceptions noted above. These organizations clearly altered how they described their religious identity and mission as they approached or after they received government funding. Given that these are the exceptions rather than the rule, such censoring would seem to be self-induced. This may be due to the organizations seeking out advice from consultants or grant writers that invoked their own assumptions concerning the government's requirements, or it could be the organizations responding to their own assumptions about what the government would want or require in a nonprofit it funds. They may have assumed that interference would occur and simply preempted it by altering how they presented themselves. Ironically, many of the words dropped in the postgovernment funding narratives are those that were most common (e.g., Christian, spiritual) among the nonprofits with public funding, making censoring seem even less necessary. This also provides some evidence that they were not simply mimicking other government-funded Christian nonprofits since they would have found the use of such terminology common. Of course, they may have referenced secular organizations instead of other Christian nonprofits.

TABLE 7.6. Before and After Text of Nonprofits Showing Some Change in Self-Description.

	Pregovernment Funding	Postgovernment Funding
Organization 1*	"A Christian ministry that seeks to advance the scriptural mandate to help people who are suffering injustice and oppression." "In addition . . . help them heal emotionally, physically, mentally, spiritually, and economically."	"In addition . . . help them heal emotionally, physically, mentally, and economically."
Organization 2**	". . . Child sponsorship arm . . . to assist Christians in providing education . . ." ". . . the purpose of empowerment towards social, emotional, spiritual and economic stability." "Ministry projects: Various projects . . . inspire spiritual hope through programs . . ."	"a faith-based relief and development organization . . ." ". . . program links sponsors with children . . . who need education, nutritious food . . ." ". . . program to help the poorest families . . . encourage economic independence . . ." ". . . designed to assist ministry needs . . ."

*Narrative from 1 year before government funding.
**Narrative from 2 years before government funding.

A Longer View

Although most of the organizations examined here did not show a change in self-descriptions, this does not necessarily mean that change has never occurred. Government-funded organizations that are less likely to express religiosity may not have always been so reserved or inclusive in their identity. The strategy here was to measure more dramatic changes that occur directly due to the receipt of government funding. However, the change may not have occurred directly with the receipt of funding, but the funding might have been the culmination of a much longer evolution within the organization. The relatively short window of observation examined here was not able to account for a less direct path of causation, although other research has suggested such a path. In his study of Habitat for Humanity, sociologist Jerome Baggett observed a tension between growth, professionalization, and religious identity. In the words of a Habitat vice president:

> You know, in the early years of the organization, the Christian emphasis
> was exactly why people came here. But there was a shift because the
> success of the organization was really beginning to create some serious
> management problems. The whole issue was the balance between faith
> and competence. . . . I would say that things have been done to increase
> competency and technical skills. But maybe we did lose a bit of the
> Christian element.[27]

Changes in the organization, such as growth and professionalization, led to a decrease in the explicit religiosity of the organization. This reduction in religiosity likely made Habitat more willing and able to partner with government agencies since the fears about restrictions on religiosity had become moot. Furthermore, the professionalization and growth that had led to that reduction in religiosity also put them in a better position to successfully compete for government funding as they had more resources and staff to put toward things like writing grant applications. In other words, the road to government funding is often a long and complex one for a Christian nonprofit, and while funding may not directly cause changes in an organization's religiosity, it very well may reflect such changes.

Lobbying and Nonprofits

The parachurch-state relationship created by government funding represents an exchange of resources in one direction. The government provides funding to a Christian nonprofit to provide some service the government is interested in supporting or outsourcing. The other major point of contact between the Christian nonprofit population and the state is in the reverse direction. In lobbying efforts, a parachurch organization spends resources to convince government officials to support legislation that the organization wants.

You might be a little confused, though. Is not one of the fundamental rules for nonprofits that they cannot engage in lobbying? Indeed, one of the first lines in the IRS's list of ways for a nonprofit to lose their tax exemption states that the organization "must restrict its lobbying activities to an insubstantial part of its total activities." The argument behind this is that nonprofits are essentially receiving a government subsidy through their tax exemption. If nonprofits use that exemption to then lobby the government, then the government and hence the general public are actually indirectly funding political positions and activities. People are free to spend their own money on such activities, but the government does not want to subsidize them. Note that this has some parallels with the debate concerning tax exemptions to churches and other religious organizations as some argue that this violates the establishment clause by providing government support for religion.[28]

Read the rule again, though, and you will notice a bit of fuzzy language. It does not absolutely rule out lobbying. It just says that the lobbying must be an insubstantial part of their activities. The IRS would evaluate the organization's lobbying based on

> . . . a variety of factors, including the time devoted (by both compensated
> and volunteer workers) and the expenditures devoted by the
> organization to the activity, when determining whether the lobbying
> activity is substantial.[29]

If based on these factors the lobbying activities were determined to be "substantial," then the nonprofit could lose its tax-exempt status and possibly pay monetary penalties. But what exactly counts as substantial? It is a classic eye of the beholder question. A million dollar lobbying campaign might not seem substantial to one person, while to another it might. It would also seem dependent on the revenue of the organization. A small amount might be substantial if it constitutes the entire budget of the nonprofit. Mainly due to the inherently arbitrary and vague nature of the substantial test, the IRS created an alternative option in the Tax Reform Act of 1973. Called the "H election" or the "expenditure test," this law defined a specific monetary limit on lobbying expenses based on the total revenue of the nonprofit.

> At the low end, nonprofits with budgets up to $500,000 can spend 20
> percent of all their expenditures on direct lobbying. An organization

with a budget between $1.5 million and $17 million can spend $225,000 plus 5 percent of the budget over $1.5 million. The formulas for grass-roots lobbying allow for one-quarter of the spending on direct lobbying.[30]

Now, in true bureaucratic form, things get complicated. First, the expenditure test did not replace the substantial test. Instead, they both exist today, and it is entirely up to the nonprofit to elect whether they want to go by the expenditure test. They can also decide to switch back and forth between the two rules from year to year. The problem with this system is that they are not entirely consistent standards. On the one hand, the expenditure test provides a very clear definition, so it is attractive because it can guarantee that an organization will stay out of trouble. However, for some organizations, it might actually be stricter than the substantial part test. Consider a nonprofit with a very large budget. It might be able to do more lobbying without it being seen as substantial than they would under the expenditure test, which limits total lobbying expenses to $1,000,000 regardless of total budget. So it becomes a question of risk . . . is worth trying to spend more on lobbying knowing that you might get burned by the IRS, or do you spend less and gain the comfort of knowing that you will be safe? It is important to note that the expenditure test is not available to nonprofits qualifying for a church exemption since they do not have to report their finances, making a test based on expenses and revenue impossible (see earlier in this chapter).

Maybe more problematic than the dueling tests of lobbying activity is the very definition of lobbying on which those tests rely. In the words of the IRS:

> An organization will be regarded as attempting to influence legislation if it contacts, or urges the public to contact, members or employees of a legislative body for the purpose of proposing, supporting, or opposing legislation, or if the organization advocates the adoption or rejection of legislation.[31]

Let us deconstruct this statement. Lobbying only includes those activities where a nonprofit states a *specific* position on a *specific* piece of legislation *and* encourages either the public (i.e., grassroots lobbying) or the legislators (i.e., direct lobbying) to support that position. This definition of lobbying does not refer to general statements about social issues that may or may not involve a particular law that is being voted on. For instance, an organization's pro-life stance is not necessarily lobbying unless it refers to H.R. #3442 or some other specific piece of law. Similarly, the lobbying definition does not count general announcements about legislation as long as the organization does not explicitly take a side. Since they lack reference to a specific piece of legislation or a call to action, all of these activities would be seen as "educational" instead of lobbying.

What this means is that nonprofits can get away with many activities that are political without them counting as lobbying as long as they present it in a particular way. For instance, a nonprofit can tell their supporters how the organization feels about a particular issue as long as that does not lead them to explicitly advocating for or against a particular law, even though that position might be implied in any existing or future legislation. Similarly, a nonprofit can provide legislators' voting records on particular issues as long as they do not explicitly state that one voting pattern is better or worse than another. They can even express a specific position on a specific piece of legislation as long as it does not encourage action (something to the effect of "I feel strongly about this, but please do not feel like *you* need to do anything about it . . ."). Some have called this the "wink-wink" rule, meaning that nonprofits can express and advocate a position in a way that technically does not violate the rules even though everyone knows that a clear position is being advanced.[32]

Educational activities are supposed to consist of "nonpartisan analysis, study or research . . . [with] sufficiently full and fair exposition of the pertinent facts to enable the public or an individual to form an independent opinion or conclusion."[33] However, in practice, this becomes a laughable statement as education becomes a sort of implied or covert form of lobbying. Consider the Life Issues Institute, which describes its mission as "serving the educational needs of the pro-life movement." It reports no actual "lobbying" expenses or activities on its annual returns from 2003 through 2005. However, its Web site was filled with "educational" materials on abortion, physician-assisted suicide, stem cell research, and organizations such as Planned Parenthood and the March of Dimes. Clearly, many of these issues have and will come up in actual legislation, and nothing in their materials leaves doubt about the position of the organization. Such implied lobbying can walk a very fine line. For example, in a 2003 press release, the organization announced the introduction of legislation banning "partial birth abortions" by a Congressman. In the press release, the president of the Life Issues Institute stated that "We are very pleased that Congressman Chabot has reintroduced this bill." Many would view this as the organization actively advocating for specific legislation.[34]

To be clear, though, this is not just an issue with nonprofits having a Christian or even a conservative Christian viewpoint. It is true that within the Christian nonprofit population, there are more organizations that might be considered conservative than liberal. However, if we were examining nonprofits in a different sector, say, environmental organizations or some other sector, there would be plenty of covert lobbying on the liberal side of political issues as well. The problem is more systemic than it is with any particular viewpoint or nonprofit. Many if not most nonprofits are inherently what political scientists call an "interest group." They are organizations run and supported by individuals who share a collective interest and would like to advance that interest in society. Hence, almost all nonprofits are trying to engage and shape some part of society, whether it is religion, the environment, education, poverty, or some other cause. It is almost impossible for the interests that form the underlying purpose for the nonprofit's existence not to overlap with positions that may be seen as political and may even come up in legislation. How can a hospital not have some view on healthcare policy or an environmental nonprofit on air quality laws or a parents-teachers association toward an education bill?[35]

Christian Nonprofit Lobbying

Having laid some groundwork for understanding lobbying among nonprofits, let us take a look at lobbying among the different Christian nonprofit sectors. Only 16 of the almost 2,000 largest organizations reported any lobbying expenses. The Advocacy & Activism has the highest number and rate of lobbying organizations, which is to be expected. Somewhat surprisingly, though, only about one-third are located within that sector, with 10 of the 16 lobbying organizations distributed in other sectors. Following up that sector is the Fellowship & Enrichment sector with four organizations reporting lobbying expenses. The Relief & Development, Radio & Television, and Education & Training sectors also have at least one lobbying nonprofit.

I took a more detailed look at the tax returns of these 16 organizations to see if I could determine what exactly their lobbying efforts were aimed toward. About half did not specify any legislation or general issue, so we cannot be sure what legislation was targeted.[36] Of those that did provide some details, family issues was the most common target. Two specified "marriage amendments" (i.e., against gay marriage), while three others simply discussed general family values, sanctity of life, pornography, and other similar policy initiatives. One organization did not specify any legislation, but given its general mission, it is probably safe to assume it involved abortion legislation. Three of the nonprofits reported lobbying expenses in the general area of domestic and international aid. One specified "hunger" policies and another "Sudan legislation." Ten of the 16 lobbying nonprofits elected to use the expenditure test discussed earlier, while 6 used the substantial part test. Of the former, five directed all of their lobbying expenses toward direct lobbying of legislators, one conducted grassroots lobbying of the general public, and four spent money on both methods. Overall, the mean amount spent on grassroots and direct lobbying was about $140,000 for each.[37] Among the six organizations using the "substantial part test," the average lobbying expense was just under $130,000.

TABLE 7.7. Percent with Lobbying Expenses within Christian Nonprofit Sectors.

	Charismatic Evangelism	Relief & Development	Education & Training	Publishing & Resources	Radio & Television	Missions & Missionary	Fellowship & Enrichment	Advocacy & Activism	Fund-Raising, Grant-Making, Other
Had lobbying expenses (N)	0	3	1	0	2	0	4	6	0
Percent within sector (N/ number of organization in sector)	0.0	1.3	0.4	0.0	1.5	0.0	2.7	6.2	0.0
Percentage of lobbying organizations (N/16)	0.0	18.8	6.3	0.0	12.5	0.0	25.0	37.5	0.0

Organizations that engage in formal lobbying, whether direct or grassroots, tend to be larger than nonlobbying organizations. The median revenue of lobbying nonprofits is just under $15 million, while it is just over half a million for those without lobbying expenses. This is partly a product of the sectors that lobbying organizations are in (e.g., Relief & Development), but it is also a function of the resources required to conduct a formal lobbying campaign. Direct lobbying, for instance, usually requires someone who can navigate government bureaucracy and politics. These people are typically professional lobbyists, even if that is not their official title. Furthermore, lawyers, policy advisors, communications directors, and other skilled professionals are also involved in many lobbying efforts at either the grassroots or the direct level. It is difficult for a small-budget organization to fund such activities.

For a variety of reasons, many might assume that nonprofits receiving government funding might be less likely to conduct lobbying campaigns. For instance, government-funded organizations might be hesitant to annoy or anger the government out of fear of losing funding the next year. Actually, though, almost one-third of the lobbying organizations are also receiving government funding. This makes sense given that both receiving funding and lobbying government require similar skills and resources. Legal specialists, professional writers, policy advisors, and connections with government officials can help with both lobbying and winning grants. Furthermore, the more a nonprofit is involved with government in one area, such as receiving funds, the more of a stake they might have in another area, such as legislation concerning the organization's activities. It could go the other way around as well. The face time with government officials and publicity received through lobbying could lead an organization to gaining a favorable reputation when government grants are being distributed.

Christian Nonprofits and the Government

Overall, very few large national and international Christian nonprofits interact with the government when it comes to receiving government funding. This does not make the interactions that do occur insignificant. Almost half a billion dollars of public funds go to the largest Christian nonprofits examined here. Clearly, government funding is likely to be more prevalent if one looks at more local nonprofits that are engaged more in social services than those of interest here. Very few of these Christian nonprofits spent money on formal grassroots or direct lobbying either. However, we must keep in mind that this only includes a *very specific type of activity*. The political impact of these organizations is undoubtedly greater than their formal lobbying expenses. Many of them are spending their entire budget addressing social issues like poverty, abortion, and marriage and family policies without actually engaging in "lobbying" as defined by the IRS. Names like James Dobson, Pat Robertson, Tony Perkins, and their respective organizations have become powerful voices in American sociopolitical issues, but these are just examples of celebrity parachurch leaders with explicitly political interests. Many more lesser known Christian leaders and their nonprofits are engaging in issues that have social and political implications. Often, these leaders and organizations may not realize or even care about those implications, but their activities and teachings do influence the ideas of their contributors and the people they interact with during their nonprofit activities. This indirect and unintentional political influence is not unlike the impact churches have on their members when it comes to social and political issues.

Concluding Thoughts

The preceding chapters have attempted to provide some insight into the population of Christian nonprofit organizations, or what has been popularly called the parachurch sector. Christian nonprofits are both reflective of and a catalyst for transformations in the religious market. While they may have been created in response to changes they had nothing to do with, now that they exist, they will have an active role in producing other changes. This has implications for churchgoers and social scientists alike.

Centers of power have shifted, boundaries have been redrawn or erased, structures have been built or dismantled, and identities have been altered. Such changes do not come without growing pains, whether it is for individuals, congregations, denominations, or the nonprofits themselves. Whether it is a religious or secular market, restructuring a market often displaces some people or organizations temporarily or permanently. However, these individuals may take some solace in the fact that this is not the first time such a restructuring has occurred nor will it be the last, yet Christianity has endured and thrived. Indeed, the rise of Christian nonprofits speaks to the adaptability of individuals and organizations to find outlets for their religious pursuits, which in itself speaks to the strong continued desire of Christians for these pursuits. It is arguable that Christianity is more mobilized now than ever before. Christian nonprofits have allowed for a great amount of creativity and flexibility not only in the activities pursued but also by how those activities are framed or conducted. While mission work, publishing, evangelism, or any other activity may not be new, Christian nonprofits have found many new ways of conducting these activities. Christianity is being presented in places and in forms never before seen primarily due to Christian nonprofits.

In their book, *The Future of Religion*, sociologists Rodney Stark and William Bainbridge argued that we too often "misread" religion by failing "to recognize the dynamic character of religious economies."[38] There may be no better example case study in this regard than Christian nonprofits and the parachurch movement. As seen throughout these chapters, Christian nonprofits have an important role in everything from church-state relations to trends in financial giving. As social scientists look to understand the American religious market today and in the future, we will again risk error by ignoring this population.

Appendix

Data Collection Methods

Most of the data presented throughout this book come from an original collection conducted by the author. The collection consisted of three stages that began in 2006. First, organizations fulfilling certain criteria had to be identified. Second, tax returns for these organizations had to be located and financial information from them entered into a database. Third, organizational narratives provided on these tax returns had to be coded and combined with the financial measures.

DEFINING THE TARGET POPULATION

While a significant amount of research has looked at local religious social service organizations, almost no systematic research had looked at the type of organizations that are more commonly mentioned as representing the parachurch sector. Specifically, little research had looked at the larger Christian organizations that have a national and/or an international reach. The goal of this book has been to fill this gap. Therefore, the target population of interest for this project was defined as large Christian nonprofit organizations based in the United States that operate on a national or an international scope and are not under the financial or administrative control of official denominational organizations. This still required some specification and operationalization, though, since "large" and "national/international" are concepts that are not entirely clear.[1]

The national or international scope requirement was defined by having operations in either a foreign country (i.e., international) or in at least two states in the United States (i.e., national). The "large" requirement is obviously always going to be relative, but it ended up being tied to the national or international scope standard. It was found that under a total revenue of $200,000, organizations were increasingly likely not to fulfill the national/international scope standard and were also more vague in their description of activities (likely because smaller organizations are still trying to figure out exactly what they are doing). Therefore, it was decided that the data collection would be limited to those organizations with total revenue greater than \$200,000.[2] The availability of scanned tax returns lags by about 2 years. When this data collection began, the most consistently available recent data came from 2004, so that is the year utilized in these data.

So to be included in these data, the organization had to

1. be a 501(c)(3) public charity
2. identify as Christian
3. have revenue more than \$200,000 in 2004
4. operate in at least two U.S. states and/or in a foreign country and
5. not be under the financial or administrative control of a church or denomination.

IDENTIFYING THE ORGANIZATIONS

With the criteria for inclusion set, the next step was to find the organizations that met the criteria. In the absence of a list of Christian nonprofits, I had to look for other sources. The closest thing to a list of Christian nonprofits is the National Center for Charitable Statistics' (NCCS) database of all nonprofits that submit annual tax returns.[3] Looking through every one of the over 303,000 nonprofits contained in the 2004 database to determine which ones fulfill the criteria would be an impossible task. Fortunately, the NCCS provides some guidance by assigning each organization a code based on its activities or mission. This coding system is called the National Taxonomy of Exempt Entities (NTEE). The NTEE has 10 broad categories:[4]

1. Arts, Culture, and Humanities
2. Education
3. Environment and Animals
4. Health
5. Human Services
6. International, Foreign Affairs
7. Public, Societal Benefit
8. **Religion Related**
9. Mutual/Membership Benefit
10. Unknown, Unclassified.

Under each of these broad categories are a variety of subcategories. Of interest to my data collection were those subcategories listed under the "Religion Related" category:[5]

1 Alliances & Advocacy
2 Management & Technical Assistance
3 Professional Societies & Associations
5 Research Institutes & Public Policy Analysis
11 Single Organization Support
12 Fund-Raising & Fund
   Distribution
19 Support—Not Else Classified
20 Christian

21 Protestant
22 Roman Catholic
30 Jewish
40 Islamic
50 Buddhist
70 Hindu
80 Religious Media & Communications
81 Religious Film & Video
82 Religious Television
83 Religious Printing & Publishing
84 Religious Radio
90 Interfaith Coalitions
99 Religion-Related—Not Else Classified.

The bold categories were those that were examined in detail to see whether organizations within them fulfilled the criteria.[6] Using the NCCS' database, queries were run to limit the returned organizations to those with total revenue above $200,000.[7] Once the names of the organizations were found, the actual digital (i.e., scanned) 990 tax return for the organization was then located using either www.guidestar.org or www.foundationcenter.org. Using the self-description located on the 990 form, it was determined whether the organization fulfilled the other criteria concerning national/international scope, Christian identity, and were not official denominational organizations.[8] Any organizations that fulfilled these criteria were then added to a list of included organizations.

Because it is possible that some Christian nonprofits would not have been identified using just the methods described above, particularly because some Christian nonprofits may be classified with a different code (e.g., Education), four other sources were also consulted. The first was the membership list of the Evangelical Council for Financial Accountability. The ECFA has just over 2,000 members and many are large national organizations. Also, the over 500 organizations listed on the Christian "watchdog" Web site www.ministrywatch.org were also examined for eligibility. Keyword searches (e.g., "Christian," "ministry," "bible," "god," "faith") were also conducted on www.charitynavigator.org and the Associations Unlimited database to identify any other potential organizations for inclusion. While a handful of organizations were solely identified by one of these four sources, the large majority of organizations identified were simply confirmations of organizations already identified through the NCCS' database.

ENTERING FINANCIAL DATA

After creating the list of included nonprofits, the first step of data collection was to enter the financial information of each organization from its 990 tax return for the year ending in 2004.[9] All of the revenue, expense, and asset lines on page 1 (Revenue, Expenses, and Assets) and page 2 (Functional Expenses) of the 990 form were entered into a database. For those organizations required to fill it out (specifically, those not claiming church status), information on revenue from the previous four years and lobbying activity from Schedule A of the 990 form were also entered.

After this information was entered, internal accuracy checks were conducted by using the totals entered from the forms against computed totals created from entered parts. For example, Total Revenue was entered directly from the 990 form, but another "Total Revenue" was computed using parts entered from the 990 form that goes into the Total Revenue number. Any discrepancies were then checked against the forms and corrections made. In some cases, the issue was due to an error in the original form. Because it was sometimes impossible to know what exactly was incorrect in the forms (i.e., was the total incorrect or were one of the subparts incorrect? If the latter, which subpart?), these cases were left as they were on the original forms.[10]

CODING STATEMENTS OF PURPOSE

The financial data collected from the 990 forms provided critical information on the identified organizations. However, some key concepts of interest could not be measured by financial numbers alone, such as the organization's activities and how each organization expresses its religious identity. For both these measures, I looked to the "Statement of Program Service Accomplishments" provided in Part III on page 2 of the 990 forms. Each form was coded as having 1 of 27 primary activities. These 27 activity codes were contained within the nine larger sectors featured in the preceding chapters. These primary activity codes were created inductively based on informal examinations of many organizations and their 990 forms.

Each form was coded independently by multiple coders. This provided for the assessment of the measures' reliability using Cohen's kappa scores, which assesses the percent agreement in coding between the two coders. Kappa adjusts for the expected agreement due to chance and is therefore a more stringent measure than just percent agreement. Reliability scores for each sector, the unweighted average, and the weighted average are all shown.[11]

TABLE A.1. Reliability of Sector Codes.

	Kappa	Average Percentage of Organizations in Category
1. "Charismatic Evangelism"	.75	21.1
2. "Relief & Development"	.77	11.9
3. "Education & Training"	.63	13.4
4. "Publishing & Resources"	.79	13.5
5. "Radio & Television"	.89	6.8
6. "Missions & Missionary"	.72	16.2
7. "Fellowship & Enrichment"	.53	6.4
8. "Advocacy & Activism"	.66	4.4
9. "Fund-Raising, Grant-Making, & Other"	.54	5.6
10. "Unspecific or missing"	.61	1.3
Unweighted average kappa	.69	
Weighted average kappa	.71	

After assessing the reliability of the activity codes, the two coders then began to discuss those organizations where there were disagreements between codes. Each was then assigned an agreed-upon final code. In addition to organizational sector, both coders also assessed the religious expression and identity for each organization by looking for certain religious keywords within the self-description of program service accomplishments. These words are listed with their respective kappa scores of reliability.

TABLE A.2. Reliability of Religion Keywords Codes.

	Kappa
Bible/biblical	.88
Christ/Jesus/Jesus Christ	.90
Christian/Christianity	.91
Church/churches/congregations	.86
Disciple/discipleship	.78
Evangelism/evangelize/evangelical	.87
Faith	.83
Fellowship	.64
God	.88
Gospel	.89
Great Commission/Commission	.75
Lord	.82
Message	.74
Ministry/ministries	.74
Mission/missions/missionary	.83
Religion/religious	.81
Scripture/scriptural	.78
Spirit/spiritual	.83
Witness	.51
Word	.85

Again, any discrepancies were investigated and corrected. The coding process also assessed whether the organization operated on an international level, whether it was affiliated with some religious tradition (e.g., Lutheran, Baptist), and whether it was named after someone listed as an officer on the 990 form. The same reliability scores for each of these were computed and are shown.

TABLE A.3. Reliability of International Activity, Faith Tradition, and Executive-Named Codes.

	Kappa
International activities	
No international activities mentioned	.80
Canada	.79
South/Central America (including Mexico and Caribbean)	.90
Africa	.85
Europe (including Russia)	.86
Middle East	.78
Asia	.80
Australia (including New Zealand)	.76
Unspecific, but international activities mentioned	.70
Affiliated with faith tradition	.66
Named after executive	.85

Notes

CHAPTER 1

Page 101, Wuthnow, Robert. 1988. *The Restructuring of American Religion: Society and Faith since World War II*. Princeton, NJ: Princeton University Press.

1. Horiuchi, Heather. July 9, 2005. "Specialized Ministries a Spiritual Oasis for Youths with Disabilities." *The Washington Post*. B09; CNN Sunday Morning. April 29, 2007; Stange, Mary Zeiss. March 19, 2007. "A Dance for Chastity." *USA Today*. 15A; Neela Banerjee. December 4, 2006. "At Bosses' Invitation, Chaplains Come into Workplace and onto Payroll." *The New York Times*. A14; McKinley, Jesse. March 9, 2007. "A Youth Ministry Some Call Antigay Tests Tolerance." *The New York Times*. A10; Henriques, Diana B. and Andrew W. Lehren. June 13, 2007. "U.S. Grant for a Medical Mission Winds Up as 2 Boats Gone Awry." *The New York Times*. A1 and A20.

2. Wuthnow. 1988. *Restructuring of American Religion*; Wuthnow, Robert. 1994. *Producing the Sacred: An Essay on Public Religion*. Urbana, IL: University of Illinois Press; Monsma, Stephen V. 1996. *When Sacred and Secular Mix: Religious Nonprofit Organizations and Public Money*. Lanham, MD: Rowman & Littlefield; Chaves, Mark. 2002. "Religious Organizations: Data Resources and Research Opportunities." *American Behavioral Scientist* 45: 1523–1549.

3. Mark Chaves summed up the situation when he said that research in this sector needs to be the "highest priority" for those interested in understanding the religious structure of the United States. 2002. "Religious Organizations."

4. Stark, Rodney and William Sims Bainbridge. 1985. *The Future of Religion: Secularization, Revival, and Cult Formation*. Berkeley, CA: University of California Press.

5. Roof, Wade Clark. 1985. "The Study of Social Change in Religion." Pages 75–89 in *The Sacred in a Secular Age: Toward a Revision in the Scientific Study*

of Religion. Edited by Phillip E. Hammond. Berkeley, CA: University of California Press. Page 77.

6. See Chapter 3, 2000. "Secularization, R.I.P." in *Acts of Faith: Explaining the Human Side of Religion.* Edited by Rodney Stark and Roger Finke. Berkeley, CA: University of California Press. See also Hadden, Jeffrey K. 1987. "Toward Desacralizing Secularization Theory." *Social Forces* 65: 587–611. Swatos Jr., William H., and Kevin J. Christiano. 1999. "Secularization Theory: The Course of a Concept." *Sociology of Religion* 60: 209–228.

7. Page 155, Weber, Max. 1918 [1946]. "Science as a Vocation." Pages 129–156 in *From Max Weber: Essays in Sociology.* Translated and edited by H. H. Gerth and C. Wright Mills. New York: Oxford University Press. Although it is worth noting that Weber saw this as a much larger phenomenon that was not limited to religion.

8. Berger, Peter. April 25, 1968. "A Bleak Outlook Is Seen for Religion." *The New York Times.* 3.

9. Wuthnow, Robert. 1976. "Recent Pattern of Secularization: A Problem of Generations?" *American Sociological Review* 41: 850–867; Bellah, Robert N. 1976. "New Religious Consciousness and the Crisis of Modernity." Chapter 16 in *The New Religious Consciousness.* Edited by Glock and Bellah; Cooper, John Charles. 1971. *Religion in the Age of Aquarius.* Philadelphia, PA: Westminster.

10. Warner, R. Stephen. 1993. "Work in Progress toward a New Paradigm for the Sociological Study of Religion in the United States." *The American Journal of Sociology* 98: 1044–1093.

11. Finke, Roger and Rodney Stark. 2005 [1992]. *The Churching of America 1776–2005: Winners and Losers in Our Religious Economy.* New Brunswick, NJ: Rutgers University Press.

12. For a thorough presentation of these ideas, see Stark and Finke. 2000. *Acts of Faith.*

13. Some are surprised that there is not a more precise number, but the Census Bureau does not collect religion information and there is no requirement for congregations to register with agencies like the IRS. As a result, we must rely on other estimations.

14. However, in what might seem to be a paradox at first, the minority of large churches hold the majority of individuals. This is because the collective members of all the many small congregations are still dwarfed by those of the relatively few large congregations. There is also a trend toward increased concentration of members in large churches. Chaves, Mark, Mary Ellen Konieczny, Kraig Beyerlein, and Emily Barman. 1999. "The National Congregations Study: Background, Methods, and Selected Results." *Journal for the Scientific Study of Religion* 38: 458–476. See also Chaves, Mark. 2006. "All Creatures Great and Small: Megachurches in Context." *Review of Religious Research* 47: 329–346.

15. Page 103, Stark and Finke. 2000. *Acts of Faith.*

16. Chaves, Mark. 1993. "Denominations as Dual Structures: An Organizational Analysis." *Sociology of Religion* 54: 147–169.

17. Page 40, Winter, Gibson. 1968. *Religious Identity: A Study of Religious Organization.* New York: Macmillan.

18. As Mark Chaves states, "individuals do not directly 'belong' to any Protestant denominations." 1993. "Denominations as Dual Structures." *Sociology of Religion* 54: 147–169.

19. Page 154, Ibid; Page 1, Greeley, Andrew M. 1972. *The Denominational Society: A Sociological Approach to Religion in America.* Glenview, IL: Scott Foresman.

20. Because he relied on the Encyclopedia of Associations as a primary data source, many of Wuthnow's examples of these special purpose groups were professional or social associations, such as the Fellowship of Christian Athletes, Fellowship of Christian Peace Officers, Christian Chiropractors Association, and so forth. While this is definitely one subsector, we will see that these "special purpose groups" extend far beyond this activity or purpose; Pages 100–101, Wuthnow. 1988. *Restructuring of American Religion.*

21. See, for example, Martin, William. 1999. "The Christian Right and American Foreign Policy." *Foreign Policy* 114: 66–88.

22. For instance, the charitable Choice and Faith-Based Initiative legislation providing the opportunity for religious organizations to receive public funding. See, for example, Foley, Michael W., John D. McCarthy, and Mark Chaves. 2001. "Social Capital, Religious Institutions and Poor Communities." Chapter 9 in *Social Capital and Poor Communities.* Edited by Susan Saegert, J. Phillip Thompson, and Mark R. Warren. New York: Russell Sage Foundation. Bartkowski, John P. and Helen A. Regis. 2002. "The Promise and Peril of Charitable Choice: Religion, Poverty Relief, and Welfare Reform in the Rural South." *Southern Rural Sociology* 18: 222–258.

This debate also included the role of congregations. See Chaves, Mark. 1999. "Religious Congregations and Welfare Reform: Who Will Take Advantage of 'Charitable Choice'?" *American Sociological Review* 64: 836–846.

23. Page 194, Lindsay, D. Michael. 2008. *Faith in the Halls of Power: How Evangelicals Joined the American Elite.* New York: Oxford University Press.

24. Krapohl, Robert H. and Charles H. Lippy. 1999. "Parachurch Movements: Sustaining Modern American Evangelicalism." Chapter 12 in *The Evangelicals: A Historical, Thematic and Biographical Guide.* Westport, CT: Greenwood Publishing Group; Page 63, Sheler, Jeffery L. 2006. *Believers: A Journey into Evangelical America.* New York: Penguin Group.

25. Willmer, Wesley K., J. David Schmidt, and Martyn Smith. 1998. *The Prospering Parachurch: Enlarging the Boundaries of God's Kingdom.* San Francisco, CA: Jossey-Bass Inc.

26. This could simply be a philosophical objection (i.e., you think it demeans religious faith), or it could be an empirical one (i.e., you do not believe this model accurately represents how congregations behave and/or how individuals come to their decisions about what they believe or who they affiliate with).

27. This does not mean that these traditional organizations are going to become obsolete, as does occasionally happen in other markets. There are reasons to believe that denominations and especially congregations offer religious goods and services that are not easily replaced. However, as we will see in later chapters, there have been and likely will be "growing pains" as this restructuring of the religious market proceeds.

28. Page 101, Wuthnow. 1988. *Restructuring of American Religion.*

29. Wuthnow referred to collecting data on these organizations as "nearly an impossibility" given their "diverse range of styles, administrative forms, locations, sizes, and levels of organization." Ibid.

30. Warner, R. Stephen. 1994. "The Place of the Congregation in the Contemporary American Religious Configuration." In *American Congregations*. Edited by James P. Wind and James W. Lewis. Chicago: The University of Chicago Press.

31. We could split hairs about the meaning or boundaries of "religious" organizations. Here, however, I include those that are explicitly religious in their mission (e.g., church planting, mass evangelism) and those that are not explicitly religious in mission but are so in identity. That is, those pursuing superficially secular activities but claiming a religious motivation for their organization. A fair argument could be made that secular actors are also part of the parachurch sector since many congregations will interact with such organizations and secular organizations represent a very important competitor in the religious market. See, for example, Hungerman, Daniel M. 2009. "Rethinking Religious Competition." Presentation at the annual meeting of the Association for the Study of Religion, Culture and Economics. Washington, DC. However, the common usage of "parachurch" is limited to religious organizations. Secular actors might be said to constitute their own "nonchurch" category.

32. Willmer, Schmidt, and Smith, for instance, reject broad definitions of the parachurch that include denominations and other "traditional" religious organizations. See page 24. 1998. *Prospering Parachurch*.

33. Those claiming some tradition even though they are not formally a denominational organization might be called extradenominational, while those not claiming any tradition might be called nondenominational.

34. Page 17, Willmer, Schmidt, and Smith. 1998. *Prospering Parachurch*.

35. A literal approach to specifying the parachurch might include all of these nondenominational organizations regardless of their profit orientation. This would include some producers of Christian music or books, as well as some Christian counseling or day care centers. See, for instance, Brown, Charles. 2005. "Managing Tension between Religious and Professional Commitments in the Christian Popular Culture Industry." Presentation at the Annual Meeting of the Society for the Scientific Study of Religion. Rochester, NY. See also Chaves. 2002. 1523–1549.

36. Weitzman, Murray S., Nadine T. Jalandoni, Linda M. Lampkin, and Thomas H. Pollak. 2002. *The New Nonprofit Almanac and Desk Reference*. New York: Jossey-Bass. These numbers do not include organizations with less than $5,000 in annual receipts, which are not required to register.

37. Outside of the 501(c)(3) category, there are several other types of 501(c) nonprofits. For instance, 501(c)(19) status represents veteran's organizations. Some of these other 501(c) categories differ from 501(c)(3)s in that contributions to them are not always deductible from individuals' income taxes, although the organization itself is exempt from taxes. The full description of the 501(c)(3)s' exempt purpose: "The exempt purposes set forth in section 501(c)(3) are charitable, religious, educational, scientific, literary, testing for public safety, fostering national or international amateur sports competition, and preventing cruelty to children or animals. The term *charitable* is used in its generally accepted legal sense and includes relief of the poor, the distressed, or the underprivileged; advancement of religion; advancement of education or science; erecting or maintaining public buildings, monuments, or works; lessening the burdens of government; lessening neighborhood tensions; eliminating prejudice and discrimination; defending human and civil rights secured by law; and combating community deterioration and juvenile delinquency." From "Exempt Purposes—

Internal Revenue Code 501(c)(3)." *Internal Revenue Service.* Retrieved May 4, 2009, from http://www.irs.gov/charities/charitable/article/0,,id=175418,00.html

38. Contrary to what its name might suggest, a nonprofit is not forbidden from making a profit in a traditional sense. That is, in any year, their donations or contributions can exceed their expenses. What matters more is what the organization does with that excess to make sure that the organization is not being run like a business where profits benefit owners or shareholders.

39. Foundation Center. "What's the difference between a private foundation and a public charity?" http://foundationcenter.org/getstarted/faqs/html/pfandpc.html

40. National Center for Charitable Statistics. "Registered 501(c)(3) Public Charities by Major Purpose or Activity (NTEE Code)." From September 2007 IRS Business Master File.

41. "Registered 501(c)(3) Public Charities by IRS Foundation Code." Internal Revenue Service, Exempt Organizations Business Master File (501(c)(3) Public Charities, 2007, September). The Urban Institute, National Center for Charitable Statistics. http://nccsdataweb.urban.org

42. Still, this is undoubtedly an underestimate, likely a gross one, since it only includes those organizations classified in the religious category, excluding religious organizations that are engaged in activities that lead them to be classified in a different category (e.g., education, health, public service). However, it does give us some general idea of the size of the population we are talking about.

43. Numbers in figure 1-3 may not add up due to rounding. This is comparable to other estimates. For instance, Berry and Arons estimate the percentage of noncongregational nonprofits to be 4%. See page 5 in Berry, Jeffrey M. and David F. Arons. 2003. *A Voice for Nonprofits.* Washington, DC: Brookings Institution Press.

44. Page 3, Berry and Arons. 2003. *Voice for Nonprofits.*

45. Salamon, Lester M. 1994. "The Rise of the Nonprofit Sector." *Foreign Affairs* 73: 109–122.

46. Interested readers can find more methodological details in the appendix. Clearly, any attempt to narrow zero in on one group means another will be excluded. In this case, it is non-Christian nonprofits and small local Christian nonprofits that are excluded. The exclusion of both is partly practical in that it allows for a more focused data collection and presentation. Any attempt to present and discuss the theology, history, and dynamics of non-Christian organizations will inevitably come off as superficial and incomplete. As Smith, Emerson, and Snell put, "American Christianity is plenty big enough to make sense of." Similarly, while possible, comparisons between small local organizations and those operating in multiple nations might not always be meaningful or useful. All of this may trade breadth for focus, but I believe the following chapters and these data benefit from this sacrifice. A book that gives a wide-ranging view of the religious nonprofit world would not be that useful if it could not provide enough detail and/or analysis on any aspect of it.

47. Ruling dates are not always the same as founding dates. Often, an organization is founded and receives official exempt status a year or two later. The exception is with very old organizations (e.g., pre-1900s) that were founded long before an official exempt status even existed. However, in the end, ruling dates still serve as a useful proxy for describing growth.

CHAPTER 2

Baptist minister John Leland quoted on page 100 of Hatch, Nathan O. 1989. *The Democratization of American Christianity*. New Haven, CT: Yale University Press.

1. One of the first books dedicated to the topic was Jerry White's 1983 book *The Church & Parachurch: An Uneasy Marriage*. Portland, OR: Multnomah Press.

2. Miller, Sharon L. 1999. "Financing Parachurch Organizations" in *Financing American Religion*. Edited by Mark Chaves and Sharon L. Miller. Walnut Creek, CA: AltaMira Press.

3. Warner, Stephen R. 1993. "Work in Progress toward a New Paradigm for the Sociological Study of Religion in the United States." *The American Journal of Sociology* 98: 1044–1093.

4. The other being the ever-present "gap in the literature."

5. Winter, Ralph. 1980. "Protestant Mission Societies and the 'Other Protestant Schism'." Pages 194–224 in *American Denominational Organization: A Sociological View*. Edited by Ross P. Scherer. Pasadena, CA: William Carey Library; Primer, Ben. 1979. *Protestants and American Business Methods*. Ann Arbor, MI: UMI Research Press; Chaves, Mark. 1998. "Denominations as Dual Structures: An Organizational Analysis." In *Sacred Companies: Organizational Aspects of Religion and Religious Aspects of Organizations*. Edited by N. J. Demerath III, Peter Dobkin Hall, Terry Schmidt, and Rhys H. Williams. Oxford: Oxford University Press.

6. Page 141, Hatch. 1989. *Democratization of American Christianity*; Nord, David Paul. 2004. *Faith in Reading: Religious Publishing and the Birth of Mass Media in America*. New York: Oxford University Press.

7. Young, Michael. 2006. *Bearing Witness against Sin: The Evangelical Birth of the American Social Movement*. Chicago: University of Chicago Press; Boylan, Anne M. 1988. *Sunday School: The Transformation of an American Institution, 1790–1880*. New Haven, CT: Yale University Press. They were originally called "Sunday" schools not because of their association with churches but because their target audience, the poor working classes, only had time for education on Sundays as it was their only day off from work.

8. Page 35, White. 1983. *Church & Parachurch*; Willmer, Wesley K., J. David Schmidt, and Martyn Smith. 1998. *The Prospering Parachurch: Enlarging the Boundaries of God's Kingdom*. San Francisco, CA: Jossey-Bass Inc.

9. Bullock, F. W. B. 1963. *Voluntary Religious Societies 1520–1799*. St. Leonards-on-Sea, England: Budd & Gillatt.

10. Thompson, H. P. 1954. *Thomas Bray*. London: Society for the Propagation of Christian Knowledge.

11. Excerpts from Thomas Bray's "*A General Plan of the Constitution of a Protestant Congregation or Society for Propagating Christian Knowledge*," from W. O. B. Allen and Edmund McClure. 1898. *Two Hundred Years: The History of the Society for Promoting Christian Knowledge, 1698–1898*. New York: E. & J.B. Young and Co.

12. A letter to the editor of the *Boston Mirror* on June 30 in 1810 noted that the "amiable and disinterested example" of the British and Foreign Bible Society had "called into being" Bible societies across New England.

13. *Columbian Centinel*. September 3, 1796. "Bible Society." Boston, MA.

14. *Connecticut Journal.* April 18, 1811. "The Connecticut Religious Tract Society." New Haven, CT.

15. *Centinel of Freedom.* 1796.

16. Young. 2006. *Bearing Witness against Sin.* The nondenominational structure of parachurch organizations proved particularly necessary for these movements as they allowed individuals to unite for a cause when their churches and denominations were crippled by division on these issues. It is not surprising that the same motivation provokes the creation of many contemporary parachurch organizations, although the issues may have changed to abortion, sexuality, and family values.

17. New York Missionary Society. November 8, 1797. "Report of the Directors of the Missionary Society." Meeting of the New-York Missionary Society. Emphasis added.

18. Primer. 1979. *Protestants and American Business Methods*; Chaves. 1998. "Denominations as Dual Structures"; Winter, Gibson. 1968. *Religious Identity: A Study of Religious Organization.* New York: The Macmillan Company.

19. Warner, Lloyd, Darab B. Unvalla, and John H. Trimm. 1967. *The Emergent American Society: Vol. 1, Large-Scale Organizations.* New Haven, CT: Yale University Press; Galambos, Louis. 1970. "The Emerging Organizational History in Modern American History." *The Business History Review* 44: 279–290; Finke, Roger and Rodney Stark. 2005 [1992]. *The Churching of America 1776–2005: Winners and Losers in Our Religious Economy.* New Brunswick, NJ: Rutgers University Press.

20. Page 43, Kidd, Thomas S. 2004. *The Protestant Interest: New England after Puritanism.* New Haven, CT: Yale University Press; Page 64, Finke and Stark. 2005 [1992]. *Churching of America 1776–2005*; Page 18, Primer. 1979. *Protestants and American Business Methods*; Page 208, Latourette, Kenneth Scott. 1941. *The Great Century in Europe and the United States of America A.D. 1800-A.D. 1914. Vol. IV in A History of the Expansion of Christianity.* New York: Harper & Brothers Publishers; Page 72, Young. 2006. *Bearing Witness against Sin*; Page 37, Boylan, Anne M. 1998. "Presbyterians and Sunday Schools in Philadelphia, 1800–1824." *Journal of Presbyterian History* 76: 37–44.

21. Pages 209–210, Latourette. 1941. *Great Century in Europe and the United States of America A.D. 1800-A.D. 1914*; Primer. 1979. *Protestants and American Business Methods*; Chaves. 1998. "Denominations as Dual Structures"; Page 213, Latourette. 1941. *Great Century in Europe and the United States of America A.D. 1800-A.D. 1914*; Page 25, Winter. 1968. *Religious Identity.*

22. Pages 125–126, Dwight, Henry Otis. 1916. *The Centennial History of the American Bible Society.* New York: The Macmillan Company.

23. Ibid Pages 456–457.

24. Page 35, Primer. 1979. *Protestants and American Business Methods.*

25. Page 59, Wolfe, Alan. 2003. *The Transformation of American Religion: How We Actually Live Our Faith.* New York: Free Press.

26. This is likely an underestimate since it does not count the individuals in various independent Baptist churches that are included in the individual claiming an "other" or "don't know" Baptist affiliation. The 2007 *U.S. Religious Landscape Survey* by the Pew Forum found similar growth in the "nondenominational" category, although it estimated the total to be about 9% of all Protestants. "Religious Affiliation: Diverse and Dynamic."

U.S. Religious Landscape Survey. The Pew Forum on Religion and Public Life. http://religions.pewforum.org/pdf/report-religious-landscape-study-full.pdf

27. Chaves, Mark, Mary Ellen Konieczny, Kraig Beyerlein, and Emily Barman. 1999. "The National Congregations Study: Background, Methods, and Selected Results." *Journal for the Scientific Study of Religion* 38: 458–476.

28. Thumma, Scott. 1999. "What Makes God Free Is Free Indeed: Nondenominational Church Identity and Its Networks of Support." Hartford Institute for Religion Research. http://hirr.hartsem.edu/bookshelf/thumma_article5.html

29. The lines represent 3-year moving averages.

30. See Chapter 5. Wuthnow, Robert. 1988. *The Restructuring of American Religion: Society and Faith Since World War II.* Princeton, NJ: Princeton University Press; Pages 244–249, Roof, Wade Clark and William McKinney. 1987. *American Mainline Religion: Its Changing Shape and Future.* New Brunswick, NJ: Rutgers University Press; Page 59, Wolfe. 2003. *Transformation of American Religion.*

31. Empty Tomb. 2004. "Table 1: Per Member Giving as a Percentage of U.S. Per Capita Disposable Personal Income, and U.S. Per Capita Disposable Personal Income, 1968–2004." http://www.emptytomb.org/table1_04.html; Ronsvalle, John and Sylvia Ronsvalle. October 23, 1996. "The End of Benevolence? Alarming Trends in Church Giving." *The Christian Century.* 113: 1010–1014.

32. Empty Tomb. 2004. "Table 1: Per Member Giving as a Percentage of U.S. Per Capita Disposable Personal Income."

33. Amerson, Philip, Edward J. Stephenson, and Jan Shipps. 1997. "Decline or Transformation? Another View of Mainline Finances." *The Christian Century* 114: 144–147.

34. Stark, Rodney and Roger Finke. 2000. *Acts of Faith: Explaining the Human Side of Religion.* Berkeley, CA: University of California Press.

35. Page 141, Ammerman, Nancy Tatom. 2005. *Pillars of Faith: American Congregations and Their Partners.* Berkeley, CA: University of California Press.

36. See, for example, Lunn, John, Robin Klay, and Andrea Douglass. 2001. "Relationships among Giving, Church Attendance, and Religious Belief: The Case of the Presbyterian Church (USA)." *Journal for the Scientific Study of Religion* 40: 765–775.

37. Page 85, Cowan, Douglas E. 2003. *The Remnant Spirit: Conservative Reform in Mainline Protestantism.* Westport, CT: Praeger Publishers; The Presbyterian Coalition. 1998. "Turning toward the Mission of God: A Strategy for the Transformation of the PC (USA)." Coalition Strategy Paper. www.presbycoalition.org/newsfile16877_1.doc. Accessed May 5, 2009.

38. Hutcheson Jr. and Richard G. 1981. *Mainline Churches and the Evangelicals: A Challenging Crisis.* Atlanta, GA: John Knox Press. Emphasis in original.

CHAPTER 3

Board, Stephen. June 1979. "The Great Evangelical Power Shift: How Has the Mushrooming of Parachurch Organizations Changed the Church?" *Eternity* 30(6): 17–21.

1. White, Jerry. 1983. *The Church & The Parachurch: An Uneasy Marriage.* Portland, OR: Multnomah Press; Fitch, David E. 2005. *The Great Giveaway: Reclaiming the Mission of*

the Church from Big Business, Parachurch Organizations, Psychotherapy, Consumer Capitalism, and Other Modern Maladies. Grand Rapids, MI: BakerBooks.

2. Fletcher, Darrell. 2008. "Parachurch—Does the End Justify the Means?" http://reformedbaptistfellowship.wordpress.com/2008/06/24/parachurch%E2%80%94does-the-end-justify-the-means/

3. Page 64, Wolfe, Alan. 2003. *The Transformation of American Religion: How We Actually Live Our Faith.* New York: Free Press.

4. White. 1983. *Church & The Parachurch*; Hammett, John S. 2000. "How Church and Parachurch Should Relate: Arguments for a Servant-Partnership Model." *Missiology: An International Review* 28: 199–207.

5. "The Emerging Para-Church." February 19, 2008. Blog entry at http://themelancholicpipe.blogspot.com/2008/02/emerging-para-church.html

6. Board. June 1979. "Great Evangelical Power Shift."

7. Shin, Sam. 2008. "The Church and the Parachurch." Blog entry at http://blogogetics.com/2008/09/the-church-and-the-parachurch/

8. Denominations can be equally protectionist toward each other when threatened by competition. Consider radio and television broadcasting. For a long time, the members of the National Council of Churches (NCC) protected their access to broadcasting by persuading radio and television stations that they were the only legitimate representative of Christianity. Therefore, they argued that they should be the natural recipients of the stations' free "public service broadcasting" airtime. Furthermore, the NCC lobbied the networks to not to sell any time for religious broadcasters. The NCC praised cooperation across denominations as long as those denominations belonged to the NCC. See chapter 6 in Finke, Roger and Rodney Stark. 2005 [1992]. *The Churching of America 1776–2005: Winners and Losers in Our Religious Economy.* New Brunswick, NJ: Rutgers University Press.

9. Page 1, Vara, Richard. August 19, 1995. "Filling the Gaps: Parachurches Changing the Landscape." *Houston Chronicle.* 2 STAR Edition.

10. Page 7, 69. Young, Michael. 2006. *Bearing Witness against Sin: The Evangelical Birth of the American Social Movement.* Chicago: University of Chicago Press; Boylan, Anne M. 1998. "Presbyterians and Sunday Schools in Philadelphia, 1800–1824." *Journal of Presbyterian History* 76: 37–44; Latourette, Kenneth Scott. 1941. *The Great Century in Europe and the United States of America A.D. 1800-A.D. 1914.* Vol. IV in *A History of the Expansion of Christianity.* New York: Harper & Brothers Publishers.

11. Riew, Yong K. "The Theology of Mission Structures and Its Relation to Korea's Indigenous Student Movements." Ph.D. diss., Fuller Theological Seminary, 1985. Quoted in Paris, Jonathan. 2007. "The Reason for and the Role of the Parachurch." Found at http://www.ivevents.com/doc/5/parachurch.pdf; Page 171, Willmer, Wesley K., J. David Schmidt, and Martyn Smith. 1998. *The Prospering Parachurch: Enlarging the Boundaries of God's Kingdom.* San Francisco: Jossey-Bass Inc.; Page 17, Paris. 2007. "Reason for and the Role of the Parachurch."

12. *Cooperating in World Evangelization: A Handbook on Church/Parachurch Relationships.* The Lausanne Committee for World Evangelism. Occasional Paper 24.

13. Personal conversation.

14. Vara. August 19, 1995. "Filling the Gaps." *Houston Chronicle.*

15. Pages 95–98, Clowney, Edmund P. 1995. *The Church: Contours of Christian Theology*. Downers Grove, IL: InterVarsity Press.

16. Quoted on page 59 of Wolfe. 2003. *Transformation of American Religion*.

17. Page 413, Wright, Charles Henry Hamilton, and Charles Neil. 1904. *A Protestant Dictionary: Containing Articles on the History, Doctrines, and Practices of the Christian Church*. London: Hodder and Stoughton.

18. The word "ecumenical" and its corresponding social movements has had many meanings and goals over time. I am referring to only one aspect of that movement that looked for institutional unification; Perkins, Bill. 2000. "Reimagining Ecumenism for the 21ˢᵗ Century." The Center for Progressive Christianity. http://www.tcpc.org/library/article.cfm?library_id=110; Wolfe refers to the consequence of this "ecumenism" as a "generic conservative Christianity." 2003. *Transformation of American Religion*.

19. Hutcheson, Richard G. 1981. *Mainline Churches and the Evangelicals: A Challenging Crisis?* Atlanta, GA: John Knox Press.

20. Page 157, Wuthnow, Robert. 1993. *Christianity in the Twenty-first Century: Reflections on the Challenges Ahead*. New York: Oxford University Press.

21. See, for example, McGuire, Meredith. 1996. *Religion: The Social Context*. 4th Edition. Belmont, CA: Wadsworth Publishing Co.

22. You might call this a "face-value" definition or one that accepts self-defined religious behavior as being religious.

23. Zald, Mayer N. 1982. "Theological Crucibles: Social Movements in and of Religion." *Review of Religious Research* 23(4): 317–336.

24. Newbigen argued that the three roles of the church were as community, servant, and messenger. These overlap somewhat with the worship and outreach functions described here. The "servant" role closely corresponds to the charity outreach goal, while the "messenger" function corresponds to the conversion and communication goals. The "community" role overlaps the worship and community outreach goal described here. 1983. *The Other Side of 1984: Questions for Churches*. Geneva: World Council of Churches.

25. This does not have to be a formal organization, although many would argue that in the last century, it has indeed meant formal, often bureaucratic, organizations. Some would argue that religion is social (i.e., organized) by definition, and any entirely individualistic activity is something other than religion (e.g., magic).

26. Winter, Ralph D. 1973. "The Two Structures of God's Redemptive Mission." Pages 220–230 in *Perspectives on the World Christian Movement: A Reader*. Edited by Ralph D. Winter and Steven C. Hawthorne. 3rd Edition. Pasadena, CA: William Carey Library Publishers; Pages 36–37, White. 1983. *Church & The Parachurch*; See Acts 13–15.

27. Although clearly there is great variation within the congregational form, ranging from home-churches to megachurches.

28. See page 157 in Stark, Rodney and Roger Finke. 2000. *Acts of Faith: Explaining the Human Side of Religion*. Berkeley, CA: University of California Press.

29. Indeed, megachurches are able to conduct outreach on a much larger scale, allowing them to resist relying on partnerships and other methods of outsourcing outreach.

30. Clearly, the other factor is the level of energy or commitment of members. Many relatively small religious groups (e.g., Jehovah's Witnesses) do much more outreach than larger ones because their members have very high levels of commitment.

31. These ideas come out of the organizational ecology literature. See Hannan, Michael T., Glenn R. Carroll, and Laszlo Polos. 2003. "The Organizational Niche." *Sociological Theory* 21: 309–340. See also McPherson, Miller. 1983. "An Ecology of Affiliation." *American Sociological Review* 48: 519–532; Hsu, Greta, Michael T. Hannan, and Ozgecan Kocak. 2009. "Multiple Category Memberships in Markets: An Integrative Theory and Two Empirical Tests." *American Sociological Review* 74: 150–169.

32. Miller, Kent D. 2002. "Competitive Strategies of Religious Organizations." *Strategic Management Journal* 23: 435–456. Finke and Stark. 2005. *Churching of America 1776 2005.*

33. Hannan, Michael T. and John Freeman. 1977. "The Population Ecology of Organizations." *The American Journal of Sociology* 82: 929–964.

34. McPherson, Miller, Lynn Smith-Lovin, and James M. Cook. 2001. "Birds of a Feather: Homophily in Social Networks." *Annual Review of Sociology* 27: 415–444. When it comes to homophily in identity groups, race and ethnicity is the strongest basis of division. Age and religion are often the second and third strongest factors, followed by education, income, and gender. It is worth noting that churches are no different when it comes to social homophily. Obviously, they are homogenous theologically, but they are often very homogenous on demographic variables, especially race and ethnicity. See, for instance, Dougherty, Kevin D. 2003. "How Monochromatic Is Church Membership? Racial-Ethnic Diversity in Religious Community." *Sociology of Religion* 64: 65–85.

35. Sometimes, groups that appear to be activity based, say a hunter's club or an environmental social group, tend to have people who are very similar to each other. The activity is often secondary to the identity or at least is indistinguishable from it.

36. Nelson, Reed E. 1993. "Authority, Organization and Societal Context in Multinational Churches." *Administrative Science Quarterly* 38: 653–682. From the communities of "desert ascetics" in the third century to mendicant orders, the Catholic Church provides many examples of movements that could be considered "parachurch." However, many of these were usually within the official boundaries of the institutional church. See Finke, Roger and Patricia Wittberg. 2000. "Organizational Revival from within: Explaining Revivalism and Reform in the Roman Catholic Church." *Journal for the Scientific Study of Religion* 39: 154–170; Ralph Winter refers to this as the "enviable Roman Catholic synthesis" of church and parachurch structures.

37. Work, Telford. 1999. "Reordering Salvation: Church as the Proper Context for an Evangelical *Ordo Salutis*." Pages 182–195 in *Ecumenical Theology in Worship, Doctrine, and Life: Essays Presented to Geoffrey Wainwright on His Sixtieth Birthday*. Edited by David S. Cunningham, Ralph Del Colle, and Lucas Lamadrid. New York: Oxford University Press; Winter, Ralph D. 1980. "Protestant Mission Societies and the 'Other Protestant Schism.'" Pages 194–224 in *American Denominational Organization: A Sociological View*. Edited by Ross P. Scherer. Pasadena, CA: William Carey Library.

38. Page 34, quoted in Hall, Timothy D. 1994. *Contested Boundaries: Itinerancy and the Reshaping of the Colonial American Religious World*. Durham, NC: Duke University Press.

39. McPherson. 1983. "Ecology of Affiliation"; Hannan and Freeman. 1977. "Population Ecology of Organizations"; Hannan, Carroll, and Polos. 2003. "Organizational Niche."

40. Although not shown for simplicity's sake, the niches of the different parachurch organizations and the religious groups could also overlap.

41. Note that having a local component does not make an organization local in scope. It may have a national office and be operating nationally, but it also has many local chapters.

42. McKee, Jonathan. "When 'Us vs. Them' Trumps Kingdom Mentality: The Church/Para-church Fight Brought to the Table." Published online by *The Source for Youth Ministry* (www.thesource4ym.com).

43. See page 12 in Williams, Bud. 2002. "Theological Perspectives on the Temporary Community/Camping and the Church." Christian Camping International. http://www.cciworldwide.org/resources.htm

44. Chaves, Mark. 1998. *National Congregations Study. Data File and Codebook.* Tucson, AZ: University of Arizona, Department of Sociology. There is also a response for "publishing houses." However, since this could include denominational publishers, so I do not include it here. Data are weighted to represent congregations regardless of their size ("weight2" in the data file). These are admittedly somewhat dated data. There was a 2006 update to this survey, but it unfortunately did not include all of the questions being examined here.

45. Pages 82–90, 203–204, Ammerman, Nancy Tatom. 2005. *Pillars of Faith: American Congregations and Their Partners.* Berkeley, CA: University of California Press.

46. Of course, such an argument will be more convincing if an alternative is provided. Simply telling someone that they cannot do something they want without providing some other way to satisfy their interests could be ineffective.

47. Page 86, Ammerman. 2005. *Pillars of Faith.*

48. This is referred to as a "federated structure." John D. McCarthy and Mayer N. Zald. 1977. "Resource Mobilization and Social Movements: A Partial Theory." *American Journal of Sociology* 82: 1212–1241.

49. Board. June 1979. "Great Evangelical Power Shift."

50. Ritzer, George. 2004. *The McDonaldization of Society.* Thousand Oaks, CA: Sage Publications.

51. Economists refer to this as a form of "contract failure." For more information, see Henry B. Hansmann. 1980. "The Role of Nonprofit Enterprise." *The Yale Law Journal* 89: 835–901.

52. Latourette. 1941. *Great Century in Europe and the United States of America.* Vol. IV in *History of the Expansion of Christianity*; Page 98, White. 1983. *Church & The Parachurch.*

53. Boylan, Anne M. 1979. "Sunday Schools and Changing Evangelical Views of Children in the 1820s." *Church History* 48: 320–333.

54. Page 107, Clowney. *Church*; Christian and Missionary Alliance. "A Brief History." http://www.cmalliance.org/whoweare/whoweare-past.jsp

CHAPTER 4

Stafford, Tim. October 6, 1997. "When Christians Fight Christians." *Christianity Today* 41: 28–34.

1. There are several other taxonomies of parachurch/nonprofit activities. Willmer, Schmidt, and Smith presented a 16-point system: Arts/Culture, Associations, Audiovisual/ Media, Camps/Conferences, Constituency-Based Ministries, Consulting, Counseling/ Guidance, Education, Environmental/Agricultural, Evangelism, Health Care, Legal Assistance/ Political Action, Missions, Printed Media, Relief and Development, and Social Services. Most of these have direct equivalents to the nine that will be presented here (e.g., both have a Relief & Development category). The main difference is due to some collapsing of categories to create a more manageable system for analysis. For instance, the various media categories are collapsed into one Publishing & Resources category in the sectors presented here. Willmer, Wesley K., J. David Schmidt, and Martyn Smith. 1998. *The Prospering Parachurch: Enlarging the Boundaries of God's Kingdom.* San Francisco, CA: Jossey-Bass Inc.

2. It is important to remember that, by design, we are just looking at the larger Christian nonprofits that exist. The number of nonprofits would obviously be higher and the financial numbers would be different if we could include all the smaller organizations as well and those that are not operating on a national or an international level. It is worth noting how religiously focused many of the sectors' activities are.

3. Monsma, Stephen V. 1996. *When Sacred and Secular Mix: Religious Nonprofit Organizations and Public Money.* Lanham, MD: Rowman & Littlefield. Ebaugh, Helen Rose, Janet S. Chafetz, and Paula F. Pipes. "Collaborations with Faith-Based Social Service Coalitions." *Nonprofit Management and Leadership* 18: 175–191.

4. Finke, Roger and Rodney Stark. 2005 [1992]. *The Churching of America 1776–2005: Winners and Losers in Our Religious Economy.* New Brunswick, NJ: Rutgers University Press.

5. The same can be said of congregations led by a charismatic individual.

6. Page 92 in Aldrich, Howard. 2005. *Organizations Evolving.* Thousand Oaks, CA: Sage Publications.

7. Abbotsford Christian Academy. December 29, 2005. Pastoral Reference Letter. http://www.strengthteam.com/abbotsford_letter.htm on June 15, 2009. Pine Grove United Methodist Church. February 26, 2007. Pastoral Reference Letter. http://www.strengthteam. com/pine-grove_letter.htm on June 15, 2009.

8. Sandler, Lauren. 2007. *Righteous: Dispatches from the Evangelical Youth Movement.* New York: Penguin Books.

9. February 2007. *National Drug Control Strategy.* The White House.

10. Barrett, William P. November 19, 2008. "America's 200 Largest Charities." *Forbes. com* http://www.forbes.com/2008/11/19/americas-largest-charities-pf-charities08-cx_wb_ 1119charity_land.html

11. http://www.ministrywatch.com/profile/feed-the-children.aspx#analyst

12. Ibid.

13. Padgett, Tania. December 11, 2006. "The Bible Gets Up to Speed." *Newsday.* B06; Diamant, Jeff. December 27, 2006. "Sacred but also Familiar; There's a Trend among Its

Publishers to Make the Bible's Language More Accessible to Readers." *Los Angeles Times.* E16. At least one watchdog group has criticized the American Bible Society for sitting on such a large endowment: "donors may be disappointed by the ministry's strategy to not utilize these substantial resources as quickly as possible to achieve its stated mission of putting the Bible in the hands of everyone on earth." "Donor Alert: American Bible Society." Ministry Watch. June 2008. June 18, 2009, at http://www.ministrywatch.com/pdf/MWDA_100608_ABS.pdf

14. Barr, Bob. January 11, 2006. "It's that Time, Robertson; Exit the Stage." *The Atlanta Journal-Constitution.* A13.

15. MinistryWatch.com notes that "some observers fear for the future of CBN once Pat Robertson passes of the scene." "Christian Broadcasting Network, Analyst Comments." Ministrywatch.com. June 18, 2009, at http://www.ministrywatch.com/profile/christian-broadcasting-network.aspx#analyst

16. Sheler, Jeffrey L. 2006. *Believers: A Journey into Evangelical America.* New York: Viking.

17. Horner, Sue S. 2002. "Trying to Be God in the World: The Story of the Evangelical Women's Caucus and the Crisis over Homosexuality" in *Gender, Ethnicity & Religion: Views from the Other Side.* Edited by Rosemary Radford Ruether. Minneapolis, MN: Fortress Press.

18. These include serving as the legal representation for the Dover, Pennsylvania school district during its "intelligent design" case and as the counsel for a U.S. Marine facing criminal charges for the deaths of Iraqi civilians in Haditha.

19. Crowley, James. November 12, 2004. "James Dobson: The Religious Right's New Kingmaker." *Slate Magazine.* www.slate.com/id/2109621

20. Fineman, Howard. May 11, 2005. "Daddy Dobson." *Newsweek.* www.msnbc.msn.com/id/7735880/site/newsweek/page/0/; Kirkpatrick, David D. January 1, 2005. "Evangelical Leader Threatens to Use His Political Muscle against Some Democrats." *The New York Times.* A10.

21. Richardson, Valerie. February 28, 2009. "Dobson Resigns as Focus Chairman." *The Washington Times.* http://www.washingtontimes.com/news/2009/feb/28/dobson-resigns-as-focus-chairman/

22. As mentioned earlier, this often but not always corresponds to when the organization was created.

23. Although those people who would normally attend a local church but substitute it entirely for a radio/television church are likely few and far between. Most either supplement their regular worship with such resources or would not have gone to a local church regardless of whether the televised church existed.

CHAPTER 5

John Leland quoted on page 100 of Hatch, Nathan O. 1989. *The Democratization of American Christianity.* New Haven, CT: Yale University Press.

1. Lindner, Eileen W. 2007. *Yearbook of American and Canadian Churches.* National Council of Churches. Abingdon Press.

2. Smith, Christian, Michael O. Emerson, and Patricia Snell. 2008. *Passing the Plate: Why American Christians Don't Give Away More Money*. New York: Oxford University Press.

3. Hechter, Michael. 1987. *Principles of Group Solidarity*. Berkeley, CA: University of California Press; Finke, Roger, Matt Bahr, and Christopher P. Scheitle. 2006. "Toward Explaining Congregational Giving." *Social Science Research* 35: 620–641.

4. See, for example, pages 62–64 in Wolfe, Alan. 2003. *The Transformation of American Religion: How We Actually Live Our Faith*. New York: Free Press. Also, Board, Stephen. June 1979. "The Great Evangelical Power Shift: How Has the Mushrooming of Parachurch Organizations Changed the Church?" *Eternity* 30(6): 17–21.

5. Pages 99–120, Primer, Ben. 1979. *Protestants and American Business Methods*. Ann Arbor, MI: UMI Research Press.

6. At one time, the "commercial manner" test was thought to be a useful way to determine whether a nonprofit was really nonprofit. However, with the increasing commercial activity among nonprofits, this test is not very useful. Some have argued that commercial nonprofits should fill in some need that for-profit organizations are not serving. Legal scholars and economists have noted that the factors making nonprofit organizations more attractive than for-profit organizations when it comes to the provisions of public goods and services are often absent in the case of commercial nonprofits. In the former cases, the donors are not directly benefiting from the services and have little ability to police the organization, so for-profit organizations have the motivation and opportunity to "pocket" the money. Due to the absence of this profit motivation, nonprofits are the better economic option for donors. For more information, see Hansmann, Henry B. 1980. "The Role of Nonprofit Enterprise." *The Yale Law Journal* 89: 835–901; Brown, Trevor A. 1990. "Religious Nonprofits and the Commercial Manner Test." *The Yale Law Journal* 99: 1631–1650.

7. Froelich, Karen. 1999. "Diversification of Revenue Strategies: Evolving Resource Dependence in Nonprofit Organizations." *Nonprofit and Voluntary Quarterly* 28: 246–268; Weisbrod, Burton A. 1998. "Guest Editor's Introduction: The Nonprofit Mission and Its Financing." *Journal of Policy Analysis and Management* 17: 165–174; Herman, Robert D. and Denise Rendina. 2001. "Donor Reactions to Commercial Activities of Nonprofit Organizations: An American Case Study." *Voluntas: International Journal of Voluntary and Nonprofit Organizations* 12: 157–169.

8. Edles, Peter L. 2006. *Fundraising: Hands-On Tactics for Nonprofit Groups*. New York: McGraw-Hill.

9. McCarthy, John D. and Mayer N. Zald. 1977. "Resource Mobilization and Social Movements: A Partial Theory." *American Journal of Sociology* 82: 1212–1241.

10. Emerson, Richard M. 1962. "Power-Dependence Relations." *American Sociological Review* 27: 31–41.

11. From the Part IV-A Support Schedule of the 990 form. Nonprofits claiming a "church" status do not fill out the schedule (see chapter 7) and are not included. Only includes those founded in or before 1998. Other research has supported the idea that a diversified revenue stream can help reduce volatility in nonprofits' revenue. See Carroll, Deborah A. and Keely Jones Stater. 2008. "Revenue Diversification in Nonprofit Organizations: Does

It Lead to Financial Stability?" *Journal of Public Administration Research and Theory*; Froelich. 1999. "Diversification of Revenue Strategies."

12. This is all relative, of course. While more stable than donations, commercial revenue is often less stable than government funding, which nonprofit managers view as "money in the bank." See Froelich. 1999. "Diversification of Revenue Strategies."

13. Page 434, Carson, Emmett D. 2002. "Public Expectations and Nonprofit Sector Realities: A Growing Divide with Disastrous Consequences." *Nonprofit and Voluntary Sector Quarterly* 31: 429–436; Frumkin, Peter and Mark T. Kim. 2001. "Strategic Positioning and the Financing of Nonprofit Organizations: Is Efficiency Rewarded in the Contributions Marketplace?" *Public Administration Review* 61: 266–275. On the other hand, other research has demonstrated a negative effect of higher overhead costs on donations. See Bowman, Woods. 2006. "Should Donors Care about Overhead Costs? Do They Care?" *Nonprofit and Voluntary Sector Quarterly* 35: 288–310.

14. Pollak, Thomas H., Patrick Rooney, and Mark A. Hager. 2001. "Understanding Management and General Expenses in Nonprofits." Paper presented at the 2001 Annual Meeting of the Association for Research on Nonprofit Organizations and Voluntary Action. New Orleans, LA.

15. Granted, moving food or other supplies across the world is more labor intensive than simply transferring money.

16. Numbers from Hodgkinson, Virginia. 1999. "Financing Religious Congregations: A National View." Chapter 9 in *Financing American Religion*. Edited by Mark Chaves and Sharon L. Miller. Walnut Creek, CA: AltaMira Press.

17. Because the tax returns do not allow for easily sorting out the source of contributions, this is difficult to assess directly.

18. Pollak, Rooney, and Hager. 2001. "Understanding Management and General Expenses in Nonprofits."

19. Hodgkinson. 1999. "Financing Religious Congregations."

20. See pages 36–38 in Chaves, Mark. 2004. *Congregations in America*. Cambridge, MA: Harvard University Press.

21. Ostroff, Cheri and Neal Schmitt. 1993. "Configurations of Organizational Effectiveness and Efficiency." *Academy of Management Journal* 36: 1345–1361.

22. Efficiency in this case could be cost per widget.

23. Sowa, Jessica E., Sally Coleman Selden, and Jodi R. Sandfort. 2004. "No Longer Unmeasurable? A Multidimensional Integrated Model of Nonprofit Organizational Effectiveness." *Nonprofit and Voluntary Sector Quarterly* 33: 711–728; Herman, Robert D. and David O. Renz. 1999. "Theses on Nonprofit Organizational Effectiveness."

24. Independent Sector. October 8, 2002. "Report Demonstrates Efforts of Nonprofits to Measure Effectiveness." http://www.independentsector.org/media/measuresPR.html; Page 57, Cnaan, Ram A. 2002. *The Invisible Caring Hand: American Congregations and the Provision of Welfare*. New York: New York University Press.

25. www.charitynavigator.org

26. For example, in their study of secondary schools, Ostroff and Schmitt found that being effective does not always correspond to being efficient. 1993. "Configurations of Organizational Effectiveness and Efficiency."

CHAPTER 6

Hagee quotes from Nazareno, Analisa. June 21, 2003. "The Exceeding Great Reward." *San Antonio Express-News*. 10H.

1. Gronbjerg, Kirsten A. 2008. "Are Nonprofits Trustworthy?" *Indiana Nonprofits: Scope and Community Dimensions*. A joint project of the Center on Philanthropy at Indiana University and Indiana University School of Public and Environmental Affairs. http://www.indiana.edu/~nonprof/results/pasurvey.html

2. McNamara, Carter. 1998. "Founder's Syndrome: How Founders and Their Organizations Recover." *Nonprofit World* 16: 38–41; Block, Stephen R. and Steven Rosenberg. 2002. "Toward an Understanding of Founder's Syndrome: An Assessment of Power and Privilege among Founders of Nonprofit Organizations." *Nonprofit Management and Leadership* 12: 353–368; Hodge, Robert. "The Impact of Founder's Syndrome." Evangelical Council for Financial Accountability. http://www.ecfa.org/Documents/FoundersSyndrome_Hodge.pdf

3. Wood, Miriam W. 1992. "Is Governing Board Behavior Cyclical?" *Nonprofit Management and Leadership* 3: 139–163. This transition could be delayed if executive leadership is passed to a family member.

4. Compensating board members is quite rare and often seen as inappropriate. See BoardSource. 2007. *The Nonprofit Board Answer Book: A Practical Guide for Board Members and Chief Executives*. San Francisco, CA: John Wiley and Sons.

5. From *The Nonprofit Board Answer Book*.

6. The revisions being considered to the 990 tax form would include changes meant to make these distinctions clearer.

7. If we were to take another strategy and only count individuals listed only with the title of "director," "board member," or "trustee," then only 36% have a board of five members and 56% have a board of three members.

8. Weber, Max. 1946. *From Max Weber: Essays in Sociology*. Edited by H. H. Gerth and C. Wright Mills. New York: Oxford University Press; Nelson, Reed E. 1993. "Authority, Organization and Societal Context in Multinational Churches." *Administrative Science Quarterly* 38: 653–682.

9. Carver, John. 1992. "The Founding Parent Syndrome: Governing in the CEO's Shadow." *Nonprofit World* 10: 14–16.

10. This effect, along with the earlier discussed effect of revenue source, holds at a significant level in logistic regression analyses controlling for sector, ECFA membership, and the log of total revenue.

11. Nazareno. June 21, 2003. "The Exceeding Great Reward"; Internal Revenue Service. 2006. "Table 13. Returns of Tax-Exempt Organizations, Employee Plans, and Governance Entities Examined, by Type of Return, Fiscal Year 2006." http://www.irs.gov/pub/irs-soi/table_13_2006_dp.xls; Crenshaw, Albert B. April 5, 2005. "Tax Abuse Rampant in Nonprofits, IRS Says." *The Washington Post* E01; July 8, 2007. "The New 990: IRS Proposes a Major Redesign." *New York Nonprofit Press*. http://www.nynp.biz/papereditions/070807/thenew990.shtml; Draft Redesigned Form 990, Schedules, and Instructions. Accessed September 10, 2007. http://www.irs.gov/charities/article/0,,id=171213,00.html

12. www.give.org

13. There are some other online resources for Christian donors, but these are not usually meant to provide ratings of organizations but instead give general advice for potential donors. For instance, see www.goodsteward.com. There is also the Trinity Foundation (www.trinityfi.org) that primarily polices televangelists.

14. "Ministry Description: World Vision." Accessed September 10, 2007. http://www.ministrywatch.org/mw2.1/F_SumRpt.asp?EIN=951922279

15. The Senator was Mark Hatfield from Oregon, who was an influential evangelical himself. For instance, the Council for Christian Colleges and University has an annual leadership award named in honor of Hatfield. "Rick & Kay Warren to Receive Award at 2006 CCCU International Forum"; December 16, 1977. "30 Evangelical Groups Urge Voluntary Airing of Finances." *The Washington Post*; March 16, 1979. "Evangelical Council Promotes Voluntary Financial Disclosure." *The Washington Post*; Helgeson, Baird and Michelle Bearden. July 1, 2007. "In God's Hands or the Pastors'?" *The Tampa Tribune*. http://www.cccu.org/news/newsID.387,parentNav. Archives/news_past_detail.asp;"ECFAHistory."http://www.ecfa.org/Content.aspx?PageName= GeneralBackground

16. "Benefits of ECFA Membership." http://www.ecfa.org/Content.aspx?PageName= JoinBenefits

17. This includes various subsidiaries of parent organizations.

18. Logistic regression controlling for sector, log of total revenue, whether the organization is named after an officer, and whether the nonprofit is predominantly commercial.

19. Dan Busby, vice president of ECFA. Personal communication, September 12, 2007.

20. Logistic regression analyses show this effect to be significant even after controlling for sector, total revenue, and whether the organization is named after an officer. The latter also shows a significant negative effect on the odds of being an ECFA member.

21. The ECFA Web site has at least four different articles on the topic in its "Knowledge Center," as does BoardSource's Web site; Charity Navigator. 2008. "2008 CEO Compensation Study." *Charity Navigator*. http://www.charitynavigator.org/index.cfm?bay=studies.ceo

22. Ostling, Richard. April 6, 1987. "TV's Unholy Row." *Time*; Blumenthal, Ralph. October 11, 2007. "Professors Sue Oral Roberts President." *The New York Times*; Vanden Brook, Tom. September 30, 1996. "Educator Finds Lucrative Niche: Concordia President and Family Operate an International University." *Milwaukee Journal Sentinel*. Sherman, Amy. October 11, 2004. "Doubts Taint Aid to Haiti." *The Miami Herald*; Laden, Rich. October 19, 1997. "Nonprofits Pay Big for Talent: Some CEOs Make Six-Figure Salaries, but It's Not the Norm." *The Gazette*. Colorado Springs, CO; Cedar Rapids Gazette. August 2, 1997. "Promise Keepers Founder Paid $61,000 in 1995–1996." Cedar Rapids, Iowa City.

23. ECFA Standards and Best Practices; ECFA Seven Standards of Responsible Stewardship.

24. This phenomenon is called mimetic isomorphism. See DiMaggio, Paul J. and Walter W. Powell. 1983. "The Iron Cage Revisited: Institutional Isomorphism and Collective Rationality in Organizational Fields." *American Sociological Review* 48: 147–160.

CHAPTER 7

1. Technically, the 1894 Revenue Act also included an exemption for "charitable, religious, or educational purposes," but the Revenue Act was declared unconstitutional for reasons that did not involve the exemption.

2. Hoff, Reka Potgieter. 1991–1992. "The Financial Accountability of Churches for Federal Income Tax Purposes: Establishment or Free Exercise?" *Virginia Tax Review* 11: 71–136.

3. Ibid.

4. All of this is related to a much larger debate in the history of nonprofits concerning what should or should not deserve a tax exemption. Generally, the guidelines have become broader and more inclusive by which "charitable" includes a wide range of activities not usually associated with the colloquial use of the word "charity." See *Historical Development and Present Law of the Federal Tax Exemption for Charities and Other Tax-Exempt Organizations.* Prepared by the staff of the Joint Committee on Taxation for a public hearing before the House Committee on Ways and Means. April 20, 2005.

5. Page 82, Hoff. 1991–1992. "The Financial Accountability of Churches for Federal Income Tax Purposes?" In 1969, churches would also become subject to unrelated business income taxes.

6. We could get into much more detail about the various religious terms used in the tax code. Charles M. Whelan identified at least 15 different terms, including "religious purposes," "a religious organization describe in section 501(c)(3)," "church," "church agency," "religious order," and "a church or a convention of association of churches." However, in practice, many of these other terms fall within either the "church" or the "religious organization" categories. See 1977. "'Church' in the Internal Revenue Code: The Definitional Problems." *Fordham Law Review* 45: 885–928.

7. Whelan, Charles M. 1979. "Governmental Attempts to Define Church and Religion." *The ANNALS of the American Academy of Political and Social Science* 446: 32–51. Page 45. See also Whelan. 1977. "'Church' in the Internal Revenue Code"; Hoff. 1991–1992. "The Financial Accountability of Churches for Federal Income Tax Purposes?"

8. Shaller, Wendy Gerzog. 1989–1990. "Churches and Their Enviable Tax Status." *University of Pittsburgh Law Review* 51: 345–364; Hoff. 1991–1992. "The Financial Accountability of Churches for Federal Income Tax Purposes?"; Incidentally, this is why social scientists have such a difficult time studying churches. Since they do not have to register with any central authority, there is no complete list of churches in the United States. This makes it difficult to find and select churches for study in a scientifically meaningful way. We know that there are roughly somewhere around 350,000 congregations in United States. The good news is that we have gotten around this issue through some creative techniques that have allowed us to obtain national samples of congregations without a full list of churches.

9. Page 105, Hoff. 1991–1992. "The Financial Accountability of Churches for Federal Income Tax Purposes?"

10. Brown, Trevor A. 1990. "Religious Nonprofits and the Commercial Manner Test." *The Yale Law Journal* 99: 1631–1650.

11. Bostwick, Heleigh. "What Constitutes a Church under Federal Law?" Legalzoom. com. https://www.legalzoom.com/articles/article_content/article14814.html; Muntean, Mark A.

and Robert W. Wood. "Young Life Qualifies as a Church: A Study of the IRS Ruling." *Church Solutions Magazine*. http://www.churchsolutionsmag.com/articles/621feat3.html. The irony in Young Life's classification as a church/denomination is that it, along with its peers like Campus Crusade for Christ International, is very aware of criticisms that it competes with churches for young people and is the first to state that it is trying to complement local churches, not replace them.

12. Obviously, this is an important assumption. However, there are other reasons one could argue in favor for reversing the exemption for churches. First, it would provide the IRS the ability to actually regulate churches on the issue of financial profiteering, which churches are theoretically supposed to be accountable for just like other nonprofits. Second, it would provide financial openness within churches for their individual contributors. Finally, by leveling the playing field, it eliminates the earlier mentioned implication that nonchurch religion is less protected than church-based religion.

13. Chaves, Mark. 1998. *National Congregations Study. Data File and Codebook*. Tucson, AZ: University of Arizona, Department of Sociology. Accessed through the Association of Religion Data Archives. www.thearda.com.

14. Another notable nonfiling "church" is Campus Crusade for Christ International; http://www.charitynavigator.org/index.cfm?bay=content.view&cpid=484#1

15. See footnote 236 in *Historical Development and Present Law of the Federal Tax Exemption for Charities and Other Tax-Exempt Organizations*. Prepared by the staff of the Joint Committee on Taxation for a public hearing before the House Committee on Ways and Means. April 20, 2005. See also "Developments Relating to Churches" in *Exempt Organizations Continuing Professional Education (CPE) Technical Instruction Program for Fiscal Year 1984*. Internal Revenue Service. http://www.irs.gov/charities/article/0,,id=113074,00. html

16. "Finding Sanctuary." December 5, 2004. *Fort Worth Star-Telegram*.

17. Executive Order 13199. January 29, 2001. "Establishment of White House Office of Faith-Based and Community Initiatives." http://www.whitehouse.gov/news/releases/2001/01/20010129-2.html

18. Chaves, Mark. 1999. "Religious Congregations and Welfare Reform: Who Will Take Advantage of 'Charitable Choice'?" *American Sociological Review* 64: 836–846. Four different executive orders during the Bush presidency have created 11 different Centers for Faith-Based and Community Initiatives in the following departments: Justice, Education, Labor, Health and Human Services, Housing and Urban Development, Commerce and Veterans Affairs, Small Business Administration, and Homeland Security.

19. The one exception is K-12 religious schools, which Supreme Court decisions have stated would violate the First Amendment's establishment clause. See page 10 in Monsma, Stephen V. 1996. *When Sacred and Secular Mix: Religious Nonprofit Organizations and Public Money*. Lanham, MD: Rowman & Littlefield Publishers, Inc.

20. August 2001. "Barriers to Faith-Based Organizations Seeking Federal Support." White House Report. http://www.whitehouse.gov/news/releases/2001/08/unlevelfield4.html

21. 1970. *Walz v. Tax Commission of City of New York*.

22. Emphasis added. August 2001. "Barriers to Faith-Based Organizations Seeking Federal Support."

23. Chaves. 1999. "Religious Congregations and Welfare Reform?"; Weber, Max. 1985. "'Churches' and 'Sects' in North America: An Ecclesiastical Socio-Political Sketch." Translated by Colin Loader. *Sociological Theory* 3(1): 7–13.

24. Executive Order 13279. December 12, 2002. "Equal Protection of the Laws for Faith-Based and Community Organizations." http://www.whitehouse.gov/news/releases/2002/12/20021212-6.html

25. It is important to keep in mind that many of the religious organizations that frequently receive government funding at a higher rate are not included in my data. In particular, religious hospitals and colleges are some of the "local nonprofits" that were not in the data collection but receive many public funds either directly (e.g., grants to the organization) or indirectly (e.g., student scholarships, Medicare/Medicaid payments).

26. Ebaugh, Chafetz, and Pipes did look at attempts to acquire public funding among religious social service providers. They found that religiosity was negatively related to applying for such funding. While a slightly different group of nonprofits, this does support the idea that these religiosity gaps are based on self-selection. 2005. "Faith-Based Social Service Organizations and Government Funding: Data from a National Survey." *Social Science Quarterly* 86: 273–292.

27. Page 149, Baggett, Jerome P. 2001. *Habitat for Humanity: Building Private Homes, Building Public Religion*. Philadelphia, PA: Temple University Press.

28. "Life Cycle of a Public Charity-Jeopardizing Exemption." http://www.irs.gov/charities/charitable/article/0,,id=123299,00.html; Page 51, Berry, Jeffrey M. and David F. Arons. 2003. *A Voice for Nonprofits*. Washington, DC: Brookings Institution Press.

29. "Measuring Lobbying Activity—The Substantial Part Test." http://www.irs.gov/charities/article/0,,id=163393,00.html

30. "Measuring Lobbying Activity—The Expenditure Test." http://www.irs.gov/charities/article/0,,id=163394,00.html; Page 55, Berry and Arons. 2003. *A Voice for Nonprofits*.

31. "Lobbying." http://www.irs.gov/charities/article/0,,id=163392,00.html

32. Vitello, Paul. September 3, 2008. "Pastors' Web Electioneering Attracts U.S. Reviews of Tax Exemptions." *New York Times*.

33. Pages 11–12. 2006. "Instructions for Schedule A (Form 990 or 990-EZ)." Internal Revenue Service.

34. February 13, 2003. "Congressman Chabot Introduces Partial Birth Abortion Ban." http://www.lifeissues.org/press/2003/ChabotPBAban.htm

35. Berry and Arons. 2003. *A Voice for Nonprofits*.

36. Nonprofits using the expenditure test are not required to specify their lobbying activities. Those using the substantial part test are supposed to provide details but often do not.

37. Grassroots mean: $136,474; direct mean: $142,075.

38. Pages 2–3. Stark, Rodney and William Sims Bainbridge. 1985. *The Future of Religion: Secularization, Revival, and Cult Formation*. Berkeley, CA: University of California Press.

APPENDIX

1. See, for instance, Campbell, David. 2002. "Beyond Charitable Choice: The Diverse Service Delivery Approaches of Local Faith-Related Organizations." *Nonprofit and Voluntary*

Sector Quarterly 31: 207–230; Pipes, Paula F. and Helen Rose Ebaugh. 2002. "Faith-Based Coalitions, Social Services, and Government Funding." *Sociology of Religion* 63: 49–68; Ebaugh, Helen Rose, Paula F. Pipes, Janet Saltzman, and Martha Daniels. 2003. "Where's the Religion? Distinguishing Faith-Based from Secular Social Service Agencies." *Journal for the Scientific Study of Religion* 42: 411–426; Wuthnow, Robert, Conrad Hackett, and Becky Yang Hsu. 2004. "The Effectiveness and Trustworthiness of Faith-Based and Other Social Service Organizations: A Study of Recipients' Perceptions." *Journal for the Scientific Study of Religion* 43: 1–17.

2. Nonprofits with gross receipts less than $25,000 do not have to file annual returns. "Gross receipts" is the equivalent of revenue (e.g., contributions + profits from commercial activities) added to the expenses for those commercial activities (e.g., cost of goods sold). Those with gross receipts less than $100,000 file a shorter 990-EZ form.

3. Called the "Core File," this database is produced yearly for 501(3)c nonprofits, private foundations, and other tax-exempt organizations.

4. "Guide to the National Taxonomy of Exempt Entities." http://nccs2.urban.org/ntee-cc/

5. "National Taxonomy of Exempt Entities-Core Codes." http://nccs2.urban.org/ntee-cc/summary.htm#x

6. Another code (Religious Youth Leadership) in a different major category was also examined.

7. The database limits search results to 500 organizations, so multiple queries were required within each NTEE code and revenue group (e.g., Search 1: Code=X01 AND Revenue>1000000; Search 2: Code=X01 AND Revenue <1000000 & Revenue>500000).

8. If necessary and available, the organization's Web site was also consulted.

9. Nonprofits can go by a calendar year beginning January 1 and ending December 31 or a fiscal year, which can begin and end at any time during the year.

10. For the 990 sections of Revenue, Expenses, Assets, Functional Expenses, and Schedule A, there were 13, 27, 24, 54, and 35 organizations, respectively, that showed errors in the original forms (although some of these were the same organization with errors in multiple places).

11. The weighted average takes into account the percent cases assigned to a particular code. This prevents a small category's reliability score counting as much as a larger category. For the uncondensed activity codes, the unweighted average was .58 and the weighted average was .62.

Index

Note: Page references followed by '*f*' and '*t*' denote figures and tables, respectively.